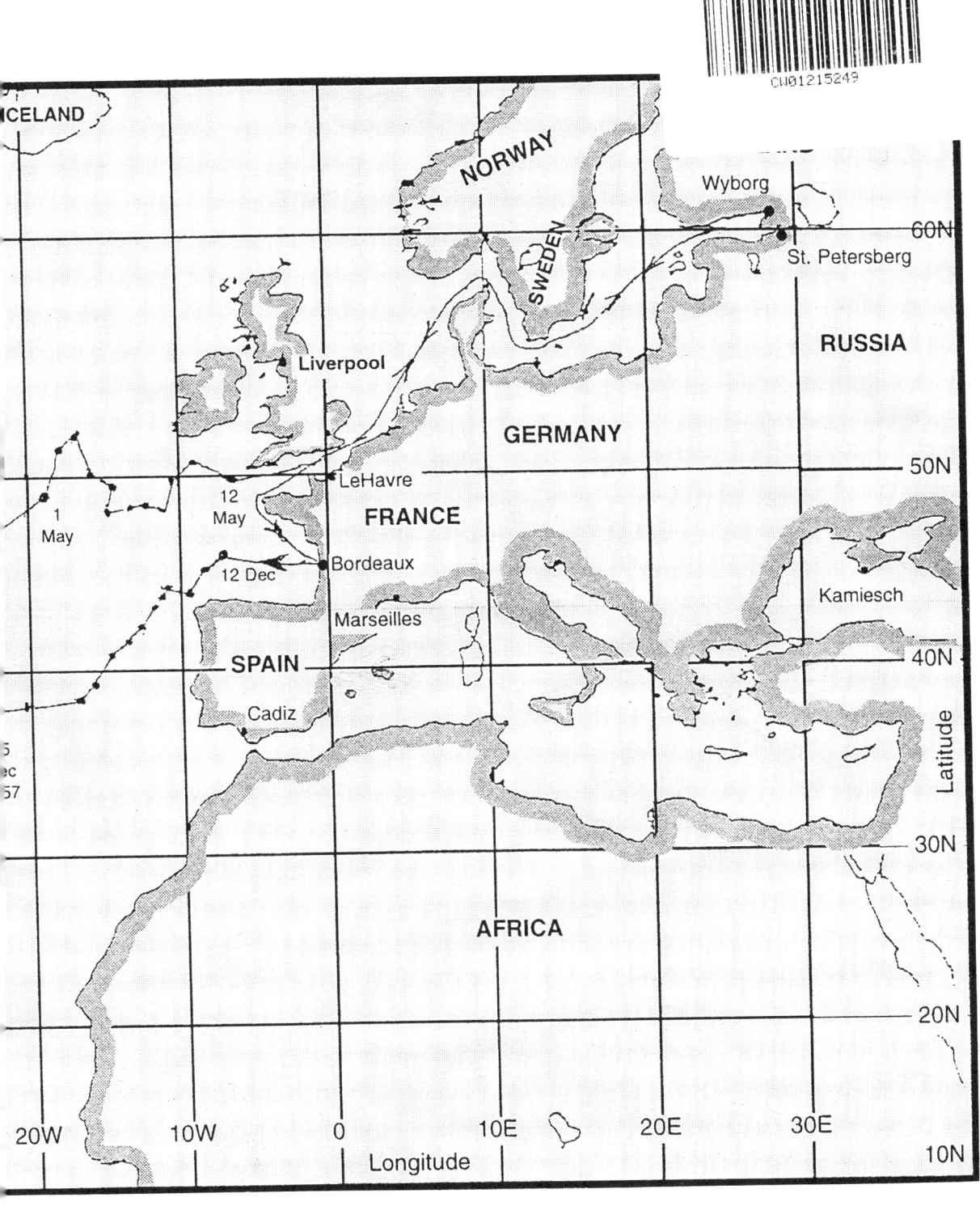

# AN ANTEBELLUM LIFE AT SEA

# AN ANTEBELLUM LIFE AT SEA

Featuring the Journal of Sarah Jane Girdler
Kept Aboard the Clipper Ship
*Robert H. Dixey*
From America to Russia and Europe
January 1857–December 1858

## L. Tracy Girdler

Original Illustrations
by
Ted Brennan

Black Belt Press
Montgomery

Black Belt Press
P.O. Box 551
Montgomery, AL 36101

Copyright © 1997 by L. Tracy Girdler. All Rights Reserved. Printed in the United States of America. No part of this book may be used or reproduced in any manner whatsoever without written permission except in the case of brief quotations in critical articles or reviews.

**Library of Congress Cataloging-in-Publication Data**
Girdler, L. Tracy, 1918–
    An antebellum life at sea : featuring the journal of Sarah Jane Girdler, kept aboard the clipper ship, Robert H. Dixey, from America to Russia and Europe, January 1857–December 1858 / L. Tracy Girdler : original illustrations by Ted Brennan.
        p.  cm.
    Includes bibliographical references and index.
    ISBN 1-881320-49-9
    1. Girdler, Sarah Jane —Journeys. 2. Voyages and travels. 3. Robert H. Dixey (Clipper ship) I. Title.
G470.G54  1996
910.4'5'092—dc20
[B]                                                                                  96-2031
                                                                                        CIP

 The Black Belt, defined by its dark, rich soil, stretches across central Alabama. It was the heart of the cotton belt. It was and is a place of great beauty, of extreme wealth and grinding poverty, of pain and joy. Here we take our stand, listening to the past, looking to the future.

*FRONTISPIECE: The writing desk used by Sarah Jane Girdler while she was aboard the* Robert H. Dixey, *shown here in the Connecticut home of Reynolds Girdler, her grandnephew. Captain John Girdler bought this cleverly built desk in the Orient in the 1830s and used it on many voyages. It is exquisitely made of rosewood, with brass handles and complex hinges. The writing surfaces are velvet-faced and the top storage file is faced with Chinese silk. Captain Girdler died in 1853, and when Sarah Jane sailed to Russia in 1857, she proudly took her father's desk and promised to make a record of the voyage. In an aft cabin, at a table tied in place, she wrote long hours with her quill pen. The ship in the painting above the desk is of Captain Girdler's last command, the* George E. Webster.

It is with great affection and respect
that the author dedicates this work to the memory of his cousin

REYNOLDS GIRDLER
of
Riverside, Connecticut.

His was the first effort to learn the story
of the lovely clipper ship whose portrait hung
on his great-uncle's dining room wall
in Jeffersonville, Indiana

# CONTENTS

| | | |
|---|---|---:|
| Foreword | | 9 |
| Preface | | 13 |
| Acknowledgments | | 16 |
| 1 | Introduction | 21 |
| 2 | A Profile of Two Cities | 24 |
| 3 | People of the *Dixey* | 29 |
| 4 | Building the *Dixey* | 44 |
| 5 | Life Aboard the *Dixey* | 52 |
| 6 | The *Dixey* in Port | 57 |
| 7 | Early Days of the *Dixey* | 60 |
| 8 | The Journal of Sarah Jane Girdler | 69 |
| 9 | The End of the *Robert H. Dixey* | 148 |
| Epilogue | | 159 |
| Genealogies | | 168 |
| Appendix A: *Dixey* Letters | | 172 |
| Appendix B: Letters of Sarah Jane Girdler | | 191 |
| Appendix C: More *Dixey* Letters | | 204 |
| Notes | | 207 |
| For Further Reading | | 216 |
| Index | | 218 |

# FOREWORD

By Caldwell Delaney
Museum Director Emeritus
City of Mobile

Mobile is an old city. Founded by the French in 1702, it was a colony of England and Spain in turn before it became American in 1813. By the last decade before the Civil War, the time of the events in this narrative, it had become a flourishing seaport and one of the larger cities in the nation.

Much of the charm of the French and Spanish city remained. Streets were still paved with shells, giving it a bright clean look. Along the old streets houses stood shoulder to shoulder with their ornate balconies overhanging the sidewalk. Just outside the city and along the bay, "villas" set in gardens of lush vegetation lent a tropical atmosphere.

Much of the spirit of the French and Spanish remained in the American city. Life was approached in a fun-loving atmosphere. The parades and balls of Mardi Gras, as now observed in this country, began in Mobile with the antics of a group of happy young bucks who cavorted on the waterfront, then roused the city with a parade.

By the time of the Civil War, Mobile had enjoyed the theater for nearly fifty years, and the great actors and actresses of the time appeared regularly in the city. So close was the association with the English stage that the London papers regularly reported what was being presented in Mobile.

In cotton-buying season English agents flocked to the city to vie for the best grades of the staple. Their offices were along St. Michael Street; and, although the buyers are long gone, the street is still sometimes referred to as the English Channel.

All this cotton furor was brought on by the opening to cultivation of the rich Black Belt of Alabama and Mississippi. When the Indians were removed in the 1830s, the spectacular era of the Cotton Kingdom opened; and, although it lasted fewer than thirty years, it wrote a page in American history which stands alone for glamorous appeal, whether reality or fantasy.

This was the time of the great columned houses looking down upon white fields of thousands of acres of cotton. And the golden harvest, when it came down the rivers to Mobile, made the old city the second-ranking cotton port of the world, surpassed only by New Orleans.

When the cotton had been baled and floated down to Mobile for sale, the planters' families followed on the white palaces which steamboats had become, for a season of gaiety in the city. They flocked to the Battle House to take up reservations made months in advance for the "winter season."

The Battle House, designed by Isaiah Rogers, was among the country's first modern hotels. It boasted such wonders as its own water and sewer system and hot baths, day or night. Foreign visitors often called it America's best-run hotel and approved the fact that it was staffed by smiling Irish rather than the usual sullen slaves to whom they had become accustomed in the South.

Most of the wealthy families of Mobile were related, by business or family ties, to the plantation families, so the crowded city was friendly and congenial

There was much for the wives and daughters of the planters to do while the men of the family tended to business or sought mysterious amusements. Shopping was the women's first need, and Dauphin Street was heaven. The population was polyglot, and its nature was nowhere more apparent than in the shops, in which the language spoken was often French, German, or Italian.

For rest and refreshment there were ice cream parlors in which the latest confections favored by Paris were always available. The coffee saloons never closed, but they were frequented more by the men, who transacted business there.

The ladies, if their connections were good enough, might even gain entry to the salon of the fabulous Madame Octavia Walton LeVert and hear her tell of her reception by Queen Victoria and Napoleon III, and of her friendships with the Brownings, Webster, President Jackson, Poe, and Longfellow, and about everybody else in the world worth knowing.

If they were fortunate, they might see the great lady resplendent in her box at the opera or theatre and join the locals in wondering if the attentive man was really Henry Clay.

They would probably be taken by carriage on excursions to the fashionable suburb of Spring Hill, where prominent Mobilians had their summer homes, or to Choctaw Point below the city where a camp of Indians lived in poverty and displayed themselves to the curious.

If they happened to linger on into April, they could join all Mobilians, not bedridden, in lining the streets to cheer the procession of the volunteer fire companies on Firemen's Day, the ninth of April. This was a spectacular display of bright uniforms, painted and polished equipment, and fine horses. The engines and hose reels were banked with red amaryllis lilies which old-timers in Mobile still call Ninth of April lilies.

The young men, for all their elegant dress still "country" boys, would drift to the waterfront where the "ladies" were not innocent plantation belles. If the lads were unwise or in their cups, they might wander into infamous Spanish Alley, from which few but its denizens ever returned.

The riverboats, tied up three and four deep, were a sight never to be forgotten. Many of the captains of these boats were well-known to the planters and their families, and they dispensed a lavish hospitality in their floating salons. Young sons, unused to such largesse, sometimes staggered into a waterfront gambling house from which an obstreperous loser could be dropped through a trap door into the river.

But all the gambling was not done in the disreputable houses of the waterfront. In the handsome Gentleman's Parlor of the Battle House, the games went on day and night, and occasionally a plantation changed hands at the turn of a card.

Such was the city to which the hardy New Englanders of this narrative came to seek and find fortunes. Their introduction was from the South, past the tall stone lighthouse, between the brick forts which guarded the entrance into Mobile Bay, and to the anchorage in the lower bay where all ocean-going ships had to wait and be served by the lighters which carried their passengers and cargo up to the city.

The anchorage was to the city what an overture is to an opera, for it contained, in bits and snatches, the personality of the community it nourished.

First, and above all, there was cotton. The lighters were so piled with bales that nothing could be seen of them but their smokestacks. Cotton drifted upon the water like white foam and washed upon the shores. Men of all nations scurried about their ships, shouting to their neighbors and to the vendors who swarmed among them, offering their wares. Two boats which served the fleet may be taken as an allegory of Mobile in its golden age of cotton. One was the Bethel, the floating chapel provided by the ladies of Mobile to save the souls of the sailors, and the other was the brothel, not provided by the ladies of Mobile.

From this anchorage the beautiful clipper ship, whose story is the heart of this narrative, was blown by hurricane winds and broken up on the outer bar, a bar which to this day bears her name.

# PREFACE

In boyhood visits to my grandfather, I was awed by the large painting of a beautiful clipper ship that hung on the dining room wall. It was the *Robert H. Dixey*, and Grandfather Girdler, with a seriocomic routine, always told how his sister Jennie had made a trip on it and described how it had been caught in a hurricane in the Bay of Biscay and "knocked down." He ended by saying that Jennie had spent three days on her "beam's end." Aunt Jennie died before I was born, but my father had known her well. He implied that, because of her ample girth, it would take a real storm to put her on her "beam's end."

I did remember that the ship was lost at Mobile in another hurricane. I knew that my cousin Winnifred Pierce was putting together the history of the ship. She explains her motivation as follows:

### By Way of an Explanation for My Interest in the Ship *Robert H. Dixey*
### By Winnifred Pierce

This story of the clipper ship *Robert H. Dixey* is an offshoot of my interest in the family of Captain Lewis Girdler of Marblehead.

In 1837, Lewis Girdler's son Captain John Girdler married Sarah Jane Gardner, one of the six daughters of Abel Gardner, Marblehead entrepreneur. Any family of six sisters is bound to pique interest and it was easy to become caught up in the doings of the Gardner girls. This was possible because of the more than forty letters—written by them, their husbands, or other members of the family—that are still available today.

Rebecca Gardner Dixey, born in 1820, was the fourth daughter of Abel Gardner. It was in 1842 that she married Richard W. Dixey, eleven years older than she and a successful master mariner. The Dixeys were an appealing couple. We know Richard Dixey to have been handsome from photographs, one to be seen in Lindsey's *Old Marblehead Sea Captains* and another, taken as a younger man, in a "thumbnail-sized" album belonging to Nancy Girdler Harrison of Spartanburg, South Carolina. Richard Dixey's great affection for his family was manifested by his taking his wife and children to sea with him whenever he could. He was a religious man and a humane ship's master, which led to his sobriquet "the Christian captain." But this did not make him a stern or undemonstrative man. In the pages of a journal kept by his niece Sarah Jane Girdler, who had been invited to join the family at sea for more than a year, we see him taking delight in sharing his interest in the natural phenomena of the sea, spending hours in port enjoying the role of tourist, engaging in Fourth of July high jinks. He was truly the fulcrum of the lives of all those around him. Sarah Jane would write, "It seems as if half the ship is gone when he is away."

As for Rebecca Gardner Dixey, we do know that she had flair. It was something that her sisters did not possess, and in family letters we sense an edge of envy for Rebecca and her ways. She would love to travel all her life. She had a sense of adventure. The monotony of weeks at sea seemed never to faze her. She was a good sailor, and she relished being in the company of her husband. And then there was always the anticipation of what lay ahead on shore. She loved to shop, to meet new people, to see the sights. We only wish she had left us more clues as to where and when she was able to accompany her husband. With seven-year-old Cowell, their son, we do know that she had been in London in 1851 and was being sent home on another ship, as Richard Dixey had been ordered to Rio, filled with fever at that time and so considered too dangerous a place to take his family. In February 1853, she was with her husband on the *Houqua*[1] as it left New York, bound for China via Cape Horn. That October, just as the port of FooChow was being opened to foreign commerce, she was there and went ashore to see the sights, as was her wont, only to have to be rescued from a mob of curious Chinese who crushed around her—the first white woman they had ever seen.

[1] Named for a Cantonese merchant.

When the *Robert H. Dixey* was launched in 1855, Richard Dixey was given command, and Rebecca Dixey must have been filled with high expectations. She could look forward to the coming years at sea with her husband. Passenger quarters were fitted out with such amenities as "comfortable couches and chairs, a good library of books and a good parlor organ" according to Sarah Jane Girdler's journal.

And so it is out of an interest in Rebecca and Richard Dixey, which has grown to be a genuine affection for the memory of the couple, that I have tried to reconstruct the life of the ship *Robert H. Dixey*, to which their fate and fortunes were so inextricably tied.

WPP

Ann Arbor, Michigan

March 1981


When I moved to the Mobile area in 1977, I started to research the story, as it was much connected to Mobile. Little did I know how deeply I would get involved in the next fifteen years. Searching back 130 years requires a "crazy" desire—even the tiniest facts become a challenge.

Cousin Win had pretty well documented the ship's factual story before I started. I have spent most of my time searching for pictures of people and places and have tried to "flesh out" the story behind the ship.

Cousin Win is not as "retired" as I am and has neither the time nor the inclination to keep pounding this story toward publication. She has asked me to make what use I can of all the work she and her helpers produced, without restriction and without further acknowledgment. In a final public tribute to her tremendous inital effort, let me say that I have loved pursuing her work and having her friendly counsel, and, although she wants no further recognition, I feel the initial impetus to the telling of this story was due to her.

TRACY GIRDLER

# ACKNOWLEDGMENTS

This story has been so long in creation that it will be hard to remember all who added to its lore. The best way to enumerate them is probably geographically, and I apologize in advance to any who were inadvertently omitted.

## MARBLEHEAD, BOSTON, AND SALEM

The Marblehead Historical Society and its many unnamed members furnished family data. In particular, Marion Gosling has added a great deal to the *Dixey* story. Hammond Bowden and others at the Lee Mansion helped much in finding letters and portraits.

The staff at the Peabody Essex Museum have supplied ship portraits and technical data. Mr. Richard Martin and Mr. Fetchko have helped, going back many years, with specific questions.

Dan Dixey, a dedicated genealogist and "Header" (a Marblehead resident), personally helped when we studied the Dixey family on site.

Reynolds Girdler of Riverside, Connecticut, in his efforts to study our family history, produced the first capsule of the *Dixey* story back in the 1960s. This provided the foundation for the further research that Win Pierce and later I have done.

Mrs. Daphne Brooks Prout of Dover, Massachusetts, a great-granddaughter of Captain Richard Dixey, supplied several key photos and documents. Several members of her family were also very helpful.

## NEW ORLEANS AREA

Diane Dixey (Mrs. J. W.) Hailey, a great-granddaughter of R. H. Dixey, has furnished us with the most meaningful and important letters. The details contained therein were a major source. It would be fair to say that without these Dixey/Minge letters, we would have had little to go on.

Diane's brother, Edgar Dixey, supplied the painting of Robert H. Dixey and his family, the only pictorial record we have of Robert. Undoubtedly photographs were made of this man, but we have not been lucky enough to find them.

Charles L. Sullivan, author of *Hurricanes of the Mississippi Gulf Coast,* was quite helpful to me in understanding the storm that claimed the life of the *Dixey.*

## MOBILE AREA

Since 1977 I have dug deeper and deeper into the ship's story, using every conceivable source. Court and tax records, school and military records, newspapers, wedding and burial records, real estate sales records—all have been valuable. Even the National Archives contains much of this story, probably more than we know.

The staff at the downtown branch of the Mobile Public Library on Government Street have been tremendously patient with me and my constant quest for details. In particular, George Schroeter, director of the Local History and Genealogy Division, and his staff have never been less than cooperative in every way. I have spent hundreds of hours among those shelves.

Caldwell Delaney, longtime director of the Museum of the City of Mobile, has stood by me all these years and guided my efforts to learn about this ship and its people. His efforts brought the principal painting of the *Dixey* to Mobile, and someday the other painting will hang alongside it. Mobile's history has been greatly advanced by the efforts of this man.

Betty Suddeth at the Fairhope Public Library and her staff helped many times, wondering what I was really looking for.

Suzanne S. Barnhill, word processor, editor, and advisor, has lent her expertise to the smoothing of rough edges and provided encouragement in holding a steady course.

## OTHERS

Mary (Mrs. Harry) Toulmin of Daphne, Alabama, a descendant of one of the transplanted Virginia Minge families, has been of great help in supplying family history.

Mrs. Ruth Lyon Russ of Spring Hill (Mobile), a granddaughter of W. H. H. (Willie) Minge, is a major source of background information. She owns several important paintings and furnished several important documents.

Eva Gatling, formerly of Fairhope, had a Minge Bible that helped us to locate Diane Hailey.

Mr. Sidney Schell of Mobile, Admiralty lawyer and counsel and an expert on clipper ships, has offered sound advice on many occasions.

A longtime friend, attorney Barker Stein of Daphne, unlocked the Stein connection to the *Dixey* story. Thomas Fettyplace Stein, Jr., and his daughters Emily S. Young and Annette Daughdrill have turned up important Peabody and Fettyplace paintings.

## MY FAMILY

Members of my family, including brothers, cousins (whom, like the First Sea Lord H.M.S. *Pinafore,* "I number by the dozens"), cousins-in-law, and their progeny, have supplied pictures, books, military commissions, letters, and other documents that all add to the fabric of this history. I am reluctant to name specific names, lest I forget someone, but they all helped, and I am grateful to them all.

It is difficult to stop searching now after all these years. Even after this book goes to press, I will doubtless always wonder whether some gem of a letter or a photo of the *Dixey* might not turn up among someone's family heirlooms—too late to be included.

# AN ANTEBELLUM LIFE AT SEA

CHAPTER

*1*

# Introduction

The tale we are about to unfold begins, like many stories, in great prosperity, and also like too many, perhaps, it ends with tragedy.

This ship and its people were examples of this young nation's best. The basic enterprise was sound. The world was supplied with a welcome and valuable product during its career.

Friday, September 14, 1860, was a lovely day in the central Gulf of Mexico. The five-year-old cotton clipper *Robert H. Dixey* was inbound to Mobile from New York. Making six knots in a smooth sea with a southwest wind, she steadily came up on the Sand Island lighthouse, outside Mobile Point.

The wind shifted more to the west as the day wore on. "Mare's tail" clouds were high in the western sky, but far off. The barometer was dropping from its dawn reading, and Captain Richard Dixey was somewhat concerned about the approaching weather.

Aboard the ship as a passenger was Mobile bar pilot Sam Smyly. He and Captain Dixey were aware of the hurricane season in the Gulf, but both felt the Mobile Bay anchorage would be secure if a real hurricane developed. They were wrong...

The decision to enter the bay was Captain Dixey's, and the bar was crossed about suppertime. The ship sailed up the anchorage as far as the depth of water would permit. She drew nearly eighteen feet and dropped anchor in twenty-three feet of water.

We have only a partial record of what steps were taken to protect the ship. We know that two anchors were set, with all chain. Double gaskets wrapped the furled sails, and the hatches were resecured for sea.

Knowing the kind of seaman Richard Dixey was, we can imagine the anxiety he felt as the midnight wind switched to the southwest and screamed "Hurricane!" By 2 A.M., the wind was likely gusting to one hundred miles per hour. The shelter from the south provided by Dauphin Island, two miles distant, kept the seas from overwhelming the ship, but what next?

The sturdy ship survived the night without damage. The passage of the eye of the storm gave a brief respite, but the worst was yet to come. By 0900 the weather gods had loosed a blast from the north that swung the *Dixey* around, and all hell broke loose.

The question can be raised: Why didn't the ship remain offshore until the storm had passed? A falling barometer and "mare's tail" clouds in the western sky caused Captain Dixey concern. Mobile Bay is a safe anchorage in most weather, and the decision was made to continue. Having proceeded into the bay, the ship was unable to sail out. The fate of the *Dixey* passed into the hands of the weather gods.

Our readers will learn a lot more about this day. This ship will cruise a hundred thousand sea miles to get to this day. Now we'll take you to the beginning . . .

14 January 1857

> Left Boston harbor Wednesday 14th about two o'clock. Stood on the quarter deck most of the afternoon in order to take the last sight of Boston. All the islands in the harbor were covered with snow and presented a very dreary appearance. It was not until we parted with the steamship off Boston lights that I began to realise that we were upon the ocean. The sea and wind were very moderate, and continued so all night. I had considerable trouble getting into my berth, which is an upper one, but after once attaining my position, was rocked gently to and fro, and slept as soundly as if I were in my bed at home.

This paragraph begins the journal of a seventeen-year-old girl, written aboard a very fast sailing ship, the *Robert H. Dixey*. She was traveling with her uncle, the ship's captain, and his wife. Her special charge was to look after her two-year-old cousin. They were off on a long voyage, and she was a seagoing nanny.

The reader will recognize that although some details are missing, the letters, journals, ship's logs, news stories, censuses, and city directories of these times have nonetheless given us a solid story of the 1850s and of the people who carried it through to its sad, sad end.

For purposes of this story, we will refer to the ship as the *Dixey*. Its story immediately breaks into the story of four families. We will give our readers a "brief" on each and try to give depth and background to the five-year antebellum period of this clipper ship.

Three of the families begin their American history in Marblehead, Massachusetts. We will profile this beleaguered but proud town. The Fettyplace, Dixey, and Girdler families all arrived in Marblehead in the 1600s. The other family, the Minges, came to Virginia from Wales in the 1600s as well and were numerous and aggressive citizens in that colony.

The Girdler family plays a part in this story only because the letters and journal of seventeen-year-old Sarah Jane Girdler are the common thread that weaves this tale into history. Sarah Jane was related by blood and marriage to the Dixey family and thus to the Minges.

*Page 1 of Sarah Jane Girdler's journal. Courtesy of the Peabody Museum, Salem, Massachusetts, where the journal forms part of a vast collection of 1850s Americana. The journal was donated by the widow of Edward Fitch, SJG's grandnephew.*

Before we get to the journal and the letters, however, we want our readers to know more about the background of the people and the ship *Dixey*. The illustrations, photos, graphs, and charts we reproduce will, we hope, leave our readers with a realistic view of life in America during the 1850s as it related to the cotton trade—when Cotton was King!

CHAPTER

*2*

# A Profile of Two Cities

## MARBLEHEAD, MASSACHUSETTS, AND MOBILE, ALABAMA, 1830–1860

Marblehead, Massachusetts, might well have been called the "Bad Luck" capital. Life there was hard at best. The rocky peninsula on which it sits is a difficult place to build. Growing food and providing pasture to support the large families that predominated were a challenge. Fishing, shipbuilding, sail making, rope making, and later shoemaking were the choices of job opportunity.

Nature had favored Marblehead with one of the finest harbors on the East Coast, sheltered from storms in all directions. The harbor was better than Boston's, which is probably why Marblehead was founded two years earlier than Boston, in 1628. But, as always happens, circumstances change. Marblehead was fine for ships the size of the *Mayflower,* but by 1830 the depth of the water began to control the commerce of this seaport. The nine-foot minimum depth of water at the harbor entrance could handle fishing schooners and small coastal craft, but the money was in larger ships, drawing up to fifteen feet by 1830. At that time, dredging was not an option for Marblehead's rocky bottom, so the commerce moved elsewhere.

Steam-powered sawing and drilling allowed the costs of larger vessels to drop and profits from larger cargos to rise. The economic forces then were the same as now—irresistible! Marblehead's value as a shipping port diminished.

In 1830 Marblehead was bigger than Mobile. In a meager way it supported about five thousand citizens. Luck was mostly bad. Fires burned large sections. In 1846 a severe storm on the Grand Banks almost wiped out the fishing fleet and took the lives of sixty-five men, leaving hundreds of children fatherless. By 1860 shoemaking was the largest industry. The town had grown a little, to 7,500, but the people were poor economically. The youth of the city had left in large numbers, seeking more opportunity. The "Headers," as they were known, had a hard time.

It would be a mistake, however, not to recognize the character that hardship had developed in the Headers. The town was built by breeding large families, and everybody worked—hard!

Most people in the town were related to most other people by either blood or marriage—sometimes both. They stood together in troubled times. The fire companies are a good example. Marblehead had at least five fire companies. Each had a name, logo, social programs, inter-company competitions, and so on. Nearly every male was a member of a company. Each house kept two or more leather fire buckets handy, and, when the bell rang, the whole town turned out to carry water.

Some of the leather buckets are on display at the Lee Mansion today. Fire engines (pumpers), pulled by hand in the early days, were gaudily painted and much admired. The first hoses were of handsewn leather with limited life and pressure capacity, but they steadily improved. At the same time ladders got longer, and horses pulled the pumpers. Anything that added to the companies' efficiency was much needed because, until coal was available, sparks from the chimneys of wood fireplaces flew onto the shake shingle roofs of neighboring houses on windy days, keeping firefighters busy.

The life expectancy was less then, but the problem of care for the old, infirm, and poor was dealt with by the locals. One modern idea that they had even in the 1700s was a lottery. In theirs, 13.5 percent was skimmed off to help the poor—showing that there is not much really new going on nowadays.

# PAINTINGS OF THE "MEDIUM CLIPPER" SHIP ROBERT H. DIXEY

*The owners of the Dixey had a more than ordinary interest in this lovely creation of the latter-day American shipbuilder's art: they had her "portrait" painted twice. Both paintings are extremely accurate technically, and students of "square rigging" of the 1850s will enjoy examining them. The differences in the rigs were caused by the changes that Captain Dixey demanded when the ship was rebuilt after the hurricane in the Bay of Biscay.*

*The first painting (above) is of the* Dixey *leaving Marseilles in March 1856—attributed to the French artist A. Roux (1765–1835) and his son, F. Roux—and shows the original rigging by Paul Curtis, East Boston. The painting was probably given by Captain Dixey to Thomas J. Fettyplace of Mobile, Alabama, one of the owners. It was purchased in 1990 by the Museum of the City of Mobile from the family of B. Devereux Barker, of Marblehead, Massachusetts, descendants of Fettyplace's mother's family.*

*The second painting (opposite) was made by an unknown American artist about 1858 and shows the "double topsail" rig as rerigged in France in December 1857. The original painting was made for the Dixey family but has disappeared. A copy was made by the same artist for Sarah Jane Girdler Belknap (Whedon). The copy was inherited by her brother Lewis Girdler of Jeffersonville, Indiana, and is now owned by T. M. Girdler III of Independence, Ohio. A lithograph exists of this second painting, and one print belongs to Mrs. Daphne Brooks Prout, a great-granddaughter of the ship's captain, and hangs in Maine. For more about the changes to the Dixey's rig, see diagram on page 48.*

Most of the prominent families of the time of the *Dixey* are still represented in the town in the 1990s. Some still live in their family homes, some of which are three hundred years old. The town was poor in 1850, but it never lacked pride. Still, the young people longed for more.

At the same time, one thousand miles to the southwest, in Mobile, Alabama, things were better. Between 1830 and 1860, three hundred thousand people from the "run-out" farm land of Virginia and other states moved to the South. Alabama got a major share. During this period Mobile grew from three thousand to thirty thousand. Some of the new residents were from Marblehead. Many came from Virginia. Many of Mobile's present population are descended from those transplanted Virginians.

It was a period of expansive commerce and industry. The low taxes, open state borders, and political stability at this time created an atmosphere that generated tremendous commercial activity. Construction of all kinds was booming. Farming, mining, lumbering, and fishing all were prosperous. Steamboats and railroads opened it all up. The invention of the cotton gin and machine-powered looms to make cotton cloth provided great opportunities. Coal, iron, lumber, and fishing were good, but—no doubt about it—Cotton was King.

Our readers are no doubt thoroughly indoctrinated with the opening of the "West." More should be told about the opening of the "Deep South" if one is to appreciate what Mobile was really like in the days of the *Dixey*.

The rapid growth of cotton as a commodity caused great hordes of people to seek the possible economic opportunities. Some of these "carpetbagger" types were not good citizens to be in the position of planning the growth of a city. And because of the small number of old families in Mobile, the 1840s and '50s were dominated politically and commercially by the newcomers.

They didn't carry six-shooters on their hips, but they looked for ways to "make it" as fast and as much as they could. True, many were hardworking, God-fearing, law-abiding citizens, but everybody was in a hurry. The builders, the bankers, the planters, and the sailors all wanted to get in and get a share. The problems they created for the future in their haste to grow in the cotton trade have caused troubles that haunt Mobile to this day.

Slipshod engineering, poor planning, loose government, unwise production—all helped Mobile generate an economic boom that was really a "bubble," unable to handle any downturn in business, whether manmade or of natural causes. Banking and insurance were two areas that caused havoc within a few years. White-collar crime was rampant in the 1840s and later. Regulatory commissions and laws were inadequate. Insurance premiums were collected but often disappeared, along with the officers of the company. Banks issued certificates backed by deposits that were overstated. Planters borrowed on crops that were never planted, on land that sometimes wasn't even cleared—a really messy situation.

The development of the steamboat and the railroad in the South was seriously hampered by the lack of trained surveyors and engineers. People bought stock in railroads that had not been properly prepared and were built sometimes to areas where rail lines would never be needed. The sale of the stock, on a commission basis, was big business, and millions of dollars disappeared. Sounds just like today!

In spite of all these problems, for a period of more than twenty years, until the Civil War blew it all apart, ships like the *Dixey* and people like Tom Fettyplace, Robert and Richard Dixey, and Collier Minge and his brothers up on their plantations helped supply the world with a useful, valuable, and important commodity.

It's a short story. Steam would soon power the ocean freighter. Nothing could stop the change. The *Dixey* was the best of the last.

CHAPTER

# 3

# People of the *Dixey*

## "FAMILY" AT THE TIME OF THE *DIXEY*

Families in 1855 behaved very much as they do now. From an intense study of all the information available in letters, newspaper stories, city directories, ship's logs, and Sarah Jane Girdler's journal, we can paint a detailed picture of how these people dealt with their human problems and tried to better their own lives and the conditions around them.

Family came first! As business succeeded, the sons (and daughters), sons-in-law, brothers, cousins, and so on, unless they were grossly inadequate, were always worked into the enterprise. Friends got first consideration in business, and, if they were in competition with outsiders, friendship clinched the deal. Summer jobs for teenagers went first to family and friends.

Free enterprise was at its zenith in those years. Problems were plentiful, but government interference with activities was minimal. The coming Civil War would bring many changes, but in 1855–1860 men were free to try to make it—and many did. The Dixey, Minge, and Fettyplace families who created this story are good examples of the most talented, hardworking citizens of these exciting times.

Later in our story we will develop the American genealogy of the Minge and

Fettyplace families which intertwine with Dixeys so constantly during and before the creation of our ship.

The Dixey story will be the theme in the early chapters, so as not to confuse our readers by meeting too many people, too fast. But the Fettyplace and Minge representatives will keep coming into the story.

It strikes your narrator that the detailed record left by these three families speaks very proudly of the character developed by the citizens of the then-sixty-year-old republic called the United States. They seem honest, hard-working, devout, and kind.

The social problems of the times troubled them all, but the principal one, slavery, was soon to boil over. The South would struggle for a long time to recover its economic and social place in the nation.

Many American families were torn by these problems. These three families would have their share of heartache and grief in the coming Civil War. But we are limiting our tale to one ship and its people, and the end of our story comes just before the war.

Now let's profile these families who relate to the *Dixey*.

## THE DIXEY FAMILY

The Massachusetts Dixey story began in 1629, when William Dixie came to the colonies on the ship *Talbot*. His cousin Thomas came some time later. They were sons of an ancient and honored family in England. Their kinsman was Lord Mayor of London and had been knighted by Queen Elizabeth I, as Sir Wolstan Dixie, in 1545. Thomas Dixie founded the line that led to our Captain John Dixey. At some time, the Colonial family changed the spelling to "Dixey" instead of "Dixie," as it is still spelled in England.

Captain John Dixey's father fought in the Revolution as a privateer. John married Rebecca Cowell, daughter of an American naval hero, Richard Cowell, in 1804. In the next twenty-two years, they had ten children. At the age of forty-four, Mrs. Dixey died under very strange circumstances. She left her four-week-old baby "sleeping in the church yard" next door to her house, and that morning she was found "drowned in Marblehead Harbor." Most people believed it was suicide, not an accident. No reason has ever been suggested, but the incident was very shocking to her large family.

Captain John Dixey was almost constantly in the employ of the Hooper family of Marblehead. The Hoopers were successful, prolific entrepreneurs, and most old families had many connections with the Hoopers by blood or marriage. The Robert Hooper for whom our Dixey son was named was typical of that family, and as a young man John Dixey was very close to him [see letter, Appendix D].

Captain Dixey had an eventful life. In 1811, he and his ship *Mercury* were captured in the Carribean by the French and he was imprisoned for a year in France. By the time he was released, the War of 1812 had begun, and the British promptly seized him and his ship again. Afer a year in prison at Ashburton near Plymouth, England, Captain Dixey was exchanged and allowed to return home—two years older, with nothing to show for his troubles, and with no ship!

Captain John Dixey commanded many ships worldwide until he was in his sixties, retiring about 1850. At that time, he moved to Sharon, Massachusetts, where he lived with several of his unmarried and widowed daughters. The family home in Marblehead was leased, and finally in 1864, after ninety years, the old place was sold and passed out of the Dixey family.

*Captain John Dixey (Courtesy Marblehead Historical Society)*

His sons Robert H. Dixey and Richard W. Dixey wrote him as often as they could. They gave him financial support and were greatly devoted to him throughout his life. He lived more than twenty years on the farm and died at the ripe old age of ninety-two.

## ROBERT HOOPER DIXEY

Robert Hooper Dixey (RHD), third son of Captain John and Rebecca Cowell Dixey, was born in Marblehead in 1817. To the best of our knowlege, he was never a commercial sailor. His interests ran more to business. We know he left Marblehead to pursue less dangerous and more lucrative work. By the 1840s he was a commission merchant in New York City and by the 1850s was in the employ of Messrs. Harbeck and Co., a French-controlled firm of international bankers and ship operators. He supervised contracting, insurance, scheduling, and acquisition and disposition of cargoes on their behalf (and also on his own) in the America-Europe trade.

Robert watched the rapid growth of cotton as a commodity during his youth and saw what a bonanza it was. He wanted in.

*An Antebellum Life At Sea*

*Portrait of Robert H. Dixey, his wife Jane Oliver Minge Dixey, and their children Anna Ladd Dixey (b. 1853) and Robert H. Dixey, Jr. (b. 1855). Painted about 1857 in France, where both children were born, and currently owned by Edgar Dixey of New Orleans.*

Thomas Fettyplace and Robert Dixey were very close in their youth, living two blocks apart. They both went to Marblehead Academy, a very early private "prep" school. It must have been one of the first coed schools of its type, although the classes were only partially coeducational: the girls sat on one side of the room and the boys on the other. The school was founded in 1788, and Robert Dixey's "Unkle Hooper" and Fettyplace's maternal grandfather Devereux were among the original trustees. They both took what would now be "college-preparatory" courses (math, English, Latin, French, and history). Although they left Marblehead and didn't go to college, they were quite well "lettered" for that period.

Tom and Robert seems to have been extremely similar in many ways. They both were aggressive and decisive in business; they both maintained an active social life in both North and South; both traveled frequently. Moreover, the search for additional wealth was constant and enjoyable for both; risk taking, if the conditions were reasonable, never bothered them.

They had many joint ventures, of which the story of this ship is only one. Dress and style were important to them—they always tried to look successful. Even at age twelve, Robert H. Dixey liked style: when he wrote his name on the attic door, he called himself "R. Hooper Dixey." This kid had a certain flair.

Tom left for Mobile in the 1830s, and Robert Dixey went to New York City. They kept in close touch through the years, as you will see.

Young Fettyplace's aunt and uncle were well established in Mobile and gave him a head start. He immediately became a "wharfinger" (dockmaster) in partnership with Duke W. Goodman, a young man from Virginia and a real "comer."

On one of Robert Dixey's trips south to see his friend Tom, he was introduced to a Mobile belle named Jane Minge, daughter of Collier Minge. Things went well between Miss Minge and the Yankee entrepreneur. In February 1852, Robert Dixey married her and carried her off to New York City.

RHD was a very personable, social, and pleasant type. His sense of humor and enjoyment of being involved with people made it easy for him to succeed in his endeavors. He loved to give presents and to see new places. Food and drink were important to him, and he always traveled first class when possible. Parties, dances, and fancy dining were all things he enjoyed.

His religion rested less heavily on his shoulders than it did, say, on his brother Richard's. Perhaps it was just his cheerful, humorous manner—he did put his faith in "the Almighty," but only on a limited, broad-minded basis. His friend Tom Fettyplace always leaned toward Unitarianism; perhaps Robert also favored it in principle.

He was a devoted husband and father. From his letters and his wife's it is clear that "Mr. D." and "Jennie" were very much in love and remained so. Their two children were loved but not spoiled. The character he tried to instill in his children served them well in later life.

Although a Yankee by birth, having spent much time in the South and married a Southern girl, RHD respected the belief that slavery was the South's problem, and Southerners should be allowed to solve it. This position was not shared by most of his family, which caused a strain in their relations—but not a breaking strain!

## CAPTAIN RICHARD WILLIAM DIXEY

Richard William Dixey (RWD), born in Marblehead in 1809, was the second son of Captain John Dixey and went to sea at an early age. At age thirty-three, he married one of the "girls next door." Rebecca Gardner, eleven years his junior, had grown up on the other side of the Old North Church, one of six sisters. Another of these was Sarah Jane, who plays a central part in this story.

RWD had two children. Richard Cowell, named for his maternal grandfather,

An Antebellum Life At Sea

*Captain Richard William Dixey (1809–1860), master of the clipper ship* Robert H. Dixey, *and his wife, Rebecca Gardner Dixey (1820–1896), who often accompanied him on long voyages. This Daguerreotype is probably the last photo of them together, and almost certainly the last picture of him. He was about 45 years old, and she was about 33. They looked much like this in 1857 when the* Dixey *went to Russia with the baby Fannie aboard and cousin Sarah Jane Girdler along to be her nanny. Captain Dixey was about 5 feet, 5 inches tall, average for the time, heavily built and extremely strong. We have no knowledge of any health problems during his life time. Rebecca Dixey lived in good health until 1896, and died in Marblehead. Photo courtesy of Mrs. Daphne Brooks Prout, great-granddaughter of Captain Dixey.*

was born in 1844. In 1854 a daughter, Fannie, was born. This unfortunate child lived only five years, much of the time in poor health. Her symptoms suggest what we now know as cystic fibrosis.

Captain RWD commanded many large and fast ships in worldwide trade. He was a superb navigator. Until his death in 1860, he kept special logs for Lt. M. F. Maury, USN, to aid in creating the "Ocean Wind and Current Charts" which are still in use today.

Dixey was also known for the way he ran his ship, especially in his dealings with the crew. In today's terms, he would be considered a good personnel manager. Hiring a ship's crew was strictly the responsibility of the captain. Sometimes he designated a mate to "sign on" members of the crew, but most experienced captains had a reputation that preceded their needs and either helped or hindered in pursuing the recruitment of seamen.

In Dixey's case, having sailed in the Boston and New York areas as a captain for more than twenty years, he had minimum problems. He commanded large, fast ships, paid good wages, fed well, and seldom had any injuries aboard. Dixey's religious beliefs attracted a certain type. He was also "color-blind" in the sense that he did not discriminate on the basis of race, and seamen knew that he didn't permit abuse by anyone. Necessary discipline was maintained, but treatment was humane and equitable. Bahamian natives of all shades of color seemed to be attracted to Captain Dixey's ships and passed the word to their friends and relatives. By the time of the *Dixey*, the majority of his deck hands were islanders. Since they knew and trusted him, he tried to keep them employed. As often as not, his crew members would "ship over" (sign on for another voyage) with him if they could, a rare circumstance for the times.

We know that RWD had some artistic calling, as he left three drawings, two of which appear to be of "Old Ironsides." The first must have been drawn while he was a teenager, as it is scratched into an attic door in the old Dixey family home, which still stands on Washington Street in Marblehead. Many of his brothers and sisters scratched their names in the same door. The second work [adjacent] is a pencil sketch of the same ship, signed by Captain Dixey and dedicated to "Mr. Richard Beck, esq." We know that Beck was a cotton "weigher" in Mobile at that time. RWD probably got to know him well. Beck died in Mobile in 1871. The sketch hangs in the Museum of the City of Mobile.

We know from the Maury logs that RWD was a real pro. Maury was trying to determine the wind and current pattern of the oceans as the months and seasons elapsed. He was not interested in extraneous comment in these logs, but he left a special column for captains to write comments. It is hard for this writer to imagine how Captain Dixey could have resisted making note of some happenings. For example:

> 1857, noon April 5 until noon April 6, this ship sailed 295 nautical miles.

Although this day's sailing represented an average speed of nearly fourteen statute miles per hour, Captain Dixey failed to comment on this splendid

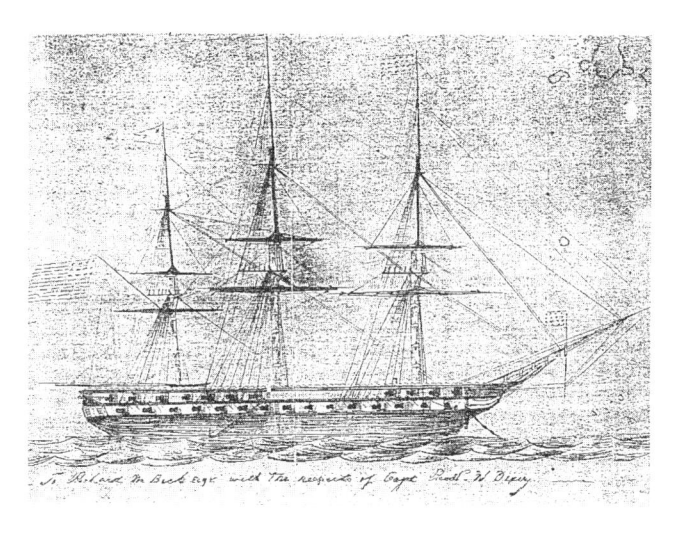

*RWD's pencil sketch of "Old Ironsides," dedicated to "Mr. Richard Beck, esq." Photo courtesy of the Museum of the City of Mobile, which now owns the sketch.*

run in the Maury log. This happened in the Atlantic with the wind abeam; it must have been an exciting "sleighride" that day. The writer became aware of this run when plotting this trip based on the Maury log. How could Captain Dixey have been so modest?

Captain Dixey has to have been the absolute "top of the line" in his profession. His long experience in command of state-of-the-art vessels, his personality and style of command, his true compassion for all creatures, combined into the best example, bar none, of the nineteenth-century seaman.

Captain Dixey was cited several times for risking his ship to come to the aid of others in bad weather. The maritime societies of Philadelphia and Liverpool, among others, honored him publicly. Sarah Jane's journal [Chapter 8] will give our readers many examples of this. He tried to aid any ship in apparent need. Sharing food and water was common, even though by doing so he often depleted his modest reserves to a dangerous level.

Captain Dixey was fully aware of all his responsibilities. Until his dying day, which our readers will share, he stood to his duty to his men and his ship, trusting in God.

## THE MINGE FAMILY

The first Minge to appear in American history is believed to have arrived in Virginia in the early 1600s, probably from Wales. In 1617 King James II granted the "Southampton 100," and about eighty thousand acres of it went to the Minges, who became one of the most powerful and wealthy clans of southern Virginia. For the next five generations, the Minges were among the leaders in the colony. A James Minge was clerk of the House of Burgesses in 1676.

In the 1830s, the Minges formed a useful political connection with John Tyler, who was becoming very aggressive as a landowner at that time and acquiring enormous plantations. By the time he was elected vice-president, he had purchased much land in Charles City County. Tyler was the archetype of the Virginia plantation owner. Massachusetts Senator Daniel Webster said of him: "Tyler is a political sectarian of the slave driving, Virginia Jeffersonian school, principled against all improvements, with the interests and passions and vices of slavery rooted in his moral and political constitution." Tyler had hundreds, perhaps thousands, of slaves. He was aware of all the advantages as well as the disadvantages of slave holding. Strange as it sounds,

Tyler freed many slaves and employed them as sharecroppers on some of his plantations. He was doing this as early as the 1830s. Perhaps he saw something coming in the future. Little is known of the economics of these experiments.

Much of the Virginia land that Tyler purchased was owned by several sons of John Minge. The Minges were looking south and saw cotton in their future. David, George, and Collier Minge all moved to southern Alabama in the 1830s, mostly to land around Demopolis. Among them they acquired more than fifty thousand acres of virgin land near a navigable river. They immediately planted cotton. Brother Collier lived largely in Mobile, where he brokered their crops and looked after the business and financial affairs, while up in the country the younger Minges concentrated on clearing land and growing crops.

*Left, copy of painting of Collier Harrison Minge (1799–1865) by T. W. Sully, 1836, owned by Ruth Lyon Russ (Mrs. G. Price Russ, Jr.), Mobile, a granddaughter of William Henry Harrison Minge. Minge was a grandson of Benjamin Harrison and a nephew of William Henry Harrison. Right, copy of painting of Sarah Harrison Minge (1770–1812), mother of C. H. Minge. The name of the painter and the location of this painting are unknown, but a photo was supplied by Mrs. G. Price Russ.*

One Minge plantation in Alabama, of twenty thousand acres, was named "Weyanoke" after the family home in Virginia. Its main house took seventy-five men seven years to build. After the Civil War this house was used not only as a home but also as a school and a hotel. It finally burned to the ground, and by the end of the nineteenth century, nothing remained.

Collier Minge is the connection of the Minge family to our story of the ship *Dixey*. Collier Minge and his children will appear often in our story, all the way to its end.

Collier Minge had excellent political connections, at least for a while. His mother,

Sarah Harrison, was a sister of President William Henry Harrison, old "Tippecanoe." Vice President John Tyler, who had become a friend of the Minges, quickly succeeded Harrison. In 1844 he appointed Collier Collector of Customs for the Port of Mobile, a very desirable job, but Minge held it for only two years. He was succeeded by someone allied to the Polk administration. John Tyler also sold a trained household "body servant" and his wife to Collier Minge. They are referred to in a letter of 1855 from Collier Minge to Robert H. Dixey. The servants' names were John and Leana Preston.

Collier Minge's oldest child was Jane Oliver Minge, called "Jennie." She married a Dixey from Marblehead and thereby ties these families together. She seems to have been a cool, levelheaded girl with a keen interest in everything, a great sense of humor, and a loving personality. Her letters reveal her soft heart, but she didn't lack spunk. "Women's lib" was unheard of in her time, but it is clear that Jennie's beliefs were not to be ignored by anyone.

Her letters were so long and detailed that we have done some editing, but the charm of this young lady comes through. She was a warm and loyal friend. After the death of Robert Dixey, she kept homes in both Mobile and New Orleans. She was very close to her family in Mobile and often visited the Dixeys in Sharon and Marblehead, Massachusetts.

Her funeral in 1885 brought out Mobile's leading families in large numbers. She lies near Captain Richard Dixey in Magnolia Cemetery.

## THE FETTYPLACE FAMILY

Even though the core of this story is about a ship, a ship has to be created by people. Several members of the Fettyplace family are involved in the story of this ship.

Originally from Normandy, the first "Pheteplace" we know about was a gentleman-in-waiting to William the Conqueror. Many generations later, a William Fettyplace came to Marblehead and married a Hannah Diamond. From this point we know quite a bit about the family. This William had seven children, including Edward (1721–1805). Edward was a member of the "committee of correspondence," served as captain in the Continental army, and fought at the Battle of Bunker Hill—a real patriot. This Edward had a son Edward (1748–1827), who married Mary Jane Williams in 1775 and immediately started producing Fettyplaces. Twenty-five years later, Mary Ann was born. She ties us to the ship.

The youngest of seven, she was spoiled and by age twenty-one was a lot for her mother to handle. She fell in love with Lt. Walter Smith, USA. He was stationed at Fort Sewell, a small post at the mouth of Marblehead Harbor. The spark of love was strong, and the pair made wedding plans. Even though her family was much opposed, Mary Ann wouldn't hear of anything else. She even threatened suicide. She won her point, and in May of 1821 the couple were married. Smith was shortly transferred to Fort Morgan, Alabama.

This move ties the story to Mobile, where Lt. Smith moved after resigning from the Army in the 1830s. Walter Smith became a leader of Mobile, both in business and socially. He commanded the Ninth Alabama Militia, before the Civil War, as a brigadier general. He headed the city banking commission and was Deputy Collector of the Port, a school commissioner, a director of several insurance companies, editor of the *Advertiser*, and a real solid citizen. Walter and Mary Ann had eleven little Smiths, several of whom were Confederate officers and substantial Mobilians.

Mrs. Smith's brother Thomas Fettyplace, up in Marblehead, had several children. Several will be a part of our story. One in particular will be a principal actor. You will hear much about Thomas J. Fettyplace (Tom), born in Marblehead (1816–1871), who was a close boyhood and lifelong friend of Robert H. Dixey. Like Robert, Tom never sailed, fished, or made shoes for a living. Not many men from that town at that time could say that. Like Robert's, his interests were in sales and service lines. His aunt lived in the booming town of Mobile, and, at age twenty-two, he went down there to make his fortune. He was successful.

Henry K. Fettyplace, Tom's younger brother, heard about the boom and soon came down to join the fun. The brothers never married, but they usually lived together, building a series of homes and always selling at a profit when they moved. Henry was principally dealing in coal. Two of their sisters, as well as their aunt, Mrs. Smith, lived in Mobile at the time of our story.

Tom was one of the original investors in the ship *Robert H. Dixey*. He and Robert were the only ones of them who still owned shares in her at the end; each had 25 percent. At the time of loss, all sixteen shares were owned by Mobilians, all associated with shipping in some way. Both Robert and Tom also owned shares in many other ships, as was common at this time.

*Thomas J. Fettyplace (1816–1871). Photo courtesy of Mrs. Annette Daughdrill, Baton Rouge, Louisiana.*

Tom and his brother Henry lived in Mobile until the war. They were substantial citizens and amongst the "in" people. Henry was a member of one of the earliest secret Mardi Gras societies, the Cowbellion de Rakin Society. The membership was a closely guarded secret, but since the society has long been dissolved, it won't harm its memory to reveal Henry Fettyplace's membership.

Tom Fettyplace owned much land in Mobile and its environs. His five-acre home and gardens in Spring Hill were a showplace at the time. His sisters, Louisa and Sarah, made extended visits to Mobile. Louisa married a cotton broker, Herbert C. Peabody, but Sarah returned to Salem, Massachusetts, without finding a mate.

After the war, both Tom and Henry Fettyplace moved back to Salem, Massachusetts. Little is known of the specifics of their move, but postwar Mobile was rocked by troubles for both business and politics. They kept their businesses in Mobile, which were substantial, and traveled back and forth often to look after their interests. Soon after they moved, Henry died in Salem. Tom was already having health problems, and Henry's death was a staggering blow. Tom's health deteriorated steadily. His death is attributed to "bronchitis"—possibly tuberculosis and/or angina. In 1871 he died while in Mobile. He was temporarily buried in Magnolia Cemetery there, but later his remains were moved to Salem, where he lies next to his closest friend, his brother Henry.

Among Tom's belongings was the French painting of the *Dixey*. On his death it passed into his mother's family, the Devereuxs. This painting has changed hands several times but now hangs in the Museum of the City of Mobile, a suitable final resting place. The *Dixey* had called at Mobile eight times in her five years of life. She had carried thirteen million pounds of Mobile cotton from the Port of Mobile. Truly "Mobile" should have been painted across her stern, not "Boston."

## HERBERT CHEEVER PEABODY

We mentioned earlier that Tom's sister Louisa had come down to Mobile. At age thirty-three, she married a recent widower, Herbert Cheever Peabody. He had just lost his wife to yellow fever and had two small children, Horace M. and Emily. Louisa raised them and had a long married life with Peabody. We bring this up because Peabody furnished us with the best glimpse we'll get of Mobile during the *Dixey* period.

Peabody had come to Mobile from Salem in the 1830s, as did another young man, Samuel St. John. When St. John left Mobile, they corresponded, and these letters are preserved in the Wilson Library of the University of North Carolina at Chapel Hill. These letters, which we have studied extensively, were mostly written between 1857 and 1859 and are filled with specifics of the times, especially about cotton.

Peabody had succeeded as a broker in Mobile in the 1840s, but, being perhaps a little greedy, he left to try out the New Orleans market. This venture was unsuccessful, and, after several poor years, he returned to Mobile. Things had changed, and he couldn't get a seat on the Cotton Exchange! This was a low point for Herbert Peabody.

His brothers-in-law, Tom and Henry Fettyplace, supported him during the *Dixey* years and after. He worked as a clerk in Henry's coal office and collected slow accounts, but he hated every minute of it. His friend St. John had a lawsuit going on in Mobile at this time, and Peabody "looked after" his interest. His letters to St. John are intimate, sad, depressing, and sometimes funny, but they tell us what life was like in the South of 1858.

His work for Thomas Fettyplace was apparently more satisfying. Tom traveled often to New York and Boston (by steamer and train as they became available). In his absence, Peabody became his "resident associate" in many family and business matters.

Peabody and his family lived with Tom and Henry both in their house on Conception Street in Mobile (just north of Bienville Square) and later in their lovely home in Spring Hill, across Tuthill Road from the still standing Marshall/Hixon House. Peabody's son, Horace, went off to fight for the Confederacy with the famous Mobilian General Archibald Gracie, alongside Robert E. Lee. His daughter, Emily, married Louis Stein, son of Albert Stein, the builder and owner of the Mobile waterworks. When she had a son, she named him Thomas Fettyplace Stein, out of affection for the man who had helped her father through a very difficult period of his life.

*Emily Peabody Stein, daughter of Herbert C. Peabody and mother of Thomas Fettyplace Stein. Photo courtesy of Emily S. Young, Mobile, Alabama.*

*An Antebellum Life At Sea*

# SARAH JANE GIRDLER

Sarah Jane Girdler (another Jennie) was born in Marblehead in 1839 to Captain John Girdler and his second wife, Sarah Jane Gardner, the second of four children by that marriage. Her father's first wife, Emma Knight, had died in childbirth, leaving Samuel Knight Girdler, her half-brother. Both Sam and his younger half-brother Richard went to sea, like their father and most young men in Marblehead in the 1840s and '50s. You will meet Sam later on. Captain John was a Master Mariner. He commanded ships worldwide, making several voyages "around the Horn" to California and one time getting stuck in San Francisco during the gold rush when his crew went prospecting. He was a cautious skipper. Some thought him unlucky, but he always gave his best.

Captain Girdler's health wasn't too robust. He had a lot of stomach ailments and suffered much. In 1853, after an eighteen-month trip around the world in the bark *George E. Webster,* he sickened and died. His youngest child, Lewis, was four, and Jennie was fourteen.

Captain Girdler hadn't put much aside, so his father-in-law, Abel Gardner, took the family in. His widow started a school for tots, and Jennie went to work making shoes, a new industry growing fast in Marblehead. Little Lewis helped in

*Sarah Jane Girdler (age ten) and her mother, Sarah Jane Gardner Girdler, about 1849. (Courtesy of the author)*

the bakery that his grandfather owned. They were a close-knit, devout family.

When Jennie Girdler's aunt Rebecca Dixey offered her a chance to go to Europe with a load of cotton, she was ecstatic. Captain Dixey had just brought a load of cotton from New Orleans to Boston in the new, fast clipper *Robert H. Dixey*. They were going to discharge it and pick up a load of cast iron railing and miscellaneous hardware for Mobile, where they would load cotton for Europe. It was with the greatest excitement that she quit her shoemaking job and joined the ship's company. Her little cousin Fannie, age two, was to be her special charge.

Jennie was a very warm, friendly, caring person. Her character shines through, and you will feel it as you read her journal of the trip. In later life, she was happily married to Dexter Belknap, a successful businessman. She had no children but was close and helpful to her many nieces and nephews, sending many of them to college. She was a substantial citizen of Louisville, Kentucky. Some years after Belknap's death, she married a man named Whedon. With her second husband she traveled extensively and in 1907 published a book about her travels.

*Abel Gardner (1788–1872) and Jane Bray Gardner (1788–1866), parents of Sarah Jane Gardner Girdler and Rebecca Gardner Dixey. (Photos courtesy of Girdler/Fitch family)*

CHAPTER

*4*

# Building the *Dixey*

By March of 1855, the shipyards of the East Coast, especially New York City and the Boston area, were racing to their death. In only a few years, their lovely greyhounds of the ocean, the "extreme" clippers, would be idled by the hundreds. The express service to California that commanded high freight rates would not be needed. The gold strike in California was playing out. Steam engines were fast being improved. A chapter would soon end. It was in these circumstances that the *Robert H. Dixey* was built and placed in service.

In modern times, we might organize a "limited partnership" with a "managing partner" to finance and direct the building of such a ship. In 1854, the mechanics of the business were similar even if the terminology was different. Robert Dixey first conceived the idea of building a state-of-the-art "medium" clipper*. It would be the best in every way and would sail the Mobile/Europe/East Coast triangle taking cotton to Europe. He then persuaded his brother, Captain Richard Dixey, to be its captain. Richard would participate in the profit, being paid 2.5 percent of the gross income in addition to a salary and expenses.

*"Medium" as used here refers to the length/width ratio. If the ship was more

Robert Dixey then passed the word of his plan to Tom Fettyplace, who naturally wanted in. Paul Curtis, the shipbuilder they selected, came in for another share, and in no time all sixteen shares were subscribed. The original owners were all substantial businessmen from Boston, New York City, Mobile, and New Orleans. They agreed to an advance and progress payments to the builder and to the other usual terms of ship contracting. The original owners were:

| | |
|---|---|
| Robert H. Dixey, New York City | 3/16 share |
| Thomas J. Fettyplace, Mobile | 2/16 share |
| Paul Curtis, Boston | 3/16 share |
| Daniel Deshon and George Deshon, Boston and Mobile | 4/16 share |
| Edward Bergoren DeMeaux, New Orleans | 2/16 share |
| Nicholas Harleston Brown, Boston | 2/16 share |

than six times its breadth in length, it was "extreme." Anything shorter was "medium." The *Dixey*, with a length of 185 feet and breadth of 37.5 feet, had a ratio of 4.93.

Work was commenced in September 1854 and finished the following spring. The ship was registered on April 8, 1855.

The *Dixey* was built at East Boston, Massachusetts, at the yard of Paul Curtis. Curtis built some very fast ships. They were medium clippers of one thousand to fourteen hundred tons, 180 to 195 feet long on deck. The masts rose 180 feet or so above the deck. The lengths of their yards and booms were about the maximum that could be built, using the best lumber available.

The American clippers of the 1850s were built with sawn live oak frames and yellow pine planking. The crooked limbs of large live oaks were extremely valuable for the frames. The builders selected crooks that matched the shape of the hull, and, because they did not have to be bent, the natural strength of the tree limbs was undiminished. The planks of yellow pine were put in a steam box before they were clamped and fastened to the hull. The steam increased the flexibility of the wood to conform to the ship's curves. The *Dixey*'s planks were probably four to five inches thick, and her frames were about eight inches square. Captain Dixey said she was built as "heavily as an eighteen hundred ton ship" even though she was only thirteen hundred. Her bottom would later be covered with copper sheets to resist seaweed, worms, and rot.

We know that Paul Curtis's ships were the best he knew how to build, and with Captain Dixey on hand during the construction and fitting of this one, we know the

*The knarled limbs of this mighty live oak, on the site of the Collier Minge summer home on Mobile Bay, would have made good frames for a ship like the* Dixey. *From the branches of this very tree, the Minges could see the tall masts of the* Dixey *when she was at anchor with the cotton fleet across the bay. This property, just south of Marriott's Grand Hotel, has had several buildings since the Minge home and is owned by Mrs. J. F. McRae.*

best was done. The eight owners had no concern on this score. Although the *Dixey* lasted only five years, it was weather, not construction, that did her in.

The cost of the *Dixey* was more than fifty thousand dollars, and she took six months to build. The masts, yards, sails, and rigging were fabricated across the river by separate firms, but to Paul Curtis's specifications. The ship was launched and towed to its rigging dock, where, in the incredible time of three weeks, its masts, yards, stays, shrouds, and sails were installed and fitted.

My grandfather, a Marbleheader who never went to sea, always said in his jocular way that a ship is referred to as "she" because the rigging costs more than the hull. Wire rope was being used for the standing rigging in the 1850s. Stainless steel had not yet been invented, and protecting the iron wire from corrosion was a problem. It was wrapped with greased twine and painted with tar. Manila, hemp, sisal, and cotton were used for the various applications of running rigging.

The sails were mostly cotton, and the best came from Egypt. The masts and spars were pine logs, hand-planed into shape. And indeed, more expense was involved in the rig and sails than in building the hull.

Most American clippers carried spare sails of various weights and kept the crew busy changing them to try and get more speed, especially in calm periods. Many clipper captains replaced a sail only after it "blew out," and then tried to use a heavier sail.

The design of Paul Curtis's ships was developed from experience of what had worked and not worked in previous designs. The *Robert H. Dixey*'s design of hull and rigging was his most sophisticated at the time. Captain Dixey was delighted with the performance in most ways. The high masts and long yards carried a penalty for the crew, however. She rolled greatly in light breezes and with the wind dead astern.

We don't expect she could have kept up with some of the larger clippers since the inherent hull speed of any ship is a function of her waterline length. The *Robert H. Dixey* was 165 feet on the water, while the *Flying Cloud* and many others were forty to sixty feet longer. From her logs and the letters of her crew and passengers, however, only one other ship on the same course is known to have passed her (the ship *Empress* 5 May 1857 Mobile to London). The captain blamed this embarrassment on the "stretched condition" of his sails after extended heavy weather. From the frequent references in the *Dixey*'s logs and Sarah Jane Girdler's journal of ships coming "up" ahead and dropping "down" astern, it is evident that the *Dixey* passed most other vessels. After passing a French clipper that was "a very fast sailor," Sarah Jane remarks that, "We went so fast that it seemed more like flying than going through the water."

About the time the *Dixey* was rigged originally, a ship captain named Robert Bennett Forbes conceived a slightly different rig that quickly became popular in Europe. It was called the "double topsail" rig. The lowest sail on a square-rigger is called the *sail* or *course*. The sail above that is the *topsail*. In the Forbes rig, it is called the "lower topsail." Above it is set the "upper topsail." In the early rigs, the two sails were combined into one larger topsail, occupying the same space. Above the topsail (or sails) is always the *topgallant sail* (t'gallant-s'l), above which is the *royal*. On some very large square-rigged ships, a sail above the royal was called the "sky" sail, and, in a few cases, a still higher sail was called the "moon" sail.

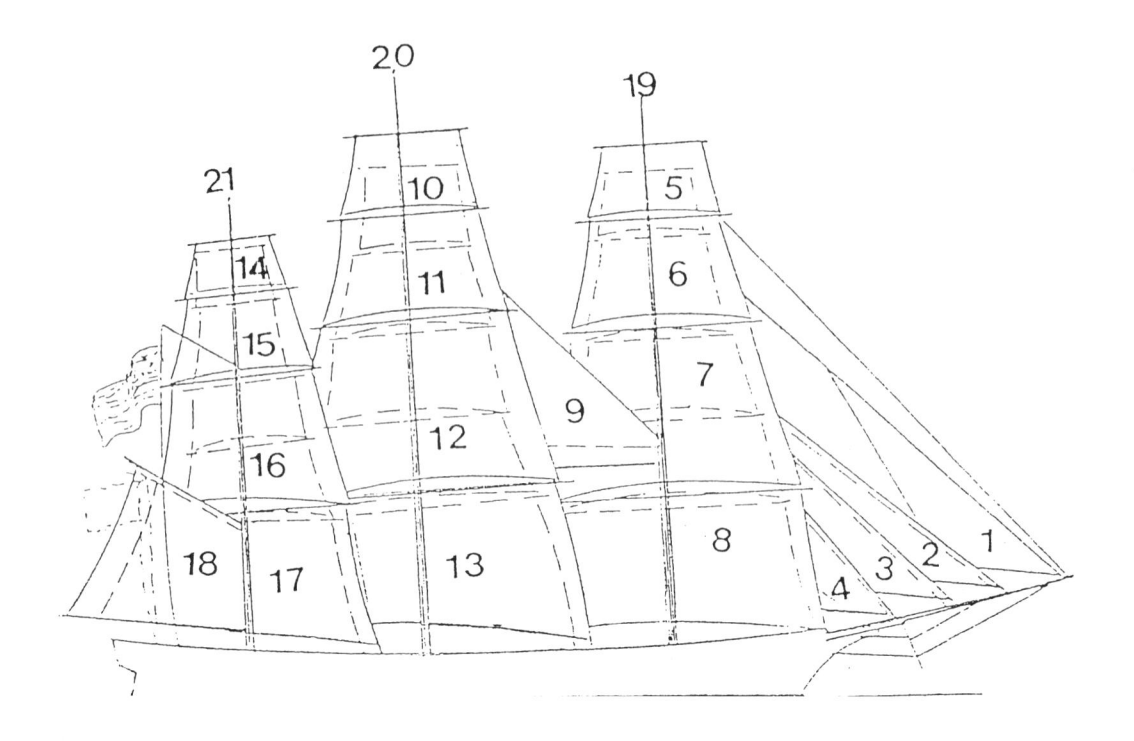

*This sketch by the author depicts the* Robert H. Dixey's *original 1855 rig in solid lines; the broken lines indicate the rig installed after the Dixey was dismasted in a hurricane in the Bay of Biscay, October 1857. A double topsail was added and all sails were reduced in size by 15 percent. The numbered sail and mast names are:*

| | | |
|---|---|---|
| 1–Flying Jib | 2–Outer Jib | 3–Inner Jib |
| 4–Fore Staysail | 5–Fore Royal | 6–Fore Topgallant |
| 7–Fore Topsail | 8–Fore Sail | 9–Main Topgallant Staysail |
| 10–Main Royal | 11–Main Topgallant | 12–Main Topsail |
| 13–Mainsail | 14–Mizzen Royal | 15–Mizzen Topgallant |
| 16–Mizzen Topsail | 17–Mizzen | 18–Spanker |
| 19–Fore Mast | 20–Main Mast | 21–Mizzen Mast |

As with most rigs, there were advantages and disadvantages to the Forbes rig. The double topsails were smaller—therefore easier to furl and reef—and gave the ship several more combinations of sail and center of lateral resistance. On the minus side, the extra yards and running rigging reduced the sail efficiency and added extra weight aloft and more work in case of sudden increase of wind or other emergency. Overall, however, the Forbes double topsails must have been clearly better, for nearly every square-rigged ship built from 1860 on, even naval vessels, used double topsails.

The *Dixey*'s original rig was more sail than she could carry in any but the lightest of air, or with the wind far aft. When she had the wind abeam or close-hauled, she had to be "shortened" down or the extreme angle of heel spilled so much wind that she lost speed.

After her dismasting in the Bay of Biscay in October 1857, Captain Dixey made several important changes in his ship's rig. First, he cut down the sizes of all sails by about 15 percent. He cut the heights of the masts by the same amount. He shortened the booms and yards proportionately. He went to the Forbes double topsail rig. He eliminated the outer jib and shortened the jib and spanker booms. He eliminated the

*The* New World, *a "Blue Swallowtail" packet (1846). Photo courtesy of Peabody Essex Museum, Salem, Massachusetts.*

signal gaff and flew the ship's colors from the spanker gaff. The illustration on page 48 shows the visual differences between the *Dixey*'s first and second rigs.

The net result of these changes was to lower the center of effort substantially and give her captain more options in suiting her rig to the existing weather. This maximized her speed and safety, an advantage when using a small crew of twenty or so men.

Captain Dixey had had excellent training and experience in fast sailing ships. Immediately before the *Robert H. Dixey* he was master of the *Houqua*, one of the earliest and most successful "extreme" clippers. A. A. Low & Bros., owners of the *Houqua,* hired only the best. Obviously, Captain Dixey was considered the best to be given command of the very famous *Houqua*. This ship was only 143 feet long and six hundred tons burden, but on her maiden voyage in 1844 the famous captain Nat Palmer raced her from New York City to China in ninety-five days, a record trip.

Before the *Houqua*, RWD captained the *New World,* the *Elvira Harbeck*, and the *Montreal*. The *New World* packet was one of the fastest on the New York–Liverpool run. For more than twenty years she served Liverpool and from 1867 to 1880 served London and New York.

The *New World* was not considered a clipper, but Donald McKay*, who built her, gave her a lot of speed for a fourteen hundred-ton packet. Mainly she carried three hundred immigrants to New York in addition to her general cargo. Students of "square-riggers" will note that the photo on page 49, taken in her later years, shows her carrying the Forbes "double topsail" rig. This change was made some years after she was built.

*McKay also built the world-famous *Flying Cloud* in 1851.

In the late 1840s, Captain Dixey also commanded the *Elvira Harbeck*, a small but fast packet barque. His last five commands were:

| | | |
|---|---|---|
| 1847 | Ship *New World*, | 1,400 tons |
| 1848 | Barque *Elvira Harbeck*, | 349 tons |
| 1851 | Ship *Montreal*, | 650 tons |
| 1853 | Ship *Houqua*, | 600 tons |
| 1855 | Ship *Robert H. Dixey*, | 1,252 tons. |

*The* Houqua *(1844–1866?). Photo courtesy of Peabody Essex Museum, Salem, Massachusetts. Most students of America's "extreme" clippers believe the* Houqua *to have been among the earliest. Captain Richard W. Dixey took her around the world in 1853/4, from New York City to San Francisco to Foo Chow (China) and back to New York. Many commercial ships in the mid-nineteenth century painted "gun ports" on their topsides to discourage pirates in the Indies. It would have been a mistake to attack the* Houqua *believing her to have used this ruse: some of her gun ports were real. She carried eight cannon and would have been a difficult prize for a pirate to take. RIGHT, daguerrotype of Captain Dixey, early 1840s. Photo courtesy Mrs. Daphne B. Prout.*

CHAPTER

# 5

# Life Aboard the *Dixey*

*The *Sea Cloud* was built for Marjorie Post (Mrs. E. F.) Hutton in Germany in 1932. It measures 315 by 50 by 18 feet. Since 1980, it has been used as a cruise ship in the Mediterranean in summer and the Caribbean in winter. The author rode it from Antigua to Cadiz in April 1984.

    The narrator of this story had the good fortune in 1984 to cross the Atlantic on a large "square-rigged" sailing ship. True, it was a yacht\*, but during the three weeks we "sailed," the magic of sea life on a large clipper was revealed to us.

    Our personal experiences of ocean crossings in many types and sizes of vessels, from the *Queen Mary*, one thousand feet long, down to a wooden tug, at 135 feet, tell us that in average weather a square-rigged ship is the quietest, smoothest-riding, most comfortable way to travel the sea. The balance of the sails reduces the ship's motion to a relaxing rise and fall, with minimal rolling or pitching. Insomnia isn't a problem!

    Now we'll tell you in some detail about life aboard the *Dixey*. Turn your clocks back to 1855, and welcome aboard!

    The diagram on page 54 shows the plan of the *Robert H. Dixey*. The "forecastle" where the crew lived was located in a separate deckhouse on the forward part of the main deck. It housed about twenty people, the working deck crew. In the stern section of the main deck was the "cabin." In it were housed eight to twenty people. The captain and officers, the passengers, and the stewards were berthed here, and below the deck near the cabin was a space for the "ship's boys." The boys were bright young men of fifteen to eighteen years who would be developed into mates and captains in time. Like midshipmen in the Navy, they had to do the meanest, dirtiest jobs. They were paid almost nothing and were held to the highest standards of seamanship and conduct. They were fed by the steward but usually ate in their quarters below.

The ship's cook fed the crew from the same galley used by the steward to feed the officers and passengers. The menu for the latter was somewhat better than the crew normally received.

The diet wasn't too bad. The oven was always hot, burning hard coal. Bread, cakes, pies, and cookies could be baked in all but the worst weather. Dried meats, fish, vegetables, and fruit were carried in quantity. Salt fish and meat needed soaking but were very nutritious. Fruit and eggs were carried for a week or two. They were replenished at every opportunity: when the ship was sailing close to land, "bum boats" sailed out and sold perishables, and fishermen would help out if the weather was calm enough. Still, sometimes several weeks went by without such fresh items.

Under the raised deck at the bow of the ship (the topgallant forecastle), she carried livestock. Pigs, chickens, geese, and the like could be eaten to vary the menu. All hands shared fresh meat, fish, and fowl, as there was no refrigeration. When a pig was slaughtered or a fish caught, it was eaten in a day or two, and everybody had some. All in all, the food aboard the *Dixey* was pretty good.

The bathing and toilet facilities were close to today's standards. Salt water tanks above the bathrooms provided a gravity flush. The tubs of copper were not too smooth, but soap was available, and, with hot water added from the stove in the dining room, you could keep about even with your hygiene.

The dining room had a large skylight that kept it airy and light in good weather. A glass-paneled door and two fairly large windows provided a view looking forward. The large dining table had ten fixed armchairs, four on each side and one at each end. At night, polished brass lamps burning coal oil swung from their brackets, giving the cabin a cheerful look.

Aft of the dining room was the lounge, which also boasted a skylight. It contained a beautiful parlor organ, fastened to the bulkhead, and two library tables, also fastened down. Several upholstered couches and chairs completed this beautifully decorated room. It was the hub of social activity.

Bookshelves and cabinets of various kinds lined the cabin bulkheads. Flush with the deck in the cabin was a hatch that led down to a storeroom where the ship's safe and valuables were kept. It also contained what the ship carried in the way of guns and ammunition.

*Deck plan of the* Robert H. Dixey, *built 1855 in East Boston by Paul Curtis, 185 feet x 38 feet; draft 18 feet. Detail based on painting of the ship and references in letters, logs, and journals of the passengers and master.*

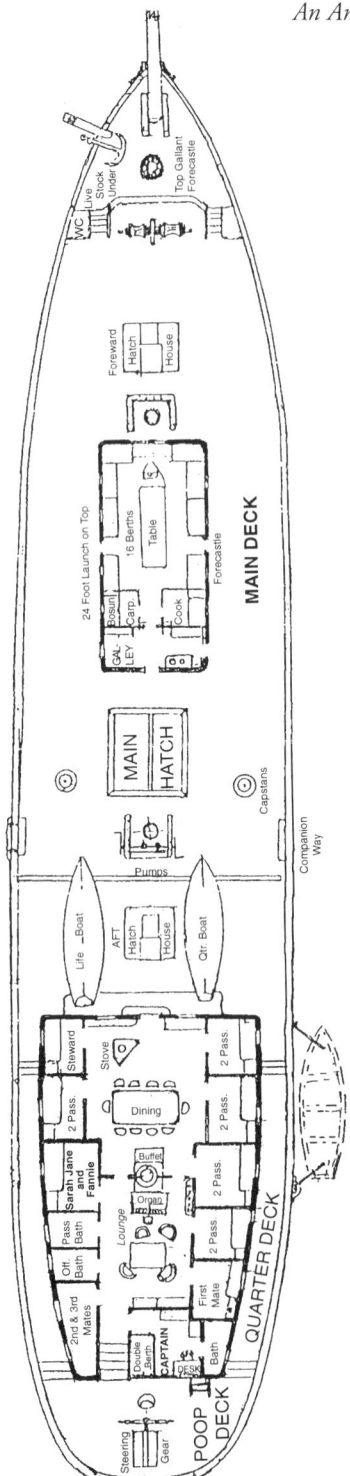

Along both sides of the cabin were small sleeping rooms, each about six feet square. The furnishings comprised an upper and a lower berth, a small chest of drawers, some wall hooks, and some rings in the bulkhead for tying trunks and boxes. A single window about eighteen inches square, hinged at the top to swing in, provided the light and ventilation for these rooms. Outside the cabin was a shutter that slid across the window to protect it in bad weather. This might sound a little spartan, but at the time it was the best Boston shipyards knew how to do. The quality of the wood craftmanship and painting was elegant even by today's standards, and Captain Richard Dixey kept the ship looking this way!

On the deck above the cabin, the large skylights provided backs for seats in which the passengers could watch the sea and pass the time in good weather. Sunbathing wasn't in vogue in those days—rather, the opposite: parasols were used to keep from "freckling." Reading, writing, sewing, singing, and, of course, talking filled the days. *Mal de mer* really wasn't much of a problem, as a sailing ship is much steadier than a power vessel and generally very quiet and smooth in its motion. The day's run (distance traveled) became of great interest. As the voyage progressed, gambling on arrivals was, even then, a popular pastime.

The captain and mates instructed the "boys" in navigation and seamanship. Sometimes the passengers would help with hoisting or trimming a sail. Checking the ship's speed by streaming a "log" was another job that amateurs could help with. Signals were usually exchanged with ships going in opposite directions. They reported these on reaching port, and newspapers published these bits of news.

The practice of carrying passengers on sailing ships was fast dying out at the time of the *Dixey*. Although there were still sailing "packets" that carried immigrants who wanted cheap transportation and would put up with primitive accommodation, steamers and sail/steam combination ships that advertised regularly scheduled trips diverted most of the business travel. The *Dixey* made several trips on which she carried no passengers.

As clippers went, in the cotton trade, the *Dixey* was one of the fastest. Her record indicates that she averaged about 150 miles per day, about six knots. The best run for which we have a record was on a trip to St. Petersburg, when she ran 295 miles during a twenty-four-hour period, a speed of better than twelve knots.

The most frustrating part of square-rigger sailing was trying to sail into port against the wind. The best square-rigged clippers could only point twelve to fifteen degrees into the wind. With the leeway (side slippage) caused by the wave action and the small keel beneath the bottom, holding even was all they could do. In light winds and shallow water, most ships would anchor and wait for a fair wind; sometimes they waited days and days.

But for all their trouble into the wind, the square-rigged clippers could really move going with it. It was many more years after the *Dixey* before a steamer on the high seas could match some of the good runs under sail. Finding the best ocean winds and currents was the life's work of Lieutenant M. F. Maury, USN. And our Captain Dixey helped supply him with data whenever he sailed "offshore." Maury's charts and recommended routes cut the average sailing time nearly in half.

While we're looking at the *Dixey* at sea, let's take a look at the economies of shipping under sail in 1855. They were very enticing!

Freight charges for cotton from Mobile to Europe (England or France) were about twenty dollars per ton. The *Dixey* carried 875 tons and thus produced a potential gross revenue of $17,500. Each voyage took an average of forty-five days en route plus fifteen days for loading and unloading. The expenses of similar ships at this time were about four thousand dollars per month, allowing for everything, including insurance (except for public liability). Fairburn's *History of American Sail* estimates the expenses for a twelve hundred-ton medium clipper as follows (revenue for miscellaneous freight was equal to that for cotton):

### EXPENSE PER MONTH

| | |
|---|---:|
| Direct Labor | 600.00 |
| Various Insurance | 400.00 |
| Depreciation (Rig and Hull) | 1,000.00 |
| Maintenance and Repair | 1,000.00 |
| Food and Supplies | 1,000.00 |
| Total | $4,000.00 |

So it is obvious that, unless the trip took twice as long, the operation would be very profitable. The *Dixey* was quite fast and frequently exceeded the estimated speed. Her average return on the fifty thousand dollars invested was in the range of forty thousand dollars per year, so she undoubtedly paid for herself several times over in her five years of operation.

The shares of ownership changed constantly; Robert Dixey and Tom Fettyplace were the only original shareholders who held on until the end.

CHAPTER

# 6

# The *Dixey* in Port

Our faithful readers should know a little more about the function of the *Dixey*, and so we will look at what happened when the ship was in port.

The *Dixey* had no steam power aboard. Steam would come soon, but in 1855 everything still had to be done with muscle. Cotton was a very light product when picked. It was bagged in the field and dragged to a mule-drawn wagon that transported it to the cotton gin, usually in the nearest village. After the gin had removed the hulls and seeds, the raw cotton was lightly baled with string and burlap. These bales measured six by four by three feet or larger and weighed five hundred pounds!

The bales were piled in warehouses or under tarpaulins, to keep off the rain, until a steamer took them downriver to Mobile. There they were squeezed by steam presses that reduced their bulk. Though their weight was still the same five hundred pounds, their volume had been reduced by about 60 percent, so that they now measured about two by three by five feet. Mobile's presses could reduce seven thousand bales a day, about equal to two large ship cargoes.

In the rush of the booming business in cotton, the early years were troubled. Stories of the 1840s and later are filled with details of business crime. The cotton wagons were weighed at the gin, then emptied and the wagon reweighed to arrive at the net weight. Keeping the planters from adding a little foreign matter was a prob-

*An Antebellum Life At Sea*

lem for the gin; it caused breakage in the machinery, and the short weight showed up in the value the planter claimed.

Foreign matter was also thrown into the bale after ginning and was harder to find on inspection. Taking samples of the bales was much needed. The city government regulated the size, weight, and quality of cotton bales, to insure customer satisfaction in Europe and elsewhere. In spite of the inspection by the city, the record indicates that the inspectors could be involved in the fraud.

The federal courts of Mobile and New Orleans settled many a claim from factors, brokers, planters, and shippers, both local and worldwide. Things got better, though, and both cities established a reputation for their cotton. By the time of the *Dixey*, when "Mobile Cotton" was stamped on the burlap wrapping of a bale, it was a commodity valued worldwide, and the price was quoted on the commodities market, even as it is today.

In 1855, at the corner of St. Michael and Commerce streets in the heart of Mobile's business district, stood the one hundred-member Cotton Exchange. It had evolved as cotton had, and, like the New York Stock Exchange on Wall Street in New York City, it dominated commerce in its town. At the time of the *Dixey*, very little cotton was sold that was not sold on its trading floor. Only members could use its facilities, and outsiders couldn't even watch.

*The Mobile Cotton Exchange as it appeared in 1885. Though this building is somewhat larger and more ornate than the 1855 version, it occupied the same corner of St. Michael and Commerce streets. Interstate 210 runs over this spot now. Photo courtesy of the Caldwell Delaney Collection.*

The Exchange consisted of factors and brokers who dealt in current crops and futures. Contracts were made up to a year in advance with the planters, through their agents, usually their factor. The planter got an advance on his crop, at an agreed price, up to a year before the actual delivery.

Most large planters dealt with the same factor year after year. For a commission, he insured the crop from the time it went into a wagon, to the gin, through shipping, compressing, storage, and delivery to the ship or rail car. Most factors had good bank credit and made frequent loans to planters. Many planters lacked business discipline and didn't fare too well. Most of the mansions on Government Street were built by wealth created dealing in cotton rather than growing it.

Many of the lovely antebellum homes on the actual plantations often housed their families in splendid poverty. Food was not often a problem, but hard cash usually was. Slave labor appeared to be low-cost, but problems were many. By the time of the *Dixey,* importing slaves had about stopped. The last load of slaves arrived on the *Clothilde* in 1859, very late in history. The slave issue would soon be resolved.

By 1855 the Port of Mobile was served by steam vessels, both sidewheelers and sternwheelers. They carried the pressed bales down to the ships waiting in the anchorage. Generally the *Dixey* crew was used to furnish the labor to lower the bales into the hold. A crew of specialists, called "cotton screwers," using special jacks and levers, packed as many bales into the ship as possible without breaking its ribs (sometimes they unknowingly did this, with deadly results).

The cargo of 3500 bales weighed about nine hundred tons, not a heavy load for this ship. It could carry at least thirteen hundred tons of metal products and sail better by being deeper in the water.

When the cotton arrived at its destination, the sailors were again required to "turn to" and bring it up to the deck, where others took it ashore. Naturally, the crew then had to load the cargo they were to take home.

Sarah Jane makes minimal reference to these commercial activities in port. She was usually doing what tourists normally do—and shopping with the captain's wife, her Aunt Becca.

CHAPTER

7

# Early Days of the *Dixey*

### MAIDEN VOYAGE

As the tug pulled the *Dixey* away from the Boston dock late on the 8th of April, 1855, the smiles were very broad on the faces of at least two of the ship's company. Robert Dixey and Captain Richard Dixey were beginning to realize a dream. The best that money could buy in a "medium" clipper was finally off to carry out its destiny.

As we have told our readers, Robert Dixey was a nineteenth-century "jet setter." He moved around a great deal in his capacity as a merchant and agent for Harbeck & Co. In the early spring of 1854 he returned to Mobile from France, bringing Jane and little seven-month-old Anna. They all stayed with her parents in their large house at 118 Conti Street (now the site of the Saenger Theatre).

Although staying with her Presbyterian family, Jane evidently decided to join her husband's family church, Christ Episcopal, where she was confirmed on March 26, 1854, by the Reverend Mr. N. H. Dobbs.

In addition to his regular business, Robert Dixey also handled the business affairs associated with financing and registering the new ship *Dixey*. He was frequently in Boston and New York as well as Mobile and New Orleans. In March 1855, he bought a small office building on Conception Street in Mobile, just off Conti, only two blocks from Tom Fettyplace's office on the same street. The site of Robert Dixey's office building is now occupied by the restaurant, Bienville Bistro. In late March Dixey went up to Boston for the registration of their ship and joined it for its maiden trip to Mobile.

On April 30, the telegraph at Fort Morgan signaled the approach of the *Dixey*. It is a reasonable assumption that all the Minges, Fettyplaces, and Dixeys who could make it gathered aboard the *Natchez,* a steamer that serviced the local anchorages, and went down the bay to welcome the sparkling new cotton clipper.

With its valuable cargo of cast-iron railings and posts, its well-trained Bahamian crew and Marblehead mates, not to mention the great speed that the ship had shown coming down from Boston, the Dixey brothers had plenty of reasons to feel very confident about their enterprise.

Collier Minge had 3,500 bales of high-priced cotton ready for France. In only six weeks, the *Dixey* had sailed from Boston to Mobile and been unloaded, reloaded with cotton, and made ready for sea.

The pregnant Mrs. Robert H. Dixey was finding her 21-month-old daughter a lot to handle and was able with very little difficulty to persuade her seventeen-year-old sister to accompany them back to France. Maria was thrilled: she was to spend two-and-a-half years with her sister and brother-in-law in France. You'll hear more about her later; she was a big help at a time when Jane needed her.

The ship reached Le Havre in early June, and the Robert Dixeys went right up to Paris. The ship remained in Le Havre where its bottom was covered with copper.* While this was being done, Robert Dixey was busy finding a cargo. Although the "Charge of the Light Brigade" had taken place a year earlier, the Crimean War was still on, and Robert got a contract to carry freight to the Black Sea for the French government.

On September 14, 1855, the ship sailed for Kamiesch, on the Black Sea. After spending two months in Marseilles looking for cargo, the ship left the Mediterranean in ballast and returned to Mobile, arriving April 27, 1856, just a year from its departure on its first cotton trip.

*Coppering the bottom of a pine-planked ship would at least triple its life. Teak wood is resistant to the worms that infest pine, but it was prohibitively expensive at this time, so copper was the best solution.

## SUBSEQUENT TRIPS

The reader should know that the data so neatly tabulated in the chart on the opposite page represent hundreds of hours of patient searching. It was necessary to examine old records of American ports, the maritime pages of many newspapers, the logs of the ship, and custom house records of several foreign ports. The dates are accurate! We believe it to be very unusual to find such detailed knowledge of the movements of a ship in the mid–nineteenth century.

Winnifred Pierce used many sources in painstakingly compiling the chart. The actual proof comes from letters of the owner, the captain's wife, some passengers and crew members, and other owners and close relatives. We are lucky that these exist to help tell the story of this ship and these times. Another valuable find, in the collection of the Local History and Genealogy Division of the Mobile Public Library, was *Passengers and Crew Arriving Port of Mobile, 1841–1860.* This book contains the following crew list of the *Dixey* on a voyage from Boston, arriving in Mobile in February 1857:

*Indicates on crew list at Bordeaux in October 1857.

†Robert Minge has not been identified. If he was related to Mrs. Robert H. Dixey, we don't know it.

#Died in Vyborg in July 1857 (heart disease).

Also on board, though not listed, were: Sarah Jane Girdler, Fannie Callamore, Mrs. Rebecca Dixey, and Fannie Dixey.

*Rich. W. Dixey, Master
*Frank Millet, 2d Mate
*Geo. Rice, Carpenter
*Wm. H. Steele, Boy
*George Williams, Boatswain
*Henry Jackson, Seaman
†Robt. Minge, Seaman
*Augustine Seliger, Seaman
*Levin Pendley, Seaman
*Janais Haliard, Seaman
*William White, Seaman
*Horatio Kate, Seaman
*Isiah Ork, Seaman
#William Butlier, Seaman
*David L. Glash, Seaman

*Dexter Collamon, Mate
*Danl. Symmonds, 3d Mate
*John Hobart, Steward
*George Steele, Boy
*Danl. Short, Cook
*Isaac Hall, Seaman
*Allen Glash, Seaman
*Robt. Harris, Seaman
*Adolph C. Sherreff, Seaman
*William Mulligan, Seaman
*Ariel Jackson, Seaman
*Charles Jenkins, Seaman
*James Swinston, Seaman
*Alex Relley, Seaman

Given under our hands and seals, at the City of Mobile, 9 Feb. 1857. Richd. W. Dixey, Sam Rinyers, Chas. F. Quina.

# CHRONOLOGY OF THE VOYAGES OF THE *ROBERT H. DIXEY*

## 1855

### MARCH
Launched at East Boston

### APRIL
3 Permanently registered at Boston
8 Depart Boston
30 Arrive Mobile

### MAY
25 Cleared for LeHavre

### JULY
4 In port at LeHavre

### AUGUST
Coppered at LeHavre

### SEPTEMBER
14 Depart LeHavre for Constantin

### NOVEMBER
12 Arrive Kamiesch
29 Depart Kamiesch

## 1856

### FEBRUARY
19 Arrive Marseilles

### MARCH
16 Depart Marseilles

### APRIL
27 Arrive Mobile

### MAY
31 Depart Mobile

### JULY
Arrive LeHavre

### AUGUST
8 Depart LeHavre
21 Arrive Cadiz

### SEPTEMBER
6 Depart Cadiz

### OCTOBER
28 Arrive New Orleans

### DECEMBER
10 Depart New Orleans

## 1857

### JANUARY
13 Permanently registered, Boston
14 Depart Boston

### FEBRUARY
4 Arrive Mobile

### MARCH
16 Depart Mobile

### MAY
24 Off Elsinore

### JUNE
5 Arrive Cronstadt
30 Depart Cronstadt

### JULY
2 Arrive Vyborg
30 Depart Vyborg

### AUGUST
20 Arrive Bordeaux

### OCTOBER
4 Depart Bordeaux
7 Dismasted in hurricane in Bay of Biscay
10 Return to Bordeaux for repairs

### DECEMBER
11 Depart Bordeaux for second time

## 1858

### JANUARY
25 Arrive Mobile

### MARCH
1 Depart Mobile

### APRIL
8 Arrive LeHavre

### MAY
20-21 Depart LeHavre

### JUNE
26 Arrive Mobile

### SEPTEMBER
4 Depart Mobile

### OCTOBER
27 Arrive Liverpool

### NOVEMBER
22 Depart Liverpool

## 1859

### JANUARY
25 Arrive Philadelphia

### MARCH
11 Arrive Mobile

### SEPTEMBER
9 Depart Mobile

### OCTOBER
17 At Liverpool
25 Depart Liverpool

## 1860

### JANUARY
16 Arrive Mobile

### MARCH
9 Depart Mobile

### MAY
23 Depart Liverpool

### JULY
2 Arrive New York

### AUGUST
15 Depart New York

### SEPTEMBER
15 Foundered in Mobile Bay

Compiled by Winnifred P. Pierce

We don't know absolutely whether any of the "hands" made all the voyages of the *Dixey,* but it is certain that she never weighed anchor or cast off her dock lines except under the command of Richard W. Dixey, her only master.

Some examples of significant correspondence relating to the *Dixey* are reproduced below and in the following chapters and appendices. Transcribing these letters was quite a challenge. To begin with, all of the source documents are old and usually faded, brittle and very fragile. They are difficult to read, but the author and the other two primary researchers on this project, Reynolds Girdler and Winnifred Pierce, all helped to decipher the handwriting. In some cases, no matter how hard we tried, passages were illegible to us. In this account, we have indicated those passages in the letters by the use of ellipsis points ( . . . ).

*From left, Tracy Girdler, Reynolds Girdler, and Winnifred Pierce, all second cousins and relatives of Sarah Jane Girdler. This photo was made in September 1976.*

## FROM COLLIER MINGE, JUNE 23, 1855

This letter from Collier Harrison Minge was written to his son-in-law, Robert Hooper Dixey, who was aboard the *Dixey* on its maiden voyage. (Minge's letter went by steamer to await RHD's arrival in France.) The envelope reads: "To Ro. H. Dixey, Esq, care of Masquillier Fils &c, Havre, France." A cancellation shows "Jun 24, Mobile." Another, smaller cancellation is very smudged but is possibly a French stamp. Also, one can make out "PAID" and the number "21."

Mobile–June 23/55

R. H. Dixey–Esq
Havre

We have the Asia's news: . . . advance for the . . . ; & 107 bales sold; but it has produced little impression on our market . . . 11_; our . . . are down again . . . there . . . 12,000 bales . . . still coming in – stock not cleared & on hand 44,000 bales – at the present prices abroad  . . .  I hope you will take the option of holding for the last red  . . . ; all well–Mother much better from 2 weeks use of Bladon[6] water, walked all over town yesterday afternoon &

Evening – do write to William[7] to the Care of A. M. McGilvercy & Co. No. 10 Strand Calcutta and try and induce him to come home in some good American ship. Or British to London or Liverpool; Oh! how we do miss dear Anna[8]; and none of us more than Sophia and "Ouley"[9] – we have no one to ring the bell for "Ouley" now. Gaum[10] . . . has to do it herself; we have not seen Mrs. Walker since you all left at our house; taken up entirely with the Govt . . . sh–t & s–ll, only hear of her by . . . for milk – a recipe in an . . . occasionally –

*Lithograph (courtesy Mobile City Museum) showing the Southern Star, the first regular passenger steamer to serve the Eastern Shore of Mobile Bay from the city of Mobile. Point Clear was then and remains a favored resort area for Mobilians, many of whom had and have summer homes there. An ad that appeared in the* Mobile Daily Register *on September 8, 1855, announces the new service:*

"DAILY SERVICE TO POINT CLEAR"
Capt. John P. Carson
Steamboat "Southern Star"
4 P M Daily except Sunday
Tue, Th, Sat & Sun 10 A M  Pt Clear direct
Mon, Wed & Sat  will stop at Battles Wharf

*An Antebellum Life At Sea*

and she has been over to Coz H– twice and they . . . and took Mrs Mr F. Smith & Mr Leacock to spend a day and 2 nights – Mrs Mr F first visit to Cousin H. Since her appl– . . . Mary has been over to see Mother when sick and once since – freights here are firm at 3/8. The "Van Guard" Capt. Morton . . . was taken up at that for 3000 . . . bales & is filling up at the same price, in different about it at that. Br $^5/_{16}$ & filling up at 3/8 – . . . – No rain . . . above; tho we have had fine rains here – Crops promising every where; we are to have a daily & direct boat to the Point[11] – now on her way from N. York; we are requested to telegraph the House[12] at New York every Saturday which we have commenced to day. Hay is 175 . . . salt in store (M– Neil & Brothers) sold at 1.35 – retailing at 1.50 from Store – good Balast from New York – . . . there . . . only – Mother I thought when the news of _ . . . came, would never stop her calculations of investment for her funds; some times she talks of an interest in ships and then in a nigger – I see that the Montreal[13] is up for Bordeaux. Dont neglect the claret Interest; in house bottles enough for a cask "Exchange $7^7/_8$ & $10^1/_8$ in New York for Sterling – _ of . . . here for Light and will go to one percent . . . soon – Love to all & Kind regards to the Capt[14] – and a pleasant passage to him – and profitable one to the Indias – or to China – hope he will go to Calcutta tho; & bring our boy[15] Home; if he cant get a charter[16] to the Crimea –

. . .

father

*There is a small bill of . . . here against the Bolivar[17] . . . right I presume*

What follows was added on as a kind of postscript by Sabilla Minge, Jennie's younger sister.

I am sorry to write that Mother has another of her headaches – she was . . . even Mrs. Bladon[18] yesterday by shopping all morning and walking to St Joseph . . . after tea – and then called for RL– who was drinking tea with Laura & the Emanuels at Mrs. Sprague's so you can . . . easily account for her ailings to day – she has been unusually well . . . water took hold of her – Mrs. Wilder . . . was here first time this morning and gave . . . an account of her visit to cousin Fannie – they were evidentally expected . . . who invited the party . . . to be found out – She has no hopes of getting  . . .  Bob Deals [?] house – he has altered the plans to suit his wife who means to live in it herself. Are we still commissioned to buy the Townsend [?] establishment if the old Lady is willing? She has the refusal . . . Au–t house on Monroe street and will take it if she cant do better. Mr Lovel [?] has gone home – we heard a serenade last night – it must have been his farewell to Miss M–ly – Many persons have left town though the weather has been finer for the whole month than I ever knew it. Mrs. Lyon roars in Demopolis[19] and about the middle of July will shake her manes at the astonished Virginians – We heard the new boat[20] had . . . and would make her first trip today – father has not heard of . . . Mr Witherspoons improvement since they moved down is really wonderful –

[Five lines here are too faint to be read.]

It is impossible to say how much we miss Anna . . . We love her – we want to see her more than you two put together. Frank Mei–ale has come back and will keep the Withers house[21] in their temporary absence. We scarcely see any ladies unless we go to church . . . no scandal or gossip going on – for a wonder people are minding their own business Fannie Hersdon is married much to our surprise. We have been intending to write you an independent letter – but really there is not much satisfaction in writing when we know you are yet on the high seas and not waiting. The flowers are doing finely. Kiss Anna, brother Robert & Nana[22]

. . . *your Sister B–*

# LETTER FROM ROBERT H. DIXEY TO THE FRENCH MINISTER OF WAR, 16 JULY 1855

91 Champs Elysées
Paris
–16th July 1855

To the Honourable *Minister of War.*
––Hon[d.] Sir

Understanding that your department were desirous of chartering first class

Ships for service in the Meditteranean & Crimea, I have the honour of proposing two new & superior Medium clipper Ships[23] of about 1300 tons American register tonnage of which I am part owner & agent & would thank you to inform me if wanted, the highest rate of charter the time required of service & I will if desired give your Department a full & complete description of these two fine Ships now in the port of Havre & nearly ready for business.[24]

If you will deign to honour me with an early response you will confer a favor & craving your indulgence for the liberty of addressing you I remain most
    respectfully
    your obt servant
    RHD

CHAPTER

*8*

# The Journal of Sarah Jane Girdler

What follows is a transcript of the journal kept by Sarah Jane Girdler from January 1857 to December 1858. The original, which belonged to Edward Fitch of Tucson, Arizona, until his death in January 1980, is now in the possession of the Peabody Essex Museum in Salem, Massachusetts, and is used with permission. So far you've merely had hors d'oeuvres, faithful readers; now comes the main course.

Our readers will soon realize that the journal coming up was transcribed verbatim from the hand-written original. Sarah Jane had about eight grades of schooling. When her father died, she had to go to work. Her spelling and punctuation are rather "loose." She wrote with a quill pen, often in bad weather and was in poor light. But you will get to know her, fondly we think.

*Sarah Jane wrote her letters at this desk (see also caption on page 4) aboard the* Dixey. *Reynolds Girdler's father inherited the desk, one of the few pieces of remaining* Dixey *memorabilia.*

69

Now we go to January 1857 and take you on an actual voyage of one year. Aboard a new and fast sailing ship, you will experience life as seen through the eyes of a 19th century teenaged girl.

## BOSTON TO MOBILE

**January 1857** Left Boston harbor Wednesday 14th about two o'clock. Stood on the quarter deck most of the afternoon ~~with Fannie Collamore[8] (a young lady passenger)~~ in order to take the last sight of Boston. All the islands in the harbor were covered with snow and presented a very dreary appearance. It was not untill we parted with the steam ship of[f] Boston lights, that I began to realise that we were upon the ocean. The sea and wind were very moderate, and continued so all night. I had considerable trouble getting into my berth (which is a upper one) but after once attaining my position, was rocked gently to and fro, and slept as soundly as if I were in my own bed at home.

Awoke the next morning feeling much refreshed, and attempted to get up, but how to get out of my berth was more than I knew, at last I was obliged to call Uncle Richard to my assistance, he rigged a board for me to slide down on and then I got along very well.

Had a strong North East wind all day, attended by a snow storm which increased as night came on. The vessel rolled so that I not having my sea legs on could not stand without holding on to something. The night bid fair

*No photo exists of Sarah Jane Girdler at the age when she sailed on the Dixey. This illustration represents her as she probably looked at age 18, and was made by Terry G. Davis, who scanned a photo of her at a later age. The computer software reversed the aging process.*

to be so strong that Aunt Rebecca took Fannie in her birth, and said I had better sleep in Fannie's (which is under mine) and well it was for me that I did so, for the ship rolled so that I should certainly have been thrown from the upper one had I been there, and as it was Uncle Richard had to put a board in to keep me from falling out. Uncle Richard said he never knew the vessel to roll so before. Some barrels that were between decks got adrift, and rolled aroung, making such a noise that I certainly thought they would make a hole in the ship's side. About eight bells I heard a loud noise, that sounded like ever so much water pouring into the ship, it proved to be a large sea which came over the weather side, and poured into the windows on the upper berths. Aunt Rebecca got wet through [and] the water come into my berth, but as I was in Fannie's I did not get wet.

By the time I had got over that fright, I was doomed to a still worse one. The wind which was blowing fresh took the main top sail and split it, making a tremendous noise, it seemed to my inexperienced ears as if all the masts were going over. I did not close my eyes for all that night. In the morning I succeeded in getting out of my berth, and set down my trunk and managed to dress myself. In trying to get out into the cabin, I fell down onto the floor and sat there while I combed my hair, and then crawled on my hands and knees out to breakfast–could not eat much as it took all the time to hold onto my cup and plate.

Haven't felt the least bit sea sick and know I shall not now, as I have got along so far without it.

*Photo of Fannie Dixey, daughter of Richard and Rebecca Dixey, born in August 1854. She made her first trip to Europe before she was a year old. As she approached two, her mother needed more help with her. When the ship took a load of cotton to Boston, Mrs. Dixey got her niece Sarah Jane Girdler to make the next trip and help with little Fannie. Without her, therefore, there would have been no trip for Sarah Jane and no journal of the trip to Russia. Photo courtesy of Daphne Brooks Prout.*

**Saturday [January 17].** The sea still continues rough but the air is warm, very different from Boston air, have spent most of the day on deck, shall be glad when I get so I can walk about deck without holding on to the ropes.

**Sunday, Jan. 18th.** This morning the air was as warm and the sun as bright as it is in June, at home, but towards noon the weather became squally, and by night we had a bad thunder storm. I sat up in my berth and looked out of the window, and certainly I never saw anything so sublime before. The lightning was very sharp and frequent, and would light up the water all around, so I could see the waves rising mountains high, and all lashed into a white form [sic], by the wind which blew tremendously. I never heared such loud peals of thunder before. The ship rolled so that although I had a large lee board in, I had to hold on with all my strength, so to keep from falling out.

**Monday, 19th.** Found on going to the door this morning that the weather still continues stormy. The waves were rolling mountains high, and then falling down covered with foam, presented an appearance which I think would rival all the Niagara Falls that ever were. The wind was dead ahead and very strong so we were lying to all day.

**Thursday, 22nd.** This morning was awoke by the rolling of the ship which was so great that I expected to be thrown out of my berth. All the drawers and other movable things in the cabin flew from one side to the other at a great rate. Such a racket I never heard before it seemed as if everything was coming to pieces. Uncle Richard says he hadn't had such a long spell of rough weather for a great while.

**Friday, 23rd.** A very pleasant day but the sea still continues rough. About eight bells this afternoon saw a small fishing vessel with flag half mast high supposing her to be in distress we bore down to her found she wanted the longitude which we gave her and then continued on our way. I stood on the quarter deck and watched her till we were out of sight. She seemed like a little cockle shell on the water she was so small first she would rise up on the top of a huge wave and then sink down out of sight but we were going so fast that we soon lost sight of her and then I went below to supper.

**Saturday, 24th.** It has been one of the most beautiful days I ever saw as warm as if it were June. I have been very busy all day cutting a dress. Our fresh provisions have lasted up to this date today we had a pair of chickens. We have a very good steward he makes the best puddings and pies I ever tasted. The mates are very pleasant. Mr. Millet *[the second mate]* and myself often have a nice time talking about home. Fannie Collamore and I have nice times together sitting on the deck we have been on the quarter deck almost all the evening. I never saw a more perfect night the sky is thickly studded with stars and the water looks as though milions of diamonds were sprinkled over its surface and sparkling brightly as the ship dashed amongst them.

**Sunday, 25th.** Today it is if possible more beautiful than it was yesterday, spent most of the day on deck, and this evening, which is a perfect one, Fannie Collamore and myself walked the poop deck part of the evening, and then sat down and sang the remainder of the evening.

**Monday, 26th.** Today has been as pleasant and warm as yesterday. This morning I did a little washing realy it made me feel as though I was at home. After supper this evening we went on the deck to have one of the darkies play on the fiddle, he played very well indeed about half past nine we past the Abaco island[10] celebrated for its "Hole in the wall" being evening of course we could not see the hole but we saw the large revolving light which looked very briliant we have just past two vessels sailing the same way with us but we sail much faster than they.

I wish some of my friends at home could spend the evening with me and then they would not wonder at my loving to be at sea.

When I stand on deck and gaze around it seems almost like a fairy scene the sky above me seems more thickly studded with stars than it does at home and, the white foam and brilliant phosphoric insects contrast so prettily with the dark ocean as the ship dashes merily on. It seems almost too pleasant to leave the open air for the close cabin.

**Tuesday, Jan. 27th.** Today has been as pleasant as yesterday and rather warmer after dinner we passed a ship[11] bound the same way with ourselves we spoke her and found her to be a ship from Bordoux [Bordeaux] she had a great many passengers on board. We passed a great many islands today and at one time I counted fourteen vessels around us in different directions. We had been going eleven knots an hour all the afternoon and at this rate I suppose we shall soon get into port.

**Wednesday, 28th.** Another splendid day so warm that it has been almost unpleasant on deck went up a few minutes in the afternoon but the sun was so hot that I soon had to retreat. Been very busy all day helping Aunt Rebecca make a dress. Just before supper went on deck to take a walk passed a beautiful little schooner which was gliding swiftly through the water under a full press of canvass looking more like a creature of life than only a schooner passed most of the evening on deck saw a large revolving light on one of the islands in the gulf of Florida. Uncle Richard hauled in a very large fish had a portion of it for dinner it tasted very nice something like halibut.

**Thursday, Jan. 29th.** This morning was as pleasant as yesterday but towards noon a squall came up which however passed over and then it was as pleasant as before. Have been very busy all day making my dress to my great joy have succeeded in finishing it. This afternoon saw some very large turtles as large as a common sized table. Aunt Rebecca while on deck this afternoon saw a water spout but it disappeared before she could call me I felt much disappointed but consoled myself with the reflection that I could probably see plenty of them before I arrived home. We are now in the Gulf of Mexico and if this wind holds expect to get into Mobile by Saturday. I have seen plenty of flying fish lately but have seen no other except the one that was caught yesterday I always supposed that there were plenty of fish to be seen at sea but I have now found out my mistake.

**Friday, 30th.** This morning was very pleasant and we were hurrying towards Mobile at the rate of twelve knots an hour, but in the afternoon a squall suddenly came up and we were obliged to reef all the sails, the rain poured down in a perfect sheet, and the thunder and lightning were terific. Now while I am writing the flashes of lightning are so vivid that they light up the whole cabin, I expect we shall have a very stormy night. It was a very exciting scene to stand at the cabin door and look at the sailors hurrying about on the rigging, taking in the sails, expecting every moment the squall would burst upon us. We had all the lightning rods hung over the side of the ship into the water, so that if the ship was struck the lightning would run down into the water.[12] If the wind had continued all night as it was in the morning I suppose we should have got into port by tomorrow afternoon but now I expect we shall not get in until after Sunday.

**Saturday, 31st.** Last night as I expected proved very stormy. I was awoke about twelve o'clock by the lightning, which lit up my room so that I could have seen to read in any part of it. I sat up in my berth and looked out my window. The lightning was very different from any I had seen before. There would be a flash in one place, and before the light of that had gone, there would be another, so that the sky looked like a perfect sheet of flames all the time. I sat watching it about an hour and then some one shut my shuter so I could see it no longer. Then the rain poured down in torents, and the wind blew tremendously.

About two o'clock there was a very bright flash of chain lightning instantly followed by a very heavy peal of thunder, which seemed to break directly over my head on one of the masts. I expected to hear the men cry fire but there was a dead silence. Then I thought perhaps everyone on deck is killed. But just then I heared the mate's voice giving some order, so I found that it was not the case. I called to Aunt Rebecca, asked her if she did not think the ship was struck, she said it sounded so, but if it had we should have heard of it. Soon Uncle Richard came down, and then we found that the lightning struck the rod and passed down that into the water, breaking of[f] that portion of the chain that was in the water. Uncle Richard, the mate and several of the men were affected by it, two men standing by the main mast were thrown down, but not hurt much. If we had not had lightning rods on the ship, in all probability it would have been burned up. How greatful we ought to be that we were preserved from such great danger. By noon the weather was very pleasant but the wind dead ahead we have made very little progress all day.[13]

# GLOSSARY OF PRINCIPAL NAUTICAL TERMS USED IN SARAH JANE GIRDLER'S JOURNAL

Come To — usually means heading into wind, to anchor or to slow the ship to pick up a pilot or just to kill time.

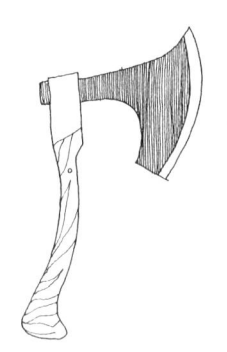

Half Mast — used at sea in an emergency to ask for aid or information, by lowering or inverting a flag. This method is still used.

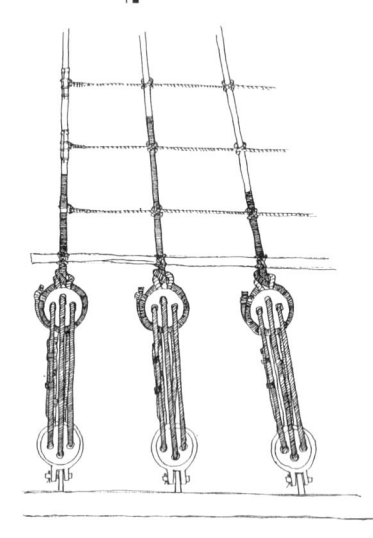

*A ship's carpenter's hatchet*

Heave To — secure sails and rudder to let ship sail itself. Used in bad weather or to kill time.

Knot — A rate of speed equaling one nautical mile per hour; about 15 percent faster than a land mile per hour.

Lee — the direction toward which the wind is blowing, thus leeward is the opposite of windward. Used in many ways at sea.

*Ratlines, shrouds and deadeyes*

Lying To — used with anchor or just killing time.

Poop Deck — the very stern of the ship. Usually raised to increase visibility forward. The steering wheel is mounted here.

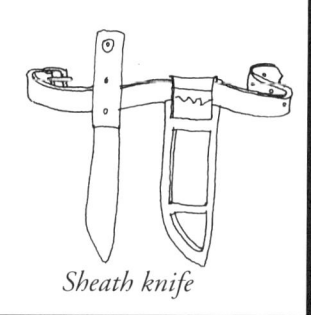

*Sheath knife*

76

Quarter Deck — stern section of deck, usually just forward of poop deck and raised above main deck.

Reef — reef and rigging are much-used sailing terms. Square-rigged vessels reduced the effect of strong winds by a process much like hemming a skirt from the top with a series of small lines across the sail that shorten the sail when tied together over the top. Some sails carry three rows of reef points for this purpose.

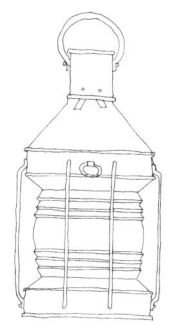

Sails — Dixey's sails are named in the chart on page 48.

Studding sails — small, light sails added to the side of regular sails and used in light breezes. Dangerous to remove in sudden squalls.

Weather Deck — the windy side, as opposed to the leeward deck.

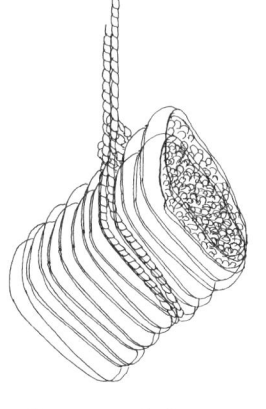

Windward — always relates to *into* the wind.

*Riding light with round wick lamp and fresnel lens*

*Anchor*

*Hoisting a bale*

*Bowline knot*

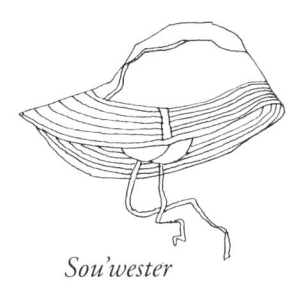

*Sou'wester*

*Illustrations by Ted Brennan*

**Sunday, February 1st, 1857.** This morning is very pleasant, but much cooler as we get further north. The wind is still ahead, and so we are obliged to beat. It seems like Sunday at home, everything is so still, there is hardly a sound to be heared, and nothing to be seen but the broad ocean all around us. Have been on deck most of the evening, it seemed almost too pleasant to go in.

**Monday, 2nd.** The weather has been very pleasant all day but the wind still continues ahead so we have not got along any to speak of. The sailors have been very busy cleaning and painting the ship so as to look nice when we get into port.

Every morning the decks are washed and rubbed with holy stones, which make them look very white and nice. This evening I have heared some singing which was about as good as any I have heared for a long time. The singer was a young Spaniard, who sung some songs in his native language with a very musical voice. We have also heared some music on a fiddle played by Albert another of our crew.[14] Mr. Millet says some of the darkies can dance the Juba[15] grandly but I have not seen any of them I hope I shall get a chance to some time.

**Tuesday, 3rd.** This morning the wind has changed fair the men have been very busy getting out sails if the wind holds fair we expect to get in tomorrow. This morning while I was writing home to mother I heard a noise on deck on going up to find out what was the matter found that we were in the midst of a school of porpoises. They were the first I ever saw. They were splendid large fish. They would dart through the water and under our keel and then come up to the surface and leap up high in the air and then plunge down into the water again. Mr. Millet tried to catch one of them with a harpoon but could not succeed.

## AT ANCHOR IN MOBILE BAY

**Wednesday, [February] 4th.** This morning when I awoke found we were in sight of land. Went on deck but found that the land was so far off that it seemed like a long low strip of white sand. About ten o'clock tool [sic] a pilot. Passed two islands on one of which is a light house that looks exactly like Mr. Darling's on the neck[16] and on the other a large Fort[17] which has 150 guns there is also a large and handsome house on this island where the officers of the fort are quartered.

We passed a great number of vessels in the bay before we came to an anchor. Just as we had got nicely anchored and the sails down a steam boat hailed us wanting to know if the Captain wished to go up to the city so he hurried to get ready and went off in her. It seems as if half of the ship is gone when he is away.

I have just been on deck to take a look round before going to bed. It is a splendid night almost as light as day. It is very damp all the ship is covered with heavy dew. There is not a soul to be seen except one

*Early drawing of the approach to Mobile Bay, viewed from the ramparts of Fort Morgan. The ship channel into the bay is to the right and the handsome building on the left is the officers' quarters. Courtesy of Caldwell Delaney.*

man pacing up and down the deck. There are between forty and fifty vessels anchored around us in every direction. The Seamans Bethel with a light on it is in sight but some distance from us. The revolving light in the light house that we passed this morning is also in sight.

Thursday a very pleasant day, quite warm. Have been on deck the greater part of the day watching the different ships and steamboats in the bay.

**Friday, 6th.** When I awoke this morning I found that Uncle Richard had returned was very much disappointed to find that there were no letters from home. Uncle Richard heared that the mails have been very irregular lately owing to the severe snow storm that they have had north so I hope that accounted for my not having any and that they are on the way. Uncle says that Boston and New York harbors have been frozen so that ships could not get in or out how different from the weather we have had all the passage which has been so warm that at times it was almost uncomfortable. How glad I am that I have escaped all the cold and snow.

**Saturday, 7th.** This afternoon Fannie Collamore left us for her home in New Orleans. I miss her very much. Uncle Richard went up to the City in the same boat with her hope he will bring back some letters from home.

If nothing happens to prevent we are all going up to Mobile next week to stay I expect we shall have a very nice time.

**Sunday, 8th.** A cold and strong north wind has been blowing all day which was so different from what we have been having that we were all glad to get 'round the stove. I have been very lonely all day have missed Uncle Richard and Fannie Collamore very much. There is a floating Bethel in the bay. If Uncle Richard had been hear and the weather had been mild we should have gone in the boat to the Bethel to hear the services. How I should like to go to Church once more. I suppose we shall go to some Church in Mobile next Sunday.

## IN MOBILE

**Saturday, 14th.** Left the ship last Tuesday afternoon for Mobile had a very pleasant time coming up. The . . . of the boat played on a very fine banjo and sang nigro songs for us and then told us funny stories so we had a nice time. We arrived at the City about ten o'clock and went directly to our boarding house. The next morning we walked out to see the City. I like the appearance of the portion I have seen very much. Our rooms at Mrs. Vaughn's were not as convenient as we wished them to be so yesterday we moved to Mrs. Ward's[18] where we now are. This house is much larger than the other. I like it much better.

The weather ever since we have been here has been as warm as it is at home in July. The trees are green and the grass is beginning to grow. This afternoon when I went out I saw some flowers in bloom in a garden. Col. Minge and family have been to see us several times. We have been there once they are all very kind and attentive. I like Miss Sabilla[19] very much. I have received four letters from home since I have been here. We expect to go to St. Petersburg Russia.

**Sunday, 15th.** This morning Uncle Richard and myself attended an Episcopal Church.[20] The building was large and handsome and beautifully dressed with evergreen. The singing was very fine. This afternoon Uncle and myself went to the colored Methodist Church.[21] The men and women were slaves but they were dressed as nicely as the white congregations North. The day has been excessively warm.

The church was well ventilated so we were quite comfortable. The negroes are beautiful singers it was a real treat to hear them sing their hymns.

**Sunday, 22nd.** Have been so busy all the week that I have not had time to write untill today. Have spent a very pleasant week. Was invited to dine with Mrs. Brown last Wednesday but prefered staying at home to take care of Fannie. Aunt Becca and Uncle Richard went. They had a very pleasant time. Spent Friday evening at Col Minges met Mr. Harbeck[22] and Mr. . . . . There had a very pleasant time.

I spend my evenings very pleasantly now. I've got acquainted with a young lady named Tailor and several gentlemen who board here and we spend the evenings in the parlor playing cards and talking. Last evening Mr. More invited

Uncle Richard and several old Sea Captains to play the game of "Old Maids" with us we had real fun seeing how hard they tried to get rid of the queen card so they need not be the Old maid. I have made several very pleasant acquaintances since I have been here. This morning Aunt Becca and Uncle Richard have gone to church. Fannie and myself are at home. The weather still continues very warm and vegetation progresses rapidly. Yesterday Aunt Becca and I went out and bought me a flounced large [?] pattern dress it is very pretty.

**Tuesday, 24th.** Today has been very warm and close much like the Northern "dog days." Towards the last part of the afternoon Aunt Becca, Mrs. Stone, Fannie and I went out to walk. The peach trees are all in blossom and everything looks finly. I have been reading two books loaned me by Mr. Mehler Earnest Sy– and Edmond Dantes sequel to the Count of Monte Christo. I like them very much. Uncle Richard has gone down to the bay tonight expects to be back tomorrow. Have been invited to go to the theatre to see the Kelley troupe, by Mr. Mehler, did not accept the invitation.

**Sunday, March 1st, 1857.** A very warm pleasant day. This afternoon about three o'clock the fire bell rang and of course all the gentlemen went to the fire. Some of them came back saying it was a large cotton yard intirely in flames supposed to be the work of an inendiary. In the evening Capt. Stone,

*The reward notice that appeared in the* Mobile Daily Advertiser *on April 14 and April 22, 1857.*

$1500 Reward.

MAYOR'S OFFICE,
City of Mobile, March 5th, 1857.

FOR the detection and proof to conviction of the person or persons who may have been guilty of feloniously setting on fire either of the Cotton Warehouses so lately destroyed; or, of any person or persons who may commit a like offence, I will pay from FIVE to FIFTEEN HUNDRED DOLLARS REWARD, reserving the right of grading the reward, after full development of the facts as to the character of the offender and importance or magnitude of the offence. [mar5 3m]    J. M. WITHERS.

lady and myself went down to see it. I never saw such a splendid sight.[23] It continued burning all night and the next day about three thousand five hundred bales of cotton were distroyed.

**Tuesday, 3rd.**[24] Was invited by Mr. Mehler to a masquerade ball last evening had a splendid time. Wore a white domino trimed with red and blue and a red masque. Mrs. Ward and sister went with us.[25]

**Thursday, 5th.** Yesterday Uncle, Aunt, Fannie and myself went to ride with Mr. Parker out on the shell road[26] to Spring Hill. Had a very pleasant drive. In the evening, went to General Smith's, met Mrs. Peabody, Sarah Fettyplace and her brothers there had a *very* pleasant time.[27]

Today has been raining hard all day seems like clearing up now. Last night Capt. and Mrs. Cook left us to go down in the bay to wait for a fair wind for sailing.

**Saturday, 7th.** The weather has been cold and like snow all day. The boat from the bay reports that it has rained, snowed, and hailed down in the bay. This evening however is warmer and I suppose will be as warm as ever tomorrow. Mr. Mehler has just given me a splendid bouquet of flowers which make the room very fragrant.

**Monday, 9th.** This morning Aunt Becca, Fannie and myself rode with Mr. Thomas Fettyplace and Sarah out to

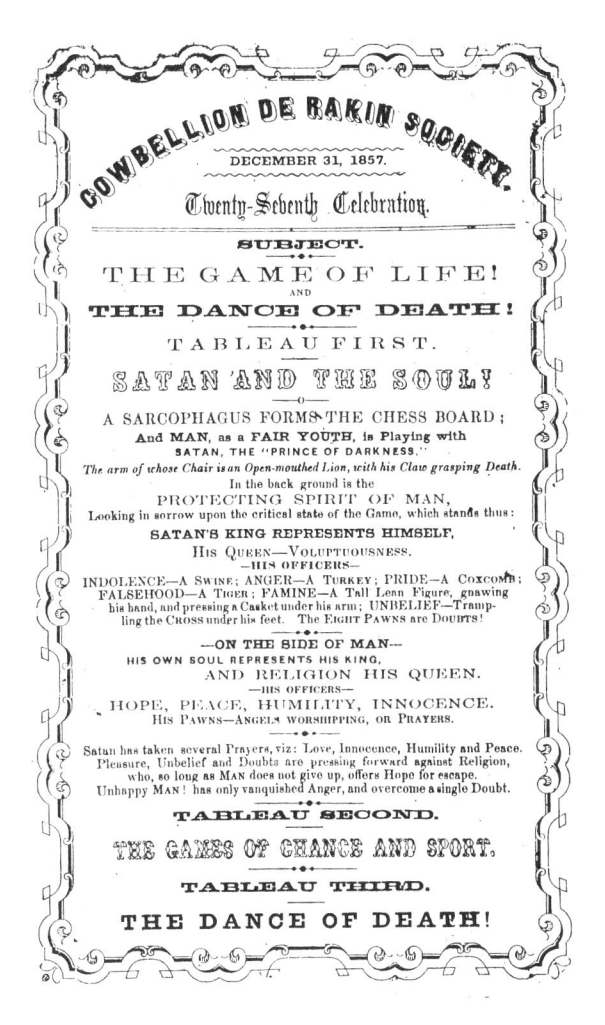

*Program for a ball held on New Year's Eve, nine months after Sarah Jane Girdler visited Mobile. The Cowbellion de Rakin Society was the* first *Mardi Gras secret society. Courtesy of Caldwell Delaney.*

Spring Hill and stopped at his place. Went over the garden which is in fine order. Picked a large bouquet of roses. He has a beautiful house with five acres and fine garden. We had a very pleasant ride. Uncle Richard has gone down in the bay expect him back tomorrow night shall then know when the ship will be ready for sea.

**Tuesday, March 10th.** It has been raining hard all day. Fannie has a bad cold. Uncle Richard returned from the bay this evening. We are waiting for more cotton to be brought and carried down before we can sail.
Wednesday, 11th. Another rainy day. This morning we had heavy thunder and lightning. This evening the rain has ceased hope it will be pleasant tomorrow.

**Thursday, 12th.** A very pleasant day but quite cold. Fannie is quite sick with a bad cold.

**Sunday, 15th.** Went to Dr. Mandervill's church[28] this morning with Col. Minge and Sabilla. Took tea at Mrs. Peabody's. Went in the evening to the Episcopal Church with Sarah Fettyplace and brothers had a very pleasant time.

**Tuesday, March 17th.** Tonight we are going down in the bay have bid farewell to all my Mobile friends.

*The* Dixey *being towed out of Mobile Bay by the* Natchez. *Illustration by Ted Brennan.*

**Wednesday, 18th.** Started in the steam boat last night at ten o'clock from Mobile. Went to bed on board the boat was awaked about two o'clock in the morning by Uncle Richard. Found we were along side the Dixey. Went on board and went to bed again. As we had a light breese this morning the ship was got under way but the wind soon went down and the ship swung round and stuck in the mud. Was towed out by the Natches.

## AT SEA AGAIN

**Thursday, 19th.** A splendid day and fair wind. Every thing seems about the same as before we arrived in Mobile. Aunt Becca has had a headache all day. I have been busy making a "cape bonnet."

**Sunday, 29th.** For several days the weather has been warm and pleasant with very light winds. Last week for several days we had a strong wind dead ahead one day and night we laid too under double reefed topsails. Saturday saw several schools of porpoises did not catch any as they did not come near the ship. Dan[29] caught a "man of war" in a bucket for us to see.[30] It was a beautiful creature looked like pearl. Some of its feathers got hurt and being afraid it would die they threw it overboard after we had looked at it.

**Tuesday, April 14, 1857.** We make very little progress toward St. Petersburg having had head winds almost all the time since we got into the "Gulf stream." We are now a little south east of the grand banks. The weather ever since we left Mobile has been warm is now quite cold so the fire in the cabin seems quite comfortable.

All day large numbers of little ice birds have been flying round the ship. They look like small ducks–now I am writing I can hear them singing. They make a noise that sounds much like our crickets at home.

**Saturday, 18th.** The wind still continues "ahead" we make very little progress. Tonight is quite stormy. The men have just finished taking in sail we are now under close reefed topsails. Yesterday morning one of our cats died very suddenly in a fit. She had two little kittens only four weeks old. They seem quite lively and will doubtless get along very well. Fannie and I have nice time petting them. We have been at sea a month today–expect we shall be another month getting to St. Petersburg.

**Monday, April 20th.** All day yesterday the barometer kept going down gradually and the weather was cold and rainy. About half past five in the afternoon just as we were going to tea the wind began to blow and the waves rose mountains high and seemed as if they would swallow the ship up.

The sails were taken in as quickly as possible but the wind blew so that it was very hard work all at once a sea came over the side of the ship making a tremendous noise and shook the ship so that it almost took me off my feet it [is] the first large sea we have shipped since leaving Boston. It frightened some of the men very much. Today has been pleasant but quite cold the wind has been fair but this evening is quite squally once in a while a squall will come which will almost blow the ship over then it will be calm again.

**Wednesday, 22nd.** Today has been very pleasant and warm quite like Spring. This evening is very beautiful. I have spent it on deck.

**Thursday, April 23rd.** Today is also very pleasant. This is my eighteenth birthday. How little I thought out my last birthday, that on this I should be on the ocean on the way to St. Petersburg. I wonder where I shall spend my next. We are now almost up to the Weslco islands. It is a perfect night. The sky is cloudless and the stars so bright that it seems almost like day. I suppose the folks at home remember that it is my birthday and have been talking about me. I got all the daguerre-o-types out to look at today. It almost seemed like talking to them. Fannie has been playing with the kittens almost all day. She carries them 'round in her arms and is not at all afraid of them.

**Monday, 27th.** Very pleasant weather but scarcely any wind. Saw a steamer in the distance supposed it to be a Havre boat bound to New York. Hoisted our private signal thinking they would report it on arriving at port and in this way our friends would hear from us. Have seen several whales this last few days but they were a long distance off.

**Tuesday, 28th.** Another pleasant day with scarce any wind. The ship only averaging between two and three knots. Just after dinner this afternoon while we were on deck a young whale came along side the ship he played round the ship for some time thus giving us a fine opportunity to see him. It was what is called the black whale.[31] They do not spout the water in the air as the sperm whales do.

**Friday, May 1st, 1857.** Today the wind is again ahead. Last night fourteen sail were in sight. We signalized with two yesterday. Today a ship passed quite near us the Europa the decks were filled with passengers. Uncle says all the ships are from the channel.

I have commenced working a skirt for Fannie today. This afternoon as I was briefly working the mate called me on deck. I ran up and saw a very large whale pursued by a thrasher.[32] The whale would dive deep down into the water trying to get rid of its tormenter but the thrasher would soon make it come up and then raising itself high in the air would pounce down on the whale with great force. It is said that while the thrasher attacks the whale above the Sword Fish assists by wounding him below. The whale was so far off that I could not have seen it [swordfish] if there had been one there.

**Wednesday, May 6th, 1857.** The wind has continued ahead over a week blowing violently and accompanied by a heavy sea which causes the ship to pitch about in every direction so that we find it hard work to move about. It seems as if we were never going to have fair winds again. We have passed great numbers of vessels coming from the channel they are all having splendid times. Tonight we passed a brig which was going very rapidly but the sea was so heavy that we could see the water roll over her cover her deck first one side and then the other while our good ship did not roll at all only pitched a little.

The weather has been very cold the past week so I have kept in the cabin close to the fire most of the time. I am afraid that we shall have a tremendous passage as we are not in the channel yet and won't be in a hurry unless the wind changes.

There has been large numbers of sea birds following us for several days

*Nautical chart of the North Atlantic approaching the English Channel*

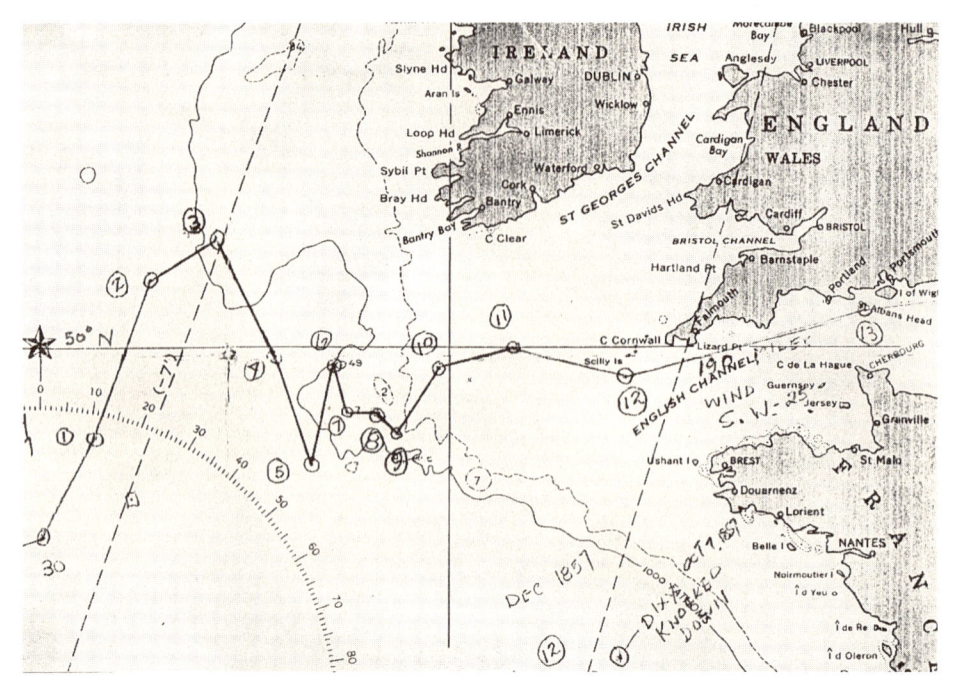

past. The mate put out a fish line but did not succeed in catching any.

Tonight I saw an enormous "gannet"[33] flying about and then diving down into the water.

**Monday, 11th.** The wind has been dead ahead from the first of the month up to this morning when it changed from "East" to "South East" but we are so far north that it does us little good. The weather is quite squally tonight. The men are now "reefing top sails."

It has been quite cold for some time so that we are obliged to keep a fire in the cabin in order to be comfortable. Uncle Richard is afraid the coal will give out if the passage is much longer. I don't know what we shall do if it does. Last night soon after I went to bed I was disturbed by a noise that sounded like the burring of a large bee or hornet. I was rather alarmed at first thinking that there may be one in my room. When Uncle came down stairs he said that the noise was on deck but did not know what it was.

In the morning they found that a drum fish[34] had been attached to the side of the ship all night and the noise was caused by the vibration of its wings. Today there has been swallows flying 'round the ship. They seemed very tired they must have flown a long distance as there is no land near us.

We had all been sitting in the forward cabin by the fire and Aunt Becca went into the back cabin and there on the window ledge sat a poor little sparrow looking very tired. We got him some canary seed but he seemed frightened and flew out at the door.

**Tuesday, May 12th.** This morning while I was dressing myself I heard Uncle tell Aunt Becca that a sail boat was bearing down towards us I hurried on deck. Found a strange man there with a basket of fresh eggs which proved very exceptable as ours were all gone. It seemed very odd to see a strange face as we have not seen one for two months. He soon left us and as the wind was fair we proceded on our course at the rate of *11* knotts an hour.

About four o'clock this afternoon we came up to a french clipper ship which although smaller than us was much sharper and a very fast sailor. When she saw that we were fast gaining on her she crowded on all her sale but it was no use the "Dixey" went by her without the least trouble. We went so fast that it seemed more like flying than going through the water.

It has been very foggy and rainy all day and as we have been passing through a fleet of fishing schooners and other vessels we were obliged to use every precaution such as blowing fog horns and keeping several men on the "look out" to prevent running into them.

*The* Dixey *passing the French clipper. Illustration by T. Brennan.*

There are several ships in sight bound the same way as ourselves they all seem to be making the most of this wind by carrying all the canvass they can–but we are fast coming up to them and will soon be past them all. We spoke a pilot this noon who offered to take us up the channel. But Uncle prefered to take us up himself.

I hope the wind will hold if it does we shall soon get into the North Sea. I think likely it will as the wind has been East here for three weeks. At least that is what the man told us this morning.

**Wednesday, May 13th.** This morning before I was up we passed a dutch ship. I went to the cabin window heared the captain speak her. Found we were in sight of land. Went on deck saw St. Albans on our lee bow. I counted fifty-four sail in sight. We were about fifteen miles from land but with the aid of a glass could see the green trees and chalk cliffs plainly. The middle of the forenoon a pilot came on board. We did not want his services however. So after giving us one newspaper he prepared to leave us by first asking if we could not give him a little tobacco having obtained that he next wanted a little tea and sugar then a piece of salt beef and pork and then some bread. I suppose he would have kept on asking to the end of the chapter but we were in a hurry to go on our way so he left us. I don't see how a man can stoop so low as to beg in such a manner but I suppose it is part of this business. About eight bells we were ten miles from "the Isle of Wight" and tacked ship and stood over to the other side.

By using the glass we could plainly see the green fields and trees also the chalk cliffs and tall tower on the top of the hill. It seemed quite refreshing to see so much green after being on the water so long.

This afternoon another pilot came on board but as we did not want him he soon left after going through the usual program of asking for tobacco, salt beef, pork, bread, etc.

He said he had seven little children at home so Aunt Becca gave him a pretty little pair of shoes that Fannie had outgrown also some "childs papers."

Tonight at eight bells we tacked again the light on the french coast can be seen very plainly. We have just taken a pilot on board to take us up to the North Sea.

As the matter of course the beef barrel had to be opened again for the benefit of his friends on board the boat. The fair wind we had yesterday did not stay with us long as it is East again. It does not make so much difference to us now as we are inside the channel and can beat up.

**Thursday, 14th.** A very pleasant day but the wind still continues East. This morning we could plainly see the towns of Worthing and Brighton. Tonight at about six bells, we passed in tacking, very near the towns of New Haven and Seatown.

New Haven is beautifully situated up a little harbor. Seatown is close to the water. They are both fine watering places. We went in so near land that we could plainly discern ladies and gentlemen walking on the beach–also the houses and churches in the towns and behind all the beautiful green hills rising in gentle undulations and the chalk cliffs, stretching on either side. The scenery here is very different from that at home. We see none of the bould ruggid rocks, pilled [sic] up in fantastic form that characterizes our sea shores. Nothing but the high white chalk cliffs, covered on top with natures own carpet of soft green verdure–which certainly is much more refreshing to the eye, than our bare rocks, after having been over eight weeks on the ocean.

The Pilot we have on board seems to understand his business very well. He puts me in mind of Lewis Evans[35] every time I look at him–only he is not near as good looking as Lewis.

**Friday, May 15th.** This morning Uncle Richard called me at five o'clock, which is much earlier than I usually arise, telling me that the morning was so fine and the prospect so delightful I had better come on deck and enjoy it accordingly. I dressed myself and hurried up. And I was amply repaid for my exertions by the delightful scene that met my gaze. In front lay the town of Hythe with its pretty little houses and pleasant roads and behind the town arose the hills covered with green verdure intersperced with patches of cultivated ground.

On the sides of one of the hills was the ruins of an old castle which greatly added to the picturesque beauty of the scene. Stretching farther to the west lay another little town snugly embosomed among the hills. On the other side you could faintly discern the dim outline of the French coast and all around was the broad blue ocean dotted over with sailing vessels and steam tuggs. There was scarcely a breath of wind so we dropt anchor and sent a boat [?] that lay along side the town to procure coals. He came back about one o'clock with a ton of coal, some beef, butter, eggs, fish and vegetables by that time there was a little wind so we got under weigh again and beat up as far as Dover.

The pilot intended to anchor us in the "downs"[36] for the night but the wind died intirely away before we reached them so we were obliged to drop anchor off Dover castle to prevent the tides taking us into the land.

Dover is a very pleasant town. I could plainly see the large houses under the hill and the broad, clean streets, winding through the town behind the town the high green hill towered up in the sky. On this hill is Dover castle–a grey ancient looking edifice so surrounded with battlements and fortifications that it seemed quite impossible to subdue it. We were so near land that we could see the soldiers on duty and even see their guns when the sun shone on the streets. In the evening when the anchor was dropt and the sails taken in so there was no noise on the ship we could hear the tap of the drums in the castle. It was Mr. Millets watch on deck and he said he could plainly hear the band play in the night.

I staid on deck till after ten o'clock. The night was so beautiful. The sky was spangled over with countless numbers of stars on the left hand was the town of Dover with its numerous lights farther to the right the two light houses on the head-way off in the distance the Calis light on the French coast besides the lights on the numerous ships anchored around us.

Not a sound could be heard save the distance strains of a violin on a neighboring vessel. It seemed almost impossible that we, lying so near the town, as to be able to distinguish every house and light, could not catch one note of the busy hum of life and activity which doubtless was sounding in it.

I have been so long on the water (fifty-nine days) that next to the pleasure of hearing the voices of my dear friends at home the noise and bustle of a town, would be the most welcomed sound that could reach my ears. But we must wait patiently untill we reach Cronstadt before we can hear that welcomed sound.

**Saturday, 16th.** This morning on awaking found we had been under way since two o'clock. There was scarcely a breath of air and the motion of the ship was hardly perceptable so slowly did we move the pilot left us about three o'clock this afternoon in a boat which was weighting for him all day. About six o'clock a slight breeze sprung up and we are now moving through the water about four knots going our course too which is quite a rarity. We have just got into the North Sea. There are great numbers of vessels of every discription all around us bound up this sea but I suppose we shall soon leave them behind us if this wind continues.

**Sunday, May 17th.** A very warm pleasant day. The water ever since we entered the North Sea has been as smooth as glass. Towards noon the wind died all away and all the afternoon we were becalmed. A tide of three or four knots was drifting us rapidly towards a shoal–so we were obliged to drop a kedge anchor until the tide turned which was about six o'clock. Then as a light breeze sprung up we got under way again.

**Monday, May 18th.** Another pleasant day so warm as to be uncomfortable in the sun. About nine o'clock we saw a dutch fishing vessel ahead of us as we approached they asked us to throw them a line which we did but they missed it and before we could throw it again we had passed them. Uncle did not intend to stop for them but they called in such a pitious tone "Cap-i-tain Cap-i-tain vater vater" that he ordered the men to back the main yard and in a few minutes they were along side again. We found they had been out much longer than they intended and had no water or anything to eat so Uncle gave them two casks of water some beef, bread and rice. They gave us some very fine sole and turbot. The sole were cooked for dinner. They are the nicest fish I ever tasted. There was a little fat faced white haired boy on board that looked just like our Louis[37] only his eyes were not quite so pretty. The poor child had not had anything to eat for some time when he saw the beef and bread coming over the side he looked perfectly delighted and *grinned* just as Lou does. All the crew of the ship had on great wooden shoes. They looked very strangely. I should not think they could move in them. They seemed very thankful for what was given them. When they left us one of them said

*Stopping for Dutch fishermen in the North Sea. Illustration by T. Brennan.*

to Aunt Becca "good bye frow." They seemed very different from the English pilots who begged for everything they could think of and then seemed to think they had nothing while these men took what was given them and seemed very thankful and did not ask for anything else. After they had gone I washed some of Fannie's and my clothes had quite a nice wash–just as I was finishing which was about twelve o'clock another boat came along. They too were out of water and provisions so we supplied them also. Their boats are the queerest looking things I ever saw. The stern and bows just alike both as 'round as a tub. Uncle asked how fast they could sail with a fair wind. They said *one knot*. This afternoon another dutch boat came by us and wanted us to wait till they could row close to us. Uncle did not like to wait but as they had no water he thought it would be cruel to leave them so we waited till they came up and supplied them also–while we were waiting for them–a row boat from an English schooner came along side with a fine codfish and some other kinds he wanted us to buy. Uncle asked him what he wanted for the fish he said a *bottle of grog* on being told we did not keep the article he said he would take some tobacco and bread so we got the codfish and tomorrow I expect we shall have a nice chowder.

The water in the tank was measured this afternoon so we are all put on an allowance of a gallon a day for if we have a much longer passage and have to supply all the fishing fleet in the Black *[sic]* Sea the water will give out before we reach Cronstadt. All the afternoon is has been almost calm but tonight a breeze has sprung up again so we are going nicely.

**Tuesday, 19th.** A very pleasant day but not quite as warm as it was yesterday–quite a nice little breeze all day.

We are now about four hundred and fifty miles from Elsinore.[38] Today I have ironed and finished working Fannie's skirt. I guess we have got rid of our fishing visitors as we have seen none today.

As we go further north the days grow much longer. It is now almost nine o'clock and the lamps are just lighted. There is day light in the sky untill after ten o'clock at night and light again at two in the morning.

We had a nice chowder today for dinner, made of the codfish we got yesterday. It seemed quite home like. The turbot we got from the men was very nice they taste like a very nice codfish. I think the sole is the nicest fish I ever tasted. It is the favorite fish among the English nobility and brings a very high price in London but the poor fishermen were so greatful for the provisions we gave them that they were glad to give us as many as we wanted.

The men are busy this week taring the rigging painting the capstan and getting everything in fine order against our getting into port.

**Saturday, May 23rd.** We have just let go the anchor at the mouth of the channel. We have been beating ever since we got around the scaw and now the wind and tide being both against us we are going to wait untill the tide turns before we go up the channel. We are only about eight miles from Elsinore. The scenery all up the sound has been delightful. On one side is the coast of Sweden on the other Denmark. I like the Swedish coast best. It is much higher than the other they both extremely fertile. All along under the sides of the green hills are little towns all surrounded by trees and cultivated ground which give quite a picturesque air to the scene. We have taken a pilot on board this afternoon he is a Sweed it is very hard to understand what he says. He tells us that the season is far advanced that they have new potatoes there already.

We have no night now the sun does not set till about nine and then rises about two and the daylight is in the sky all night. I suppose that is the reason everything grows so fast is because the sun is shining almost all the time.

**Sunday, 24th.** A very beautiful day but excessively warm. The wind and tide have been ahead all day so we could not get up channel. There are great numbers of vessels of every description anchored around us waiting like us for a chance to get in.

# DENMARK

**Monday, May 25th.** This morning when I awoke found Uncle Richard had started in a boat for the town. The tide still so strong we could not get up. He came back this evening with fresh provisions. Gave a glowing description of Elsinore. He staid at Mr. Cary's a English merchant in town liked him and family very much. They wanted us to come ashore as soon as we could get up and stay at their house.

**Tuesday.** Today the wind has been blowing violently all day. This morning a steam tug that Uncle engaged yesterday came along side to take us up town but the wind and tide were so strong against us that the boat was obliged to leave not being strong enough to tow us up. In the afternoon he came along again and said he had been ordered away for several days so he should not be able to take us up. Here we are and here we are likely to be for some time.

**Wednesday, 27th.** This morning Uncle Richard started again for town in one of the ship's boats[39] with six men to row it. He got some distance from the ship but could not get up the channel. They had very hard work to get back to the ship but after pulling a long time succeeded. This noon the wind came fair so we got under way. For a little while we got along nicely passing all the ships that were in front of us. Great care had to be taken as we were

*Mrs. Dixey descends the boarding steps while Capt. Dixey, Fannie, and Sarah Jane await their turns. The second mate and several sailors will sail them into the Danish town of Elsinore (modern spelling Helsingor). Illustration by T. Brennan.*

passing through a fleet of about five hundred vessels. First we would have to get out of the way of one then another. It certainly was a splendid sight to see so many sail all together in a passage about two miles wide.

After getting a few miles from the town the wind died away and the tide was so strong that it turned the ship round. We almost ran into two ships, first cleared them, and as the ship did not mind the helm we had to drop anchor again so here we are the same as ever. As soon as we were safely anchored Uncle Richard went up to town in a sail boat to try to get a steamer to take us up. I suppose now the wind is fair we shall not stop in Elsinore long enough for us to go ashore at any rate only for an hour or so if we could have got up there when we first came here we should have been having a nice time.

**Thursday, May 28th.** Last evening Uncle Richard again started for Elsinore in a small sail boat that came along side. This morning the steam tug that had been away returned towing a brig that had lost her bowsprite. The Captain hailed us saying he would be back in a few hours. So about two o'clock he came back bringing Uncle Richard with him. He put Uncle Richard aboard and then towed us to Elsinore on our way the wind came fair but Uncle Richard thought it would die away before we got to town so we got all ready to go on shore as soon as the anchor was dropt but we were disappointed for the wind still blew fresh so of course we could not go.

We sailed on about four miles from Elsinore then the wind died all away and we were obliged to drop anchor but it was too late to go on shore. Uncle Richard had a hard time to get ashore last night. The wind and tide were both against them and after tacking from one side to the other till quite late they found they could not get down to Elsinore so put him ashore at a little town about two miles from that place. He set out to walk to town but was stopt by a Dane. Uncle tried to make him understand that he had been to Elsinore and had his health papers but the man could not understand and would shurly have taken him to the "lock up." Fortunately a gentleman came along who could speak English so after explaining who he was he was allowed to proceed. He got to Elsinore about ten o'clock and went to the hotel but could not be accommodated as the house was full of officers so he went to his friend Mr. Cary's where he was accommodated with a nice bed and slept much better probably than he would have had he passed the night in the "lock up."

**Friday, May 29th.** This morning on awaking found we had again got under way but the wind died away and we could not go on so the anchor was again dropt. And we got ready to go on shore–Uncle, Aunt, Fannie, Mr. Baker (the pilot) and myself–with Mr. Symonds[40] and four men to see to the boat[41] we had a nice sail to the shore. We landed at a little fishing village opposite where the ship was lying and about four miles from Elsinore. It was a beautiful place with plenty of fine large trees.

The pilot, who acted as interpreter, took us to the tavern to see if we could get a carriage and ride down to Elsinore but there were nothing but wagons in the village and they were all in use. So we decided, as the wind showed no signs of changing, to go down to Elsinore in the boat and then let Mr. Symonds and the men take the boat back to the village and we ride back at night in a carriage and then go off to the ship in the boat. But before starting we went to see a large garden belonging to a nice gentleman. It seemed so nice after being on the water so long to see so many beautiful flowers and trees and birds sing so sweetly. There was a pretty pond in the garden with beautiful swans in it. Everything looked perfectly neat and nice. After spending some time admiring the garden we started for the boat passing down a beautiful green lane with large trees on each side and plenty of sheep and lams running about. The little cottages with their thatched roofs looked very strangely to me as they were the first I ever saw.

We had a pleasant sail down to the town and passed in at the side of the castle with its six high towers. Then stepped our feet in Elsinore where we had been wishing to be for so long.

We went up the street intending to go to the hotel but on our way met Mr. Carey who insisted on our going to his house. So we went and had a splendid time. I like him and his wife very much. Fannie was delighted with their three pretty children. We dined about four o'clock. It seemed very strange to see several different kinds of wine on the table. But it is the custom to have it here every day. After dinner we took coffee and then sat down again to chat. We intended to take a walk to see the town but our walk in the morning tired us so that we preferred staying in the house. About seven o'clock a nice carriage with two horses stopped at the door for us. So with many regrets at leaving them so soon we bid adieu to our kind friends and started for the little town where our boat was waiting for us. We had a fine opportunity to see Elsinore as we rode through the streets out into the country. The houses are only one story high all the rooms being on one floor. I should think they would be very cold and comfortless in winter as the rooms seem to be almost all doors and windows.

We had a very pleasant ride of about four and a half miles out to the town where we first landed, passed through several small fishing villages. They all looked very neat and the ground round seemed finely cultivated. The houses in the villages looked very different from those in town their roofs being all thatched very neatly while those in town are covered with red tiles.

The Danes seem to be a very polite people everyone we passed lifted their hat very politely.

We reached the town about eight o'clock found the boat and men waiting for us. The wind was dead ahead and the tide also against us. So we had to beat all the way. The sea was quite rough and the air very cold. I certainly thought I should freeze. Fannie went to sleep soon after we got into the boat. Everytime we tacked we had to change our seats and it was no easy matter to do so with Fannie in my arms. Uncle was afraid we should not be able to reach the ship, but after trying till about eleven o'clock we succeeded in getting along side. I never felt so glad to get anywhere in my life. We were stiff with cold and a little wet besides being very tired. I guess we all slept very sound know I did any way.

**Saturday, May 30th.** This morning on awaking found we had got under way with a nice fair breeze and were almost up to Copenhagen. Dressed myself as quickly as possible and went on deck. With the aid of a glass could see Copenhagen very plainly it seemed like a fine town. Saw the king's palace a very large building. We were in the midst of a very large fleet of vessels of every description going the same way as we but we soon left them behind the sound pilot left us this morning. Soon after he left us we entered the Baltic Sea and the wind which was fair when we were in the Sound became ahead–so we have been obliged to beat.

**Sunday, 31st.** Today is quite pleasant but cold. The wind still ahead. Passed the Island of Bonneholm this afternoon on one side of the island saw a pretty little town with three thousand inhabitants so the pilot tells us. He is a very pleasant man, a Dane, he speaks very good English.

**Monday, June 1st.** A very pleasant day but quite cold. About twelve o'clock this noon the wind came fair but very light. We are going about five knots.

The men are now busy setting "studing sails."[42] We keep coming up to fleets of vessels that were ahead of us but we sail so much faster than any here that we soon pass them.

**Tuesday, 2nd.** Today is pleasant but cold. The wind still fair we are going along nicely. This morning I cut out my calico dress that I got in Mobile.

**Wednesday, June 3rd.** Another cold but pleasant day. We are now in the Gulf of Finland. The wind is fair, but light. Uncle Richard has been taking an inventory of the things in the ship also our private property. The pilot says everything is examined very strictly and if anything is found that is not on the list it is taken away. Hope we shall not lose any of our things.

I have just met with quite an accident. Just as I was commencing to write I tiped [sic] over my ink stand spoiled some of my paper and what was of far more consequence inked part of the inside of my desk[43] so I shall have to line it again. I feel very sorry, but then accidents will happen sometimes.

I have finished my spencer[44] today. It sets very pretty.

## CRONSTADT

**Thursday, June 4th.** Today has been very pleasant not quite as cold as previously. Have been very busy all day washing, ironing, cleaning my state room besides running on deck between whiles to see the land we were passing. I suppose if nothing happens to prevent we shall get to Cronstandt tomorrow. This afternoon we passed a very high island called Hogland.[45] The pilot said it was all solid rock on which nothing grew but a kind of brush still. There is a small town on it the inhabitants get their living by carrying the brush to the main land also by fishing. It was indeed a dreary spot one in which I should be very sorry to live. There was another small rock a short distance from it on which was a light house. I saw a bark ashore on the rocks. She had probably been there some time as she was apparently diserted. I have just come down from the deck. It is five minutes to ten o'clock and is almost as light as day. The sun did not set till after nine and now the beautiful golden and crimson clouds are lingering in the west. And the moon which is almost full is already high in the heavens and looking very pale as though she

*Cronstadt (now Kronshtadt) was a naval and commercial port built by Czar Peter the Great about 1705. It lies on an island, "Ostrov Kotlin," fifteen miles northwest of the shallow harbor of St. Petersburg. Before a channel was dredged in 1875–93, cargo ships drawing more than six feet had to be unloaded at this port onto small barges that carried the freight up to the capital. In the* Dixey's *time, steamboats pushed the barges and carried such people as needed passage. The harbor was heavily built of stone, with fortifications at close intervals. These walls and fort still stand, though the cannon are long gone. It looks much as it did when the* Dixey *almost rammed the entrance. The sketch below is based on a modern chart of this harbor, edited to remove the modern naval base (Russia's largest) so that readers can visualize this port as it looked to Sarah Jane. Even in 1857, the Russians were suspicious and unfriendly toward all foreigners, and ships' crews and other visitors were much restricted in their activities ashore, even Captain Dixey. Inside this mole (harbor), ships like the* Dixey *were tied up so they could be unloaded and reloaded. The space between ships was filled with barges. The traffic was congested. Captain Dixey and his passengers had to use a ship's boat to row over to the landing to go to St. Petersburg.*

missed the company of the bright stars which usually stud the sky so thickly and seem to add new lustre to her brightness, for not one is visable owing to the light and she rides alone in solitary splendor.

There are numerous islands lying about us in every direction but so far off that nothing can be distinguished plainly. There is also a large number of vessels around us all of which we are passing. We signalized with an American bark bound down the Gulf a few hours ago. We are rapidly advancing towards our destined port. I don't know hardly whether to be glad or sorry. I am glad to think we shall be able to stand on old "Mother Earth" again but the regulations are so very strict that I expect it will be very inconvenient and annoy us sadly to obey them.

**Friday, 5th.** This morning Uncle Richard called me at three o'clock saying we were approaching the guard ship and would soon anchor. So I hurried on deck–got there just as we dropt anchor. We were lying between two forts among a numerous fleet of vessels. The forts on each side of us were large and very strong looking with large cannon at each loop hole one was an oblong form the other semmi-circular. Away off in the distance I could see the town of Cronstadt with countless numbers of ships lying at the mole.

About ten o'clock three officers from the frigate boarded us examined our papers then permitted us to go on our way. And we were soon up to the mole we let go the anchor but the chain would not pay out and we expected to dash onto the pier head but they managed to get the other anchor out just in time to swing us clear. If the ship had struck there would have been a terrible smash up. We got inside the mole late in the afternoon did not "get safely fastened untill the next day."

**Sunday, 7th.** Today Uncle Richard and I went to the English Church liked the preacher very much. The church is a very pretty one seemed quite home like. On returning to the ship found the serch officers on board. Went to my room found they had pulled everything to pieces unfolded all my clothes turned my pockets inside out and done all the mischief they could.

Found the cross belonging to my jet necklace broken off. The place where we are lying is very strongly fortified mounted cannon all around us. Last evening had a call from the head officer in the customs house opposite us. As soon as he saw the melodian[46] he sat down and played a little. He seemed full of music expect he will be off often to play on it.

**Monday, June 8th.** This morning began to discharge cotton. It is very hard work as the bales are screwed in very tightly.

This afternoon we all went on shore. It makes one feel lonly to walk in

## SEA CHANTEYS

Most wooden ships leaked. Some were as tight "as a bottle," but they were the exceptions. Pumping was a regular duty for the crew that was on watch, and very necessary to protect the cargo from water damage. Sailors sang to "keep time" as they worked, and many of the "chanteys" they sang have become famous. Captain John D. Whidden of Marblehead, who knew all the Dixeys, Fettyplaces, and Girdlers there, quotes this "pumping chantey":

Mobile Bay

Were you ever down in Mobile Bay,
Johnnie come tell us and pump away.
A-screwing cotton by the day,
Johnnie come tell us and pump away.
Aye, aye, pump away,
Johnnie come tell us and pump away.

[Quoted from Capt. John D. Whidden, *Ocean Life in Old Sailing Ship Days* (Boston: Little, Brown & Co., 1908).]

Unless the ships carried passengers, in which case the language the sailors used was a matter of more interest, the chanteys were usually very profane, sexually explicit, and not suitable for historical preservation. Students will find few actual chanteys to study.

the streets they are so wide and desolate looking. Went with Uncle Richard to the ship chandlers then after resting a while went to engage a wash woman and then stopped at our Bakers, a very pleasant man, where we were treated to a variety of very nice cakes and sherry wine and were invited to call and refresh ourselves whenever we were in town.

We went to the Greek Church but could not get in. It is said to be very fine inside. The roof is very thickly gilded looks almost like pure gold.

While we were standing trying to gain admittance I noticed several men pass by when they got opposite the church they would stop cross themselves in several places mutter something to themselves and then pass on. We had a nice row back to the ship I felt very tired walking so much. Saw for the first time a "drosky" a queer looking carriage without springs suppose we shall have a ride in one before long. This evening the gentleman from the custom house (I don't know his name) called again bringing his wife and one of his little boys. His wife is a very pleasant lady speaks but a very little English. They sang a duet together beautifully. They are coming again soon.

**Tuesday, June 9th.** I have felt quite tired all day. Aunt Becca is quite sick with a back ache. I expect we walked too much yesterday. Uncle Richard went up to Petersburg today expect him back tonight.

**Wednesday, 10th.** A very pleasant day much warmer than yesterday. This morning we had a call from Captain and Mrs. Chase we like them very much. They are living on shore in the only decent place there is there. All the other ladies here live on board ship. Uncle Richard is talking about our going up to Petersburg tomorrow don't know whether we shall go then or wait till the next day.

**Thursday, June 11th.** Concluded to go to Petersburg today and accordingly packed the trunk and got everything ready for starting, but after we were all ready the wind changed and we had quite a rain, so of course all our plans were changed and we obliged to wait until tomorrow.

## ST. PETERSBURG

**Friday, 12th.** This morning being pleasant we again got ready started about one o'clock for shore. Then took droskys for the steamboat landing. Aunt Becca and I rode in one, Uncle Richard in another, while a third containing our baggage, brought up the rear. The drosky Aunt Becca and I rode in was rather small and as this was our first ride in one we had hard work to keep our seats. The streets were all paved and the droskys have no springs so we kept bouncing up and down in a manner which alarmed us very much at first but we soon got used to it.

We were about an hour and a half going up to Petersburg in the boat. Fannie seemed quite sick and slept almost all the way. Just before we arrived she suddenly awoke and vomited all over her clothes. We could not get any water for a long time but finally a gentleman who could speak a little English came and said he would send us some. So we managed to wipe her clean. On arriving at Petersburg we again took droskys this time Uncle and I riding together with Aunt Becca following. While riding along Uncle and I happened to turn our heads around together and saw Aunt Becca and Fannie in a very perilous position another drosky was attempting to cross them. Both horses going very fast but there was not room and when we looked the horses head was close to Aunt Becca who with the driver had their arms up pushing him back and by the other driver pulling his horse back with all his strength they managed to get by. It was a very narrow escape.

We arrived at Mr. Spinks without any further advents. They seem like a very nice family the two daughters are very pretty girls and speak five or six different languages.

**Saturday, June 13th.** Fannie has been ill all night but is better this morning. So about ten o'clock we all started in a cab accompanied by Sarah Spinks to visit the Hermitage first stopping at the American Ambassadors to procure a ticket. The Hermitage is a splendid large building. The Portico is supported by gigantic marble statues of men holding the roof on their shoulders. The first hall we went into was very fine the floor of mosaic wood highly polished. All the pillars in that room were of Finland granite polished so beautifully that it looked like very fine marble. The ceiling was painted beautifully. We went up the back staircase which was built of marble all the rooms were handsomer than anything I had ever before imagined. The walls and ceilings of all the rooms were painted beautifully every one a different pattern and supported by enormous pillars of marble.

Saw some splendid specimens of malachite made into vases, urns, and many other beautiful things. It is found in Siberia is green and very costly. It is cut into thin slices and veneered on as the lumps found are not large enough to make anything solid.

There was one large room filled with cases of different kinds of medals and many others filled with splendid paintings which would have needed months to have examined as they deserved but we were obliged to give only a hurried glance and hasten on as our time would allow no more. Peter the Great's gallery pleased me very much here was all the machinery he used, his models of ships carvings in ivory, and many other strokes of his genius. There was a stick the same height as himself. Uncle Richard could just reach the top of it with his fingers. His favorite horse and dogs stuffed, the chariot he used to ride in, a clumsy looking one covered with gilt ornaments.

A wax figure of him the size of life he was a very large man nearly seven feet high.

*The Portico of the Hermitage. (Photo by Tracy Girdler, 1993)*

*An Antebellum Life At Sea*

*On this page are contemporary views of three of the scenes admired by Sarah Jane Girdler in St. Petersburg in 1857.*

*The equestrian statue of Peter the Great—known as the Bronze Horseman and memorialized in a poem by Pushkin—was commissioned by Catherine II in 1782 and created by a French sculptor, Etienne-Maurice Falconet. It shows Peter on a rearing horse that symbolizes Russia, trampling a serpent that stands for the forces opposed to his reforms.*

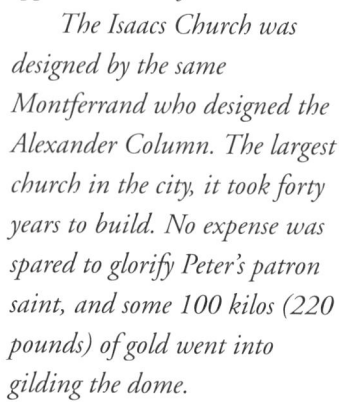

*The Isaacs Church was designed by the same Montferrand who designed the Alexander Column. The largest church in the city, it took forty years to build. No expense was spared to glorify Peter's patron saint, and some 100 kilos (220 pounds) of gold went into gilding the dome.*

*This photo, taken from a bus window, clearly shows the brick and plaster construction Jennie described as resembling stone. The "cutaway view" here was provided courtesy of German Stuka dive bombers strafing the city at the height of the Nazis' failed attempt to conquer St. Petersburg. Amazingly, the damage was still unrepaired half a century later. (Photos by the author, 1993)*

There was a glass case in this gallery filled with snuff boxes presented to the different emperors of Russia by other sovereigns of Europe. Some of them were very costly there was one I noticed particularly completely covered with diamonds.

Saw some bouquets of flowers made of precious stones one was a bunch of lilies made of diamonds and pearls which was very beautiful. There were all kinds of jewels which seemed as plenty as if they were not worth anything. There were splendid pieces of carved ivory and silver and many other things which I have forgotten.

We were shown a hall not yet finished which will I suppose surpass when completed all the other rooms in the building. It is a model of a temple in Turkey. The roof is arched and all carved in a perfect net work and gilded beautifully. There are several beautiful pieces of white marble statuary in this temple. The floor is mosaic of different colored wood. The grand stair case is considered the handsomest in the world. The hall is carved beautifully. A very handsome painting in the center of the ceiling the stairs are of solid white marble the banister of iron and brass. There are several rooms filled with beautiful statuary. On leaving the Hermitage we drove home passing on our way the winter palace, a magnificent building. We could not go in as some of the Royal family were there.

A very fine church an exact model of St. Peters at Rome. The Statue of Peter on horseback which is I think very fine. The Alexander monument,[47] the Triumphal Arch, and several other fine pieces of architecture. We passed a very handsome bridge built of iron. Also the Issac Church which is the handsomest building I ever saw there is a large dome in the center and six smaller ones around it the roof of this church is covered with gold there are fifteen tons on it.[48] After taking lunch Fannie fell asleep and Aunt Becca, Uncle, and Sarah Spinks rode to the town to do some shopping. I stayed at home with Fannie. They returned for us in a little while and then we all took a ride to see the city. The streets are very wide and paved. The houses are mostly built of brick plastered over so as to look at a little distance like stone.

The palaces, churches and other . . . are built either of stone or marble there are a great many statues and monuments placed in the streets which add greatly to their beauty. We rode through the Nevska one of the principal streets of the city where there are many fine stores then over a splendid bridge on which are four bronze statues of a man holding a horse each one in a different position. Then down by one of the public gardens the home just in time for dinner (six o'clock). We were all very tired went to bed early.

**Sunday, June 14th.** This morning Fannie and Aunt Becca both ill. Went to church with Sarah and Maggie Spinks a very fine building the marble pillars were very fine also a picture of the crucifixion which was placed behind the alter.

Did not go out in the afternoon as there were no services at church after tea (half past nine) walked out with Sarah and Maggie the sun was still shining bright it seemed like five o'clock at home.

**Monday, 15th.** This morning Aunt felt unwell. Uncle and myself went to the Academy of Arts and Sciences where we saw all kinds of stuffed birds beasts and fishes. One room was filled with wild beasts another with fish the next with birds. There was an enormous elephant one of the largest in the world and next to it a Mammoth which was almost twice as large. I never saw such a tremendous creature. It was dug out of the ice. Saw a piece of its skin which was an inch and a half thick had a very pleasant time at the Academy saw a great many curious things.

We next took a drosky and went to the museum. Here we saw another Mammoth still larger then the first the largest and the only perfect one in the world.

A great many petrifactions some of which were very curious all kinds of stones and marbles some very fine swords made in Siberia.

Models of all the machinery used in the Siberian mines. All kinds of precious stones. A large lump of malachyte just as it comes from the mines and a great many other things to numerous to mention. We then started for the museum where there is a model of the Siberian mines. We were all equipt with a lighted candle. I got a little way in but it was so very cold and damp that I retreated back to the hole and waited untill Uncle came back. We then visited a fine church the dome and walls were covered with very fine paintings and the pillars were very beautiful there were no seats in the church the congregation are all obliged to stand.

We then returned to lunch feeling very tired. After dinner Sarah, Maggie and I went to walk on the quay had a very pleasant time went on board Duke Constantine's yacht. It is just finished has been built by a young American engineer Mr. Wysby who showed us all over the boat. The cabin is very pretty. Forward of the cabin is a state room and dressing room for the Duke's wife. The Duke's state room is built on deck. He had visited the yacht this afternoon was very much pleased with it. Saw his cocked hat which he had thrown on the table.

**Tuesday, June 15th.** After lunch took a calasky[49] and drove to the bazar which is a very large square building with stone all the way along on each side bought me a pair of boots which I like very much. Everything is very high here furs are cheaper at home than they are here. After leaving the bazar drove all round the public garden it looked very pretty was very large. After a long and pleasant ride we returned home. Found Capt. and Mrs. Chase and Capt. Gidding there after dinner we . . . to go to ride. Uncle Richard had a bad cold so he did not go. Capt., Mrs. Chase, Aunt Becca and Capt. Gidding rode in one calasky Maggie Spinks and myself in another had a delightful drive out among the islands through the gardens. There are two palaces on the islands saw them both they are very pretty. There are a good many very pretty cottages and villas on the different islands we reached home after seven o'clock it was still light the sun about setting.

**Thursday, 17th.** This morning Aunt Becca and Mrs. Chase went out shopping at the Russian magazine[50] came home with some very pretty Moscow bed spreads and robes. There were about twenty American captains up to lunch today. Capt. Lanegan who we saw in Mobile was there. After Aunt Becca came back we packed the trunk and started in the six o'clock boat for Cronstadt. I rode down to the boat in a drosky with Capt. Gidding had a nice ride we arrived in safety at the ship. This evening everything about the same as usual. About half the cotton out–two of the men sick in the hospital two at jail because they would not work. Mr. Symonds is well so are all the rest that were sick when we left.

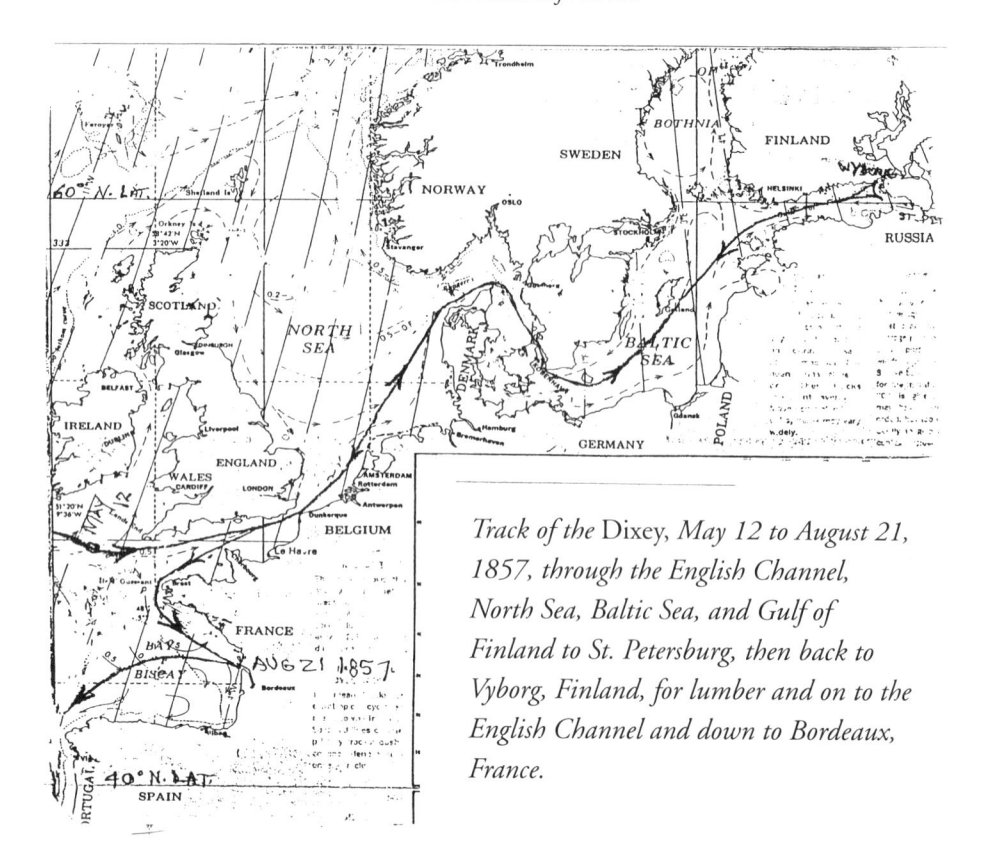

*Track of the* Dixey, *May 12 to August 21, 1857, through the English Channel, North Sea, Baltic Sea, and Gulf of Finland to St. Petersburg, then back to Vyborg, Finland, for lumber and on to the English Channel and down to Bordeaux, France.*

## CRONSTADT

**Thursday, 18th.** A very pleasant day. Fannie has a very bad cold so has Aunt Becca. I have a sore throat and cold in head. Uncle Richard is also affected with a cold. This afternoon Miss Susan Kenny from ship Caroline Nesmith[51] came on board to spend the afternoon she seemed like a very pleasant girl. We had a nice time.

**Friday, 19th.** The weather has been unpleasant all day. First we would have a heavy shower, then it would look pleasant, but would soon pour down again. Have not been out or had any callers.

**Saturday, 20th.** The weather changed pleasant this afternoon so after tea I went in the boat to the Caroline Nesmith to see Miss Kenny but did not go on board as they had only a side ladder. She came to the side of the ship so we had a little chat there and then I came back. Then Aunt Becca and Uncle Richard went on shore with Mr. Millet to help him buy a moscow[?] dress for his wife. They came back a little after ten o'clock made several quite pretty purchases.

**Sunday, 21st.** This morning the weather seemed showery but not . . . for the rain I went to church with Uncle Richard heared very fine sermon.

In the afternoon received a call from Capt. Hill he used to be well acquainted with my father thought I was very like him. In the evening Miss Kenny and her brother came on board and spent the evening we had a nice time.

**Monday, 22nd.** This morning Capt. Griffith of the Winsor Forrest called he intends to bring his wife soon. This afternoon we called on board the Lindsay to see Mrs. Gray we were hoisted up in a chair had a very pleasant call. Mrs. Gray is a very pleasant lady very pretty. After making a long call we went on shore had my foot measured for a pair of black velvet slippers embroidered with silver and lined with fur expect they will be very handsome.

**Tuesday, 23rd.** A very pleasant day. The cold I caught at Petersburg has been much worse the last few days. I have coughed a good deal all day.

This morning Capt. Bunker, wife and little girl and Mrs. Ethan called on board. They are all pleasant people. Aunt and Uncle have just gone on shore to dine with Mr. McSweeny the minister. Fannie and I being sick stayed at home. I was invited to board the Caroline Nesmith to pass the afternoon shall go some other time.

**Wednesday, June 24th.** Uncle Richard has been up to Petersburg today just returned says he must go again tomorrow. We have stayed at home all day have had no one to see us. Brother Sam is twenty-two years old today.[52]

**Thursday, 25th.** Uncle and Aunt have been to Petersburg today Mr. Millet[53] went on board the Nesmith and brought Miss Kenny, and her dog Fannie, on board to spend the day. We have had a nice time together after Uncle and Aunt came home went back with Miss Kenny to her ship and stayed a little while liked her father and mother very much. My cough is much better.

**Friday, 26th.** This morning as soon as done breakfast went on shore. We picked out some slippers and a few other things then accompanied by the pilot went into the Greek Church which is quite pretty there are several fine pictures around the altar. Saw a little baby about a week old baptised. We then went to the bakers he was out but the girl gave us some cakes. We got home about dinner time after dinner Uncle Richard again went to Petersburg and we went to make some calls.

We had hard work to get to the ships as there were a great many lighters in the way. We first called on board the Aldinah[?] saw Mrs. Bunker and little girl we intended to call on Mrs. Watts of the James Nesmith but found her at Mrs. Bunkers so made the two calls in one. Fannie was delighted with the little girl wanted to stay all the afternoon. We then went on board the Waltham to see Mrs. Ethan found Mrs. Griffith, Mrs. and Miss Kenny, made a pleasant call then returned home.

We have finished discharging our cargo suppose we shall go around to Wyburg the first of next week. The search officers have just been on board the officer at the custom house that plays on the melodian came with them so we told him we did not want the men to pull our things to pieces so he sent them out of the cabin did not let them touch anything.

**Saturday, 27th.** Uncle Richard did not return from Petersburg untill six o'clock this evening. I spent the evening with Miss Kenny on board the Caroline Nesmith had a very pleasant time. Mr. Millet came for me in the evening.

**Sunday, 28th.** Today is quite stormy raining hard and blowing a perfect gale. Uncle Richard and Mr. Millet were the only ones that ventured to church.

**Monday, June 29th.** Today the wind is quite high Aunt Becca and the pilot went on shore this afternoon came off with their hands full of bundles.

**Tuesday, 30th.** Went on shore this morning had a nice walk. After we came back had a call from a Mr. Wilkins the American counsel here.

After dinner went on shore again did not stay long as the ship was hauling out of dock. Got out without any accident was towed down to the guard ship by a steam tug are now lying at anchor waiting for a fair wind.

**Wednesday, July 1st, 1857.** This morning the wind was still ahead. About five o'clock the wind changed so we got under way. There was a large fleet of vessels that started before us so were far ahead of us but we soon came up and passed them went along at the rate of nine knots an hour. About ten o'clock it began to rain hard and the wind changed so we were obliged to beat.

## VYBORG

**Thursday, 2nd.** Towards morning as we neared Wyburg[54] the weather grew so thick that the pilot could not see where we were so we had to run back a little when it grew lighter we beat again and managed to get into the little harbor about seven o'clock we are almost surrounded by land. The passage we came through being very narrow. There is a large rock on one side of us that reminds us of Marblehead. We are about six miles from Wyburg after we are partly loaded we shall drop down still further. It is really a very pretty scene and the lumber in the yard smells very nice. We have seen several boats rowing around here all are rowed by women saw one boat with a man sitting down holding his hands with the women rowing him.

**Friday, July 3rd.** This morning commenced working on Aunt Becca's skirt. In the afternoon went on shore to take a walk took one of our sailors who can speak the Fin language with us as guide and interpreter. We went back into the woods and got a nice bouquet of wild flowers then went to the farm house adjoining had a nice drink of fresh milk as we were going to the boat met the harbor master who invited us into his house so we went in to rest ourselves were seated with milk and cakes the gentleman was very pleasant quite fond of music took us into his office to see his organ while we were looking around to see where it was he went up in a corner and commenced turning away at a hand organ. It was very large, sounded quite different from those we hear at home. There was a Norwegian Captain there also so he turned the organ and the other gentleman played on his violin played very finely, too. After hearing the music we returned to the ship found a whole cabin full of ladies and gentlemen who had come to see the ship only one of the ladies and the gentlemen could speak English.

After supper as it was the night before the "fourth," Aunt Becca feeling very patriotic ordered the steward to bring her a fog horn and commenced blowing lustily much to the astonishment of the crews in the neighboring vessels who climbed up in the rigging to see what was going. Uncle Richard caught the enthusiasm and brought out his pistols. Every time he would fire Aunt Becca would respond by a loud peal from the horn which would echo among the hills, making a loud noise. The mate fired his pistols off several times, then took Uncle Richard's gun, so we managed to have quite a time.

Our ship is the largest that was ever in this harbor so of course there are a great many on board to see it.

**Saturday, "July 4th," 1857.** Today is the anniversary of our independence. I have thought a great deal about our dear friends at home. I suppose they are having a nice time at this time. The steward gave us a very nice dinner today. Soup, roast chickens, beef, cranberry sauce, plum pudding, huckle berry pie and other nice things.

After dinner we all went on shore took a nice walk and got a beautiful bouquet of flowers. Met two young ladies who talked with the pilot in German one of them gave Fannie a very pretty bouquet. All the young girls here wear hats some of them are perfect beauties made of dark straw.

**Sunday, 5th.** Today is very pleasant. This afternoon a large party of ladies and gentlemen came on board our friends of yesterday among them. After tea a country woman and her husband came on board. I took them into the cabin when she went out she took my hand and kissed it. It is the custom among the lower classes here to do so. Soon after two little girls came on board with their father they looked perfectly amazed at the size of the ship as indeed everyone does that comes on board. I showed them Fannie's dolls they had a fine time looking at them. I suppose they never saw anything like them before.

**Monday, 6th.** Today is the warmest we have had since we have been this way really quite like summer time. We washed a little this morning some gentlemen came down from Wyburg to see the ship.

**Tuesday, 7th.** Today is still warmer than yesterday have put on my summer clothing. Uncle Richard went up to Wyburg with the pilot yesterday returned this afternoon.

We took him early then went in the boat to make some calls. First went to Mr. Stinkle's but he and family were out then went to see Mr. and Mrs. Colman but they were also away so we went over to the other island to see the folks that called on Sunday. Found them all at home had a very pleasant time. We all took tea in a pretty arbor in the garden. We were going to take a row round the island but we stopped talking so long that it was too late so we defered it for some other time.

**Wednesday, July 8th.** Today is also warm. Called on Mr. and Mrs. Colman had a nice time took tea in the summer house then went to walk on the top of two large rocks where we had a fine view of the surrounding country. Did not get back to the ship untill after eleven o'clock. Mr. and Mrs. Colman are very pleasant people also Mr. Colman's sister who with himself are English although born in Petersburg the sister can speak but very little English but Mr. Colman speaks very fluently. This morning the mate went into the forecastle for something found a English boy nicely packed away there. He had run away from a English schooner that is loading here. He says the mate beats him so he cannot stay. Uncle told him he had better go back he felt very badly about it I suppose he will be cruelly beat if he does go.

**Thursday, 9th.** Today the wind has been blowing very violently all day so we could not go out or have any company. The men have been preparing to paint the ship suppose they will commence tomorrow.

**Friday, July 10th.** Today is not as warm as the first of the week this evening Adelia and Sophie with Mrs. Seseman's children came to ask us to take a row around the island they took tea with us then we started in one of our boats had a very pleasant row the water was so shallow that we were almost afraid to go but we did not meet with any accident. The scenery along the sides of the water are beautiful. One part is said to resemble Switzerland. On our way back it commenced raining a little but only a few drops fell so we did not get much wet.

**Saturday, 11th.** It rained all the morning but cleared up beautifully towards afternoon we took coffee with Mr. and Mrs. Stinkle had a very pleasant time.

**Sunday, July 12th.** Today is very pleasant quite warm. There is no church here and the steamer does not run to Wyburg so we are obliged to stay on board ship. After tea I was on deck and saw Sophie and another young lady coming towards the ship we sent the boat for them they came on board wanted me to go to walk so I went with them. First we went to Sophie's house she played for me on the piano and showed me some of her crayon[55] drawings. One a little boy praying was very beautiful.

Then we went to Mrs. Seseman's took tea and then we four girls took a row in a boat. Sophie rowed us across the harbor to a pretty little island where we landed and found plenty of wild flowers. Coming back Sophie taught me to row and I rowed all the way liked it very much. I did not get back to the ship till quite late.

**Monday, 13th.** This morning we went to make calls first to some of the custom house officers then to see Sophie made quite a long call then went to the Agents. His sister played very prettily for us then sang with her brother some songs in the German, Russian, and Finish languages. We got back to the ship in time for dinner. We intended to go again in the afternoon but we had a constant stream of visitors all the afternoon as fast as one party would go another would come. About nine o'clock they left us and we hurried on shore to see Mr. and Mrs. Colman found Mrs. Colman's mother, brother and two other gentlemen had a pleasant call they were regretting that the lady could not see the ship as she was to leave the next day. When Aunt Becca said come now it is not too late so they started off in our boat. They liked the ship very much.

**Tuesday, 14th.** This morning the steam boat towed us down to deeper water we can see where the other ships are lying but are some way off.

**Wednesday, July 15th.** Uncle Richard went to town today. Tonight about nine o'clock a young man from town came down in a little boat to see the ship he was quite delighted with it.

**Thursday, 16th.** This morning we all started for Wyburg. Brown one of the men has been sick almost all the way went with us and was sent to the hospital.[56] We went to the hotel took a lunch and started in company with a Prussian Captain whom we met at the hotel for the garden belonging to Baron Nickoli which is very fine and large. Met the Seseman family there had a nice time returned to the ship about nine o'clock there is nothing remarkable in the town except a very old tower. The streets are very narrow and krucked.

**Friday, July 17th.** This afternoon a large party came off to see us. Sophie and Adelia were with them they all stayed to tea before leaving Adelia gave me a very pretty ivory bracelet and Sophie a pretty pin to remember them by.

**Saturday, 18th.** This morning we went on shore to try to find some berries saw plenty of vines but the berries are just beginning to form. Got some pretty pieces of Finland granite then returned to the ship. Heared today that Brown died yesterday.

**Sunday, 19th.** This afternoon a large party of French people who live in Petersburg and are spending the summer months here came on board were very much delighted with the ship. They urged us to come and see them hope we shall have an opportunity.

**Monday, 20th.** This morning Uncle Richard started for Petersburg in the steamer don't expect him back till the last of the week. In the afternoon Mr. Falten a young German music teacher came on board he had never seen a melodian before was delighted with it after trying a few times he managed it nicely and played splendidly. There was a little boy with him that was the perfect image of Cowell.[57]

**Tuesday, 21st.** This morning a large party from Mr. Seseman's came down. Mr. Falten with them played again on the melodian said he dreamed about it all night we had a nice time.

After dinner Mr. Colman came with some ladies from Petersburg and also Capt. Gibson wife and children. They had so sooner gone then Mr. Watts and his two brothers came from Wyburg.

After supper Aunt Becca being tired went to bed and after she had gone three more gentlemen from Wyburg came down to see the ship they could all speak English.

**Friday, 24th.** This afternoon we went on shore with the pilot called on Mrs. Seseman had a nice time. Adelia and Sophie were away. Then we called to see the sister of the harbor master but she was out then we went to Mr. Colman's and took tea had a nice time going back to the ship in the boat one of the men was drunk we did not know it untill we saw him fall into the bottom of the boat. We did not want him to row but he insisted and they had hard work to make him leave off. I was very much afraid the boat would tip over.

**Saturday, 25th.** This afternoon Uncle Richard returned from Petersburg bringing a large basket of raspberries, strawberries and currants we had quite a job picking them.

**Thursday, July 30th.** This morning it rained quite hard. Uncle Richard went to town as all the cargo is in. In the afternoon we went to bid some of our friends "Good Bye." We took Agustus one of the black sailors up to Mr. Suseman's[58] to let Madam Williams see him she was quite delighted having never seen one before. Adelia gave me a book called Rachel Gray. It is quite pretty. We stayed to tea and waited until Uncle Richard came from town in the steamer. I felt quite sorry to part with all our kind friends. And they seemed to be very sorry to have us go. Such kind hospitable people as we have found here I never saw before and am afraid never shall again. I really felt bad at leaving them all. We did not reach the ship till nearly eleven o'clock.

## EN ROUTE TO DENMARK

**Friday, 31st.** This morning on awaking found we were under weigh went on deck just as the steamer left us we had a nice fair wind and went along finely a little while then the wind changed ahead so we were obliged to beat.

**Saturday, August 1st, 1857.** This morning the wind is still ahead. Far off in the distance to windward of us are three ships which Uncle Richard and the mate take to be the Windsor Forest, Forest Eagle, and Sharon. We passed Hogland today are fast gaining on the ships this evening the wind died all away. In the middle of the night I heared them hailing the Sharon we had drifted close together. Towards morning the wind freshened come fair.

**Sunday, 2nd.** When I went on deck this morning found we had beat the other ships we could see one far astern the others were out of sight. A very pleasant day but quite cold not much like August.

**Wednesday, 5th.** While walking on the deck this evening the wind freshened and the ship went along eleven and one half knots an hour. If the wind holds so all night we shall be at Elsinore early in the morning.

**Thursday, 6th.** Last night proved very squally we were obliged to take in sail. So instead of being in Elsinore we were more than fifty miles off. The wind has been very light all day. The pilot came on board this morning. We were off Copenhagen about ten o'clock but it was almost calm so we did not get up to Elsinore untill evening. Uncle Richard went on shore also Mr. Borker the ground pilot and the man that we got here going up he intends leaving us here.

## ELSINORE

**Friday, August 7th.** This morning we were all up early went on shore to see Mr. and Mrs. Carey while Uncle Richard was doing his business.

We went out to walk bought a pretty piece of musline to make me a spencer also some lace to trim it with. Then we went to the castle to see a very old church the carving is very curious also to the cemetery which is very fine indeed. On going back to the house found Capt. Griffith of the Windsor Forest had first arrived his wife did not come on shore with him and as he was obliged to stay all day he sent for her after dinner we ladies accompanied by Uncle Richard took a drive out into the country had a very pleasant time. Everything looks so fresh and green quite different from Russia. We stopped in the woods gathered some raspberries and blueberries. There was any quantity of half ripe blackberries but none ripe. About eight o'clock we left for the ship on going down to the pier the boat men there told us they saw a Dutch galliot[59] run across the stern of our ship and cut the painter of the large boat, which was in the water, hook it up and hoist it on board the breeze was very great and the galliot going very fast so no one could catch her. Uncle Richard could not believe it was so thought the boat must have been adrift and so picked up but when we reached the ship we found it to be true. There was no name on the vessel so we have no way of finding her.

## EN ROUTE TO BORDEAUX

**Saturday, 8th.** This morning we got under weigh the Windsor Forest was far ahead of us when we started but we soon passed and left both her and the Sharon far behind. The wind has been quite light all day and the weather very warm.

**Sunday, 9th.** This morning is very pleasant but the wind ahead. We can just see the ships they are so far behind.

**Monday, August 10th.** Today is very warm and pleasant and the wind fair but quite light. This morning we spoke a Dutch galliot four days from Elsinore. They knew nothing about our boat I expect we shall have to give up all hopes of seeing it again. This evening is very pleasant. I counted forty ships in sight. The sea was as smooth as a lake and the sky perfectly cloudless.

**Tuesday, 11th.** Today is very warm a perfect calm. This morning we passed a English brig going to Elsinore so Uncle Richard sent a letter by her to Mr. Carey. We got two very nice halibut from a fishing boat today. They tasted very nice indeed.

**Wednesday, 12th.** Today is like yesterday very warm and calm. Towards night we have a very heavy dew so the deck is as wet as if it had been raining.

**Thursday, 13th.** Like the preceding days warm and perfectly calm. This afternoon Uncle Richard not being busy made a boat rigged her with paper sails wrote the name of our ship latitude longitude, date and c. and launched her over board her sail soon filled with wind and she sailed off nicely. Caught several dog fish today Mr. Millet took the bladder out of one for me it is very pretty.

**Friday, August 14th.** This morning a fine breeze sprung up the first we have had since Monday. We went along eleven knots an hour untill four o'clock when the wind which was blowing very fresh suddenly changed ahead then back again. Acted very strangely indeed so we were obliged to take in the royals and top gallent sails. It is lightning quite sharp with some distant thunder.

**Saturday, August 15th.** Today is quite pleasant the wind fair but not so fresh as yesterday. Fannie is three years old today.[60] She has been treating all hands with jigs.

**Sunday, 16th.** Today is very pleasant quite a nice fair wind. This morning we made the Gabbard then the Galloper light and about two this afternoon the Foreland[61] and then the Goodwin light ships. Uncle Richard felt quite relieved when we made the lights, as we were among so many shoals and were drawing so much water that it made it quite dangerous, and then ordered the royals and studding sails set to. I expect we shall be well into the English channel before long.

The ocean looks as green as grass. I never saw it such a bright color before. I suppose it is owing to the numerous shoals about.

Eight o'clock PM. We have had a nice run this afternoon passed Dover, and Dungeness and are fast approaching Beachy Head. The night very pleasant the sea much smoother than it has been all day we are going ten knots an hour.

**Monday, 17th.** We passed the Isle of Wight about one o'clock this morning and are now far down the chanel. A very pleasant day.

**Tuesday, August 18th.** This morning the wind is not so fresh as yesterday. I washed and ironed today. The weather quite warm and pleasant. Partly made my white spencer.

**Wednesday, 19th.** The wind has not been fair but changed this morning so we laid our course. Finished one of my spencers and began another. This evening passed and spoke a brig bound like us for Bordeaux.

The lights on each side of us looked very pretty last night as we were sailing up the river[62] one of them was the most brilliant I ever saw.

**Saturday, 22nd.** This morning a steam tug tried to tow us up the river but there was a little sea on and the steamer could not get us up.

At noon there was less wind so we tried again and got along nicely as far as Pauillac there dropt anchor for the night. The search officers came on board they looked into all our trunks and drawers they seemed to care more about tobacco than anything else took all that the men had and sealed up in a bag reserving one plug for each man. The scenery all the way up the river was very beautiful the land appeared to be in a perfect state of cultivation could see large numbers of cows, horses and sheep feeding in the green fields. The river seemed much like the Mississippi the water the same color and some of the scenery along the banks much the same. Pauillac is a very pretty place. Uncle Richard went on shore to get his passport brought off some very nice grapes and pears also lettuce, tomatoes, etc.

**Sunday, 23rd.** This morning we were obliged to come up the river as tomorrow there will not be enough water on the bar. When I got up found we were passing close by such pretty places! Went on deck as quick as possible. We had a steam boat each side of us were going up the river quite fast.

The land on one side was low with long rows of stately poplar trees on the other were high cliffs with pretty little villages built all along up the sides. I never saw a more beautiful spot than this. We anchored about ten o'clock about three miles from Bordeaux where we must wait untill tomorrow when a pilot will take us up where we are to lay while unloading. We are now close to the shore opposite a little village so near that we can almost throw anything on land.

A gentleman came on board soon after we landed who belongs to the house we are consigned too. He brought a letter from Mr. Dixey who is in town[?] his wife and family are living here a short distance from Bordeaux. The gentleman is coming in the morning is going to bring any letters he may find for us also some peaches, pears and grapes we are just in the fruit season.

## BORDEAUX

**October 3, 1857.** I have not written in this since August 23rd when we were lying off Lormon[63] we received a note from Mrs. Dixey saying Mr. Dixey was in Paris and insisting on our coming out to their house in the country and staying there all the time the ship was in Bordeaux. So the next day we went on shore and took a carriage out to Mr. Dixey's where we met a cordial reception from Mrs. Dixey and sister.[64] They lived in a most lovely spot with a beautiful fruit and flower garden behind the house while an extensive vineyard stretches up the hill in front. We were there nearly six weeks and had a delightful time all the while. Had just as much fruit of every description as we could eat. I like Mrs. Dixey and Maria very much little Robbie[65] is a sweet little boy. There is a diligence[66] that goes from Monrepos (the place where we lived) to Bordeaux several times a day so we had fine opportunities to go to town. I have got a

*An Antebellum Life At Sea*

new pattern dress a new bonnet pooped skirt and several other nice things since I have been here. One day we all came in with some ladies and gentlemen to see the ship she was all fixed up nice and looked finely. The American Counsel came on board and took lunch with us. Last Saturday, September 25th, 1857 Aunt Becca, Fannie and myself came on board for the ship was expected to sail Tuesday and we wanted to fix all our things in nice order as we expected to have a cabin full of pasingers we did not start however untill Wednesday.

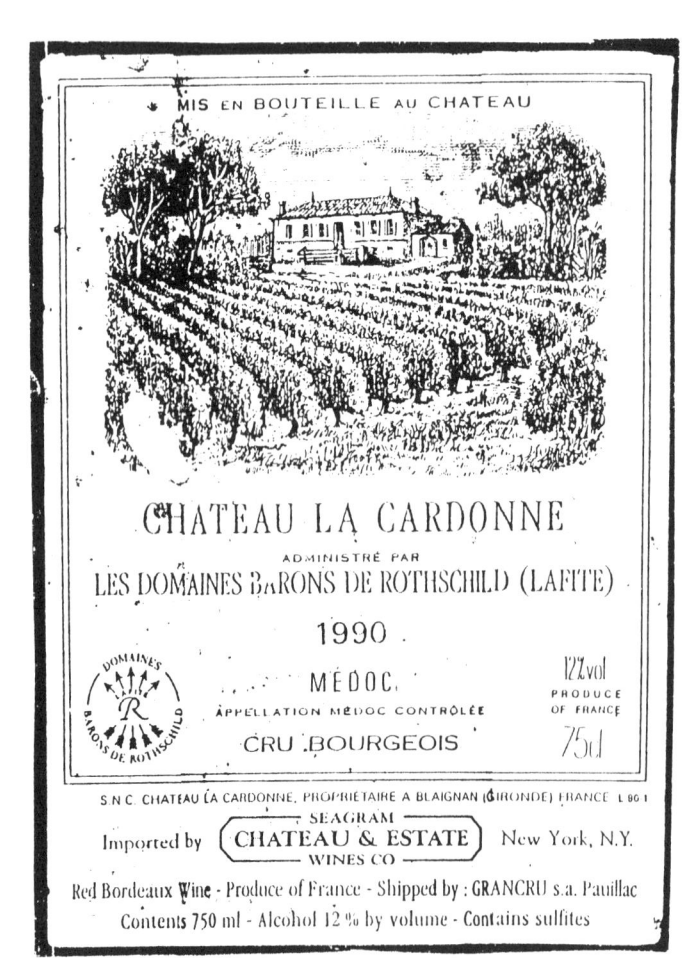

*A French diligence*

*Because the Dixey spent so much time in Bordeaux, both planned and unplanned, we wanted to go to France and find the Villa "Mon repos." Time and distance prevented this trip, but by chance we noticed on a bottle of fine red wine an illustration of a chateau, on a vineyard in the same area. The villa pictured on the wine label is of the same period and is much like the one Robert H. Dixey rented, based on Sarah Jane's description. We hope this helps our readers' sense of time and place, where Sarah Jane spent over three months. Many vineyards in the area are older than our story . . . and still produce some of France's finest wines.*

Monday morning I went with Uncle Richard, Capt. and Mrs. Conant, Mrs. Williams and Mr. Millet to the fruit market. We started before six o'clock in the morning. The fruit looked very nice and was very abundant but quite high in regard to price we got a large bag of chestnuts, some pears, figs, and apples. The next morning Aunt Becca met Mrs. Dixey and Maria at the omlibus station and they all went shopping. Fannie and I staied at home she returned to dinner after which we went with Mrs. Williams to a large basket store I bought one very pretty basket for myself also one for Mr. Millet Aunt Becca bought three. Wednesday morning we dropt down the river with the tide at noon. Mr. Dixey and family came on board. Mr. Dixey intends going down the river with us will then return to Bordeaux where he will be detailed some time by business. We anchored Wednesday night off Lomon and were there all day Thursday owing to the tides. In the afternoon the Caroline Nesmith passed us towed by a steam tug. We sent for our boat which she had brought us from Elsinore[67] and received it in good order it seems quite natural to see it in its old place on the house.

Friday noon the steam tug brought us down to Pauillac had a very pleasant time coming down the scenery on each side of us was very fine.

Saturday morning we got under weigh again but there was scarcely a breath of air. During the day we drift with the tide as far as Royan[68] where we anchored for the night. Early this morning the last pilot came on board and Mr. Dixey left us. We got under weigh with a fair breeze but the wind soon shifted ahead so we were obliged to beat. Now I am writing however it has changed again so we can nearly lay our course.

There is considerable swell on so the ship pitches some. Mrs. Dixey her two children, Maria, the servant girl and even Aunt Becca are sea sick. I feel as well as ever and am quite busy taking care of them all.

## BAY OF BISCAY

**Monday, October 4th.** Today is quite rough all the sick folks remain quite miserable.

**Tuesday, 5th.** Last night we had quite a severe squall it came up without a moments warning so we were not prepared for it the men worked very well

*A hurricane knocks the Dixey on her "beams end" where she remains until the the topmasts and topgallant masts are cut away and she can right herself. Sketch by Ted Brennan*

and succeeded in getting in all the sails but the main top gallent sail which was torn shockingly quite a squally day, very rough, have been taking in sail after sail are now under two close reefed top sails.

**Sunday, October 10th.** We are now anchored off Pauliac, and have the last few days passed through scenes of peril, which I hope will never be my lot to witness again, and which will never be forgotten. Tuesday night proved to be as we expected very stormy the sea was tremendously high, and our noble ship was tossed about on the giant waves like a little cockle shell, none of us could sleep any. Mrs. Dixey was laying on the sofa but was thrown on the floor by the rolling of the ship before daylight Maria called to me to come into her room. I found her bed on the floor so stayed with her as she was much frightened, untill day break. When I dressed myself and went to the door. The sea was tremendous the ship tottering and rolling about so we could not stand without holding on to something. The cook's fire would not burn enough to cook any dinner, everything looked dismal enough. The storm seemed increasing about nine o'clock a sea struck us and poured down through the skylight into the cabin. We all thought our last moment had come for with such high seas boats could not have lived a moment. I dressed as quick as I could all the other children, and grown persons also with the exception of Aunt Becca and myself, were in their night clothes. The two children and

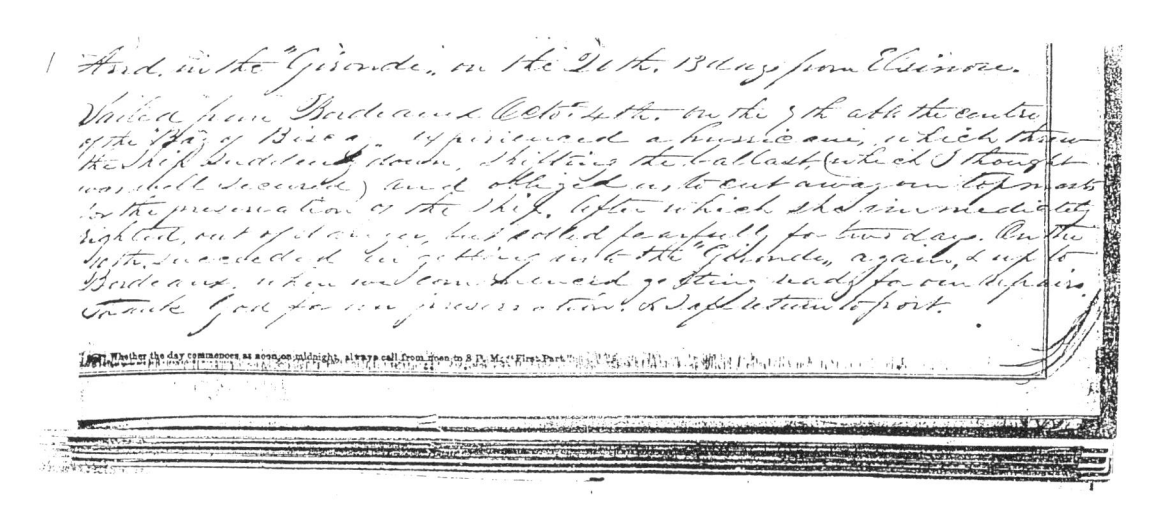

## EXCERPT FROM THE MAURY LOG KEPT BY CAPTAIN RICHARD W. DIXEY

In the portion of the Maury Log shown adjacent, Captain Dixey records the knockdown in the Bay of Biscay in the following succinct entry:

> *…On the 7th abt the centre of the Bay of Biscay experienced a hurricane which threw the ship suddenly down, shifting the ballast, (which I thought was well secured) and obliged us to cut away our topmasts for the preservation of the ship. After which she immediately righted, out of danger, but rolled fearfully for two days. On the 10th succeeded in getting into the "Gironde" again, & up to Bordeaux, when we commenced getting ready for our repairs. Thank God for our preservation & safe return to port.*

*An Antebellum Life At Sea*

*The Dixey as she looked under her jury rig after her knockdown in the Bay of Biscay, October 7, 1857. Captain Dixey cut away the topmasts to relieve the wind pressure and lost all the standing and running rigging above the lower masts. As a result, the ship righted herself and was saved. With only the spanker and foresail, she headed back toward France. A steamer spied her and came and towed her to Bordeaux for repairs.*

servants were screaming and making a most dolful noise. The steward was in the cabin with us trying to pacify them in the midst of all the confusion Mr. Millet came running down to Uncle Richard's room for his ax and hatchet. He said he only wanted it to cut a rope, but Aunt Becca and I well knew what it was for, the squall threw us down on one side, at the same moment the onions[?] between decks rolled to leward that started the balest down to leward, alas everyone thought the ship was gone but all three masts were cut away at that moment and she righted. The storm continued to rage furiously but owing to the great strength of the hull the calm energy and decision of the captain and officers, and most of all the extreme goodness and mercy of Divine Providence, we were enabled to ride out the storm all day and night and also the succeeding we were in great danger, were tossed about on the mighty waves like a straw, we spent the two days and nights in Aunt Becca's room lying on mattresses spread on the floor (we could not sit up the ship rolled so heavily). Thursday night I managed to crawl to the door such a scene of desolation as met my eye! I cannot find words to express or paint the scene. The masts were cut away, there remains hanging over the sides of the lower one, the deck covered with ropes the ship first mounting on the top of a monstrous wave, then plunging way down, till it seemed it would never rise again, the wind howling and sighing among the torn and wet rigging. Oh! It was a heart sickening sight. I thought as I stood clinging to the door, of my home and my dear friends there, and my heart grew faint within me, when I thought that I might never see them again, and earnestly did I pray to be spared to see them once more.

Friday morning the sea had gone down considerably so they rigged a foresail and spanker. The wind was fair for Bordeaux so we started for that place.

Saturday morning we passed the bar soon after took a pilot sailed up the river a few miles passed Royan where the wind died away. Then a French steam ship came along towed us up to Poliac where we now lay expect a steam tug tomorrow morning to take us to Bordeaux. When I think of all we have passed through the last few days it seems almost like a dream but a look at the poor ship dismasted and in such confusion proves the sad reality. How thankful then we ought to be that we are now safely anchored in the river, instead of being tossed about on the wild ocean, or buried in its unfathomable depths.

**November 19th, Thurs. 1857.** Since returning to this place I have not felt like resuming my journal. But tonight knowing as I do that it is Thanksgiving day at home and that many of my friends are enjoying themselves in much the same manner that they did last year when I was with them an inclination seizes me to write therefore I obey its impulse.

How little I thought last year at this time, how many scenes of peril and danger as well as pleasure I should pass through before another Thanksgiving. If I had known then that today I should be so far away from them all in a strange land and among strange people (with the exception of my Aunt and Uncle) my heart then so light would have grown heavy and my pleasure as well as their's would have been deepened but I suppose it is better not to know what is in store for us.

Today has been passed very differently from last year then I was in North Chelsea having a nice time today has been unpleasant so we were in the house all day. Maria and I have been darning stockings. This afternoon I received a letter from Mother,[69] Aunt Becca one from Bethia[70] was much rejoiced to hear that all the folks were well. I have been hoping and fearing all the week hoping I should receive a letter and fearing I might be disappointed. But now it has arrived so I have a Thanksgiving day after all in hearing from all the loved ones at home.

## [CREW LIST OF THE *ROBERT H. DIXEY*, DECEMBER 1857]

The list below was received from the authorities at the port of Le Havre, France, in 1981. It was requested by a marine historian in California who was working on the story of this ship. With some possible inaccuracies due to the translation, it shows:

Bordeaux, 7 December 1857 (arrived 12 Oct 1857; going to sea tomorrow)

| | |
|---|---|
| Richard W. Dixey, Captain | Dexter Collamon, First Mate |
| Franklin Millett, Second Mate | Daniel Symonds, Third Mate |
| George Williams, Bosun | George Rice, Carpenter |
| Daniel Franklin, Cook | John W. Hubbard, Steward |

Sailors: Henry Jackson; Isaac K. Hall; Robert Stringer; August Setegill (or Seliger); Robert Harris; Lewis Finelly; Adolf H. Schiff; Ariel Jackson; Horatio Slate; Charles Jenkins; William H. Little; Edward H. Bryant; Alex Brown; Morrison Blair; John Sparks; Franklin Smith; August Careforend; Tom Richard; Joaquin ?; Samuel K. Girdler; Charles Allenson

Total ship's crew    29

The document shows certification of the death at Vyborg, Finland, of a seaman, William Butlier, of heart disease, on 15 July 1857.

Known to be aboard, but not listed on this French document, were the following nine passengers:

Mrs. Rebecca Dixey (Mrs. Richard W.); Miss Fannie Dixey; Miss Sarah Jane Girdler; Mr. Robert H. Dixey; Mrs. Robert (Jane) Dixey; Miss Anna L. Dixey; Master Robert Dixey, Jr.; Miss Maria Minge; A French servant girl

Total aboard for the return to the United States: 38

## AT SEA—HOMEWARD BOUND!

**Friday, Dec. 11th, 1857.** We are again on the wide ocean, and must for the next month be tossed about at the mercy of the wild waves. The pilot left us this morning, and our good ship is gliding gracefully through the blue waters of the bay, now so calm and clear, that one can hardly realize them to be the same that tossed and roared so angrily when we last saw them. I hope and trust that the storm king will not give us such a polite greeting as before. It is very cold today.

**Saturday, December 12th.** The wind is fair the weather very pleasant and moderate yesterday got up the main royal and studding sails today main top gallent studding sails the breeze is very light as we go along about six knots.

**Sunday, 13th.** Today is still fair we are getting along nicely and will I suppose if this wind holds soon be out of the bay.

**Monday, 14th.** Today has been nearly all the time a dead calm sometimes a little puff of wind would come first from one quarter then from another so the men were all the time hauling the yards first one way then back again. Have both watches on deck in the afternoon now.

**Tuesday, 15th.** It was a dead calm all night towards morning the wind sprang up ahead we are now going about eight knots. See three ships down to leward on the wind, bound into the channel, they must be having a splendid run.

**Wednesday, December 16th.** Last evening we had quite a squall reefed topsails but loosed them again at ten o'clock when we were again becalmed the weather very thick and rainy. This morning there is a little more wind but not fair. Mrs. Dixey and Maria are a little sea sick owing to the excessive rolling and pitching of the ship.

**Thursday, 17th.** Today the wind is still ahead blowing strong with a very high head sea. In the afternoon as it looked very squally Mr. Millet's watch reefed topsail then the mainsail and fore sail. This evening reefed the spanker but now the wind is going down and things begin to look pleasant again. Friday, 18th. About ten o'clock last night the barometer comenced going down and it began to look squally close reefed topsails the storm increasing took in everything but two topsails. The sea was tremendously high the wind blowing furiously and the ship rolling and pitching so that none of us could sleep. Ria had her bed on the floor with Anna so I laid in the lower berth by her side towards morning the wind went down some and became fair the sea has been very high all day have royals and [?] sails set are going along finely.

Fannie is sick today seems rather feverish.

**Saturday, December 19th.** The wind still fair but very light still some sea on so there is considerable motion. Fannie has not been dressed today she seemed so feverish tonight we gave her a mustard foot bath.

**Sunday, 20th.** Today is pleasant and quite mild doesn't seem much like Christmas week. The wind is very light first on one quarter then the other or directly aft the sailors have been kept busy all the morning owing to their fickleness.

**Monday, 21st.** Last night the wind freshened considerably so we went from ten to twelve knots all night and are going eleven knots now, with royals and top gallent sails furled steering within two points of our course there is some sea on and we are quite crank.

**Tuesday, 22nd.** We are still going at quite a smart pace but rather to the westward of our course. Several schools of porpoises passed us today and yesterday. Had several squalls reefed topsails. This evening we are about eighty-five miles from the Western Islands[71] and our course leads us directly among them but the night is rather thick and squally and Uncle Richard could not get a sight of the sun today therefore does not know exactly where we are so does not deam it prudent to run among them and will soon tack and stand off untill morning.

**Wednesday, December 23rd.** Last night was very squally close reefed topsails fore and main sails. All the morning have been having squalls of wind and rain. A little while ago a whirlwind passed very near us we are now under close reefed topsails every thing else furled. This morning a whale passed across the bow the first seen this passage.

This morning Sam[72] hurt his leg badly he was hoisting the spanker and a rope slipt out of his hand caught his leg and threw him down if Uncle Richard had not caught the rope his leg must have been broken as it was he hurt his knee so badly that he could not stand on it and has been in bed all day. This afternoon Mr. Millet killed one of the pig's[73] quite a fine large one it is too.

This evening the weather has cleared up and the wind is fair again there is considerable sea on yet.

**Thursday, 24th, Christmas Eve.** Today has been very pleasant a nice fair wind though rather moderate. Washed a little this morning. Fannie has been dressed again today for the first time this week. This evening some of the men have been dancing and . . . "Juba" for us, it was really quite amusing to see Uncle Tom dancing.

It doesn't seem possible that this is Christmas Eve, how little I thought last year at this time that I should be so far away from home now. How I should like to see them all now. I wonder if mother or any other of my dear friends are thinking of me now.

I have been in the hatch house[74] this afternoon to see Sam, his leg is very stiff and he rather blue, said he should feel better if I would sing so we sat there some time singing all the old tunes we could think of, especially those about home. Poor boy he is much worse off than I am for he is not only home sick, but sick several other ways, has two sore fingers a lame leg and a bad humor all over his body. I think he is to be pitied.

Last year I was very busy helping dress the church and a nice time I had too. And very pretty did it look. I wonder who dressed it this year and if I shall ever help again I hope so, but time only will show.

**Friday, December 25th, 1857.** Well Christmas is almost over and still I can hardly realize that it has commenced. How very different it has been passed from any other Christmas. Last year I took tea at Lizzie Steven's played whist in the evening had a delightful time. Today I am on the wide ocean far far from my home and friends. I wonder if I shall ever see another Christmas and where I shall be. But I suppose it is best not to know.

The steward gave us a nice dinner today. Mock turtle soup, roast pork and chickens, squash, indian pudding, plum pudding squash mince and huckle berry pie and many other nice things. The men all had a nice dinner today as well. . . . It has been a perfect calm all day there is a ship in sight there was some talk of getting the quarter boat[75] out and making a call but at last it was decided not to. Mr. Collamore[76] took Uncle Richard's little boat and rowed all around the ship in her. She looked very pretty in the water. Have just been to see Sam he feels some better I am in hopes he will be well soon. It has been almost calm all day. But this evening the wind sprung up ahead.

**Saturday, 26th.** Today has been like yesterday almost calm. This evening three of the men were order[ed] by Mr. Millet to do something on the deck. They grumbled considerably about it. Uncle Richard was there and gave them quite a severe talking [to]. Soon after one of them[77] took his turn at the wheel. Mr. Millet asked him how he headed the man answered without saying, Sir, he told him to say Sir but he refused so Mr. Millet gave him a severe beating the mate was just going below but turned back and helped him so between the two the man had a hard time of it. Uncle Richard went up to talk to him he was rather saucy at first but was soon made to hold his tongue. Uncle Richard loaded his gun and pistols so as to have them in readiness in case he should stir up the rest of the white men to rebellion though he thought there would be no use of them, even if they did, as the blacks were all devoted to him and could with the officers soon silence them. But it is always best to be on the safe side.

**Sunday, December 27th.** Last night passed off very quietly whatever the men thought on hearing of Morison's beating they kept to themselves. So I reckon that it will teach them better manners and no harm ensue. I hope so at any rate.

The day is perfectly lovely the wind fair though very moderate and the air so mild and balmy as in June one can hardly realize that it is mid-winter and that at home the snow is probably covering everything out of doors with its cold white mantle and the air so cold and biting that the warmest clothing is in recridition [sic]. But although this weather is undoubtedly the most pleasant yet I would gladly exchange it for the other could I only be at home again among my dear friends. How long it seems since I saw them last and when I think of the many changes that must have taken place before I see them again. I feel sad for I feel that some of those I called my friends will be so no longer having married and moved away. But I must remember that my loss is their gain–and grieve no more.

**Monday, 28th.** Today is like yesterday perfectly lovely. Last evening a nice fair breeze sprung up and all night and today we have been sailing at the rate of from eight to ten knots going along very smoothly too. Such delightful weather almost makes me forget the storms and rough times we have passed through and I can understand what it is that reconciles the sailor to his hard life.

**Tuesday, 29th.** Another delightful day though rather more moderate than yesterday. Hope the trades will continue a favorable as they have commenced. Wednesday, December 30th. Today is as pleasant as yesterday only much warmer. It is really uncomfortable in the sun. The wind is very light but fair we average about five knots an hour.

**Thursday, 31st.** This is the last day of the old year I can hardly realize it. A year ago today I was at home preparing for a party. The day was bitter cold everyone keeping as near the fire as possible. How little I thought then that I should be so far away from home now I wonder if there will be a party tonight. How I should like to take a peep at all my dear friends. It seems such an age since I last saw them. How pleasantly the old year is leaving us. The air is so mild the sky so clear, the water so blue, clear and smooth, that one can easily imagine it mid-summer.

**Friday, January 1st, 1858.** So the old year has really gone with all its

*The passengers checking the ship's speed with the "log." Illustration by Ted Brennan.*

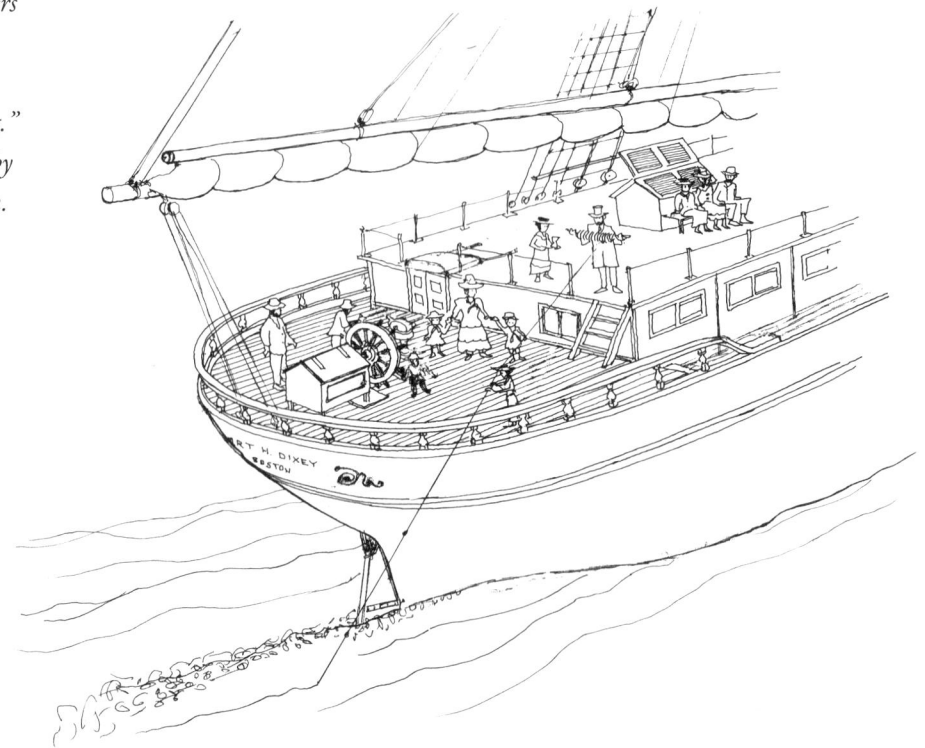

burden of smiles and tears; hopes and fears; joys and sorrows; dangers and temptations; truly a heavy burden, full enough to make him throw off the load and yield up the ghost, leaving the field to a younger and more vigorous successor though he too will in his turn bow under the heavy burden. It is a solemn thing to think that all the wrong deeds we have done, privileges slighted, opportunities neglected, the past year can now never be recalled but must remain a lasting record against us I am now a year older than on last New Year's day but sad I am to say that I am no better. All my good resolutions have failed and though I have passed through many dangers the past year they have failed to make me better.

The new year has commenced beautifully. Oh! may it prove a good one may my life this year pass like today. Calm, pleasant, happy and may I if spared to see another New Year look back on this with pleasure as being one in which I tried all the year to lead a better and more useful life.

**Saturday, January 2nd.** Today has been very pleasant with the exception of several squalls of rain which would come up very suddenly then clear up and be pleasant again saw several very beautiful rainbows. After dinner all the ladies were on deck. As the ship was going very fast we thought we would throw the log and see how fast we were sailing. So we inlisted Mr. Dixey to hold the reel found we were sailing twelve knots we had hard work pulling in the line and finely had to call Mr. Millet to our assistance. We had a fine breeze all last night at twelve o'clock found we had made two hundred and eight miles. This evening is perfectly lovely we are sailing through the water very fast we have been on deck almost all the evening singing.

**Sunday, 3rd.** We had a rain squall this morning and several beautiful "bows of promise." Since then the weather has been delightful. Uncle Richard has just worked up the sum finds we have made two hundred and forty miles.

**Monday, 4th.** It has been very warm all day with rain squalls in the morning. Made two hundred and eighteen miles today.[78] Sam and the other boys moved into the forward hatch house this morning.

**Tuesday, 5th.** Today is very warm and pleasant. Last night we had quite a squall of rain and wind. Took in studden sails and let her run since then the wind has been mostly moderate. Have made one hundred and eighty-eight miles today.

**Wednesday, January 6th.** Very warm and pleasant. This morning a young whale played around the ship some time. Saw several schools of flying fish. Last night I took a salt water bath in a fine large tub made from a hogshead with the after hatch house put over it. Have just returned from another one this evening the water is very warm and nice. Today we made one hundred and ninety-nine miles.

**Thursday, 7th.** Very warm and pleasant again today. Have made two hundred and thirteen miles. Passed some Gulf weed today the first we have seen. Friday, January 8th, 1858. Another delightful day quite warm. Have made two hundred and ten miles. A young whale has been playing around the ship

*An Antebellum Life At Sea*

nearly all day saw plenty of flying fish. Have just come from my salt water bath feel very cool and comfortable. Today is the anniversary of [Andrew] Jackson's victory.[79] I suppose they are having fine times at home now. This afternoon an American brig crossed our stern she was a long way off but we exchanged signals.

**Saturday, 9th.** This last day of the week is like all the preceding very pleasant and warm. Have made two hundred and eighteen miles. The evening is perfectly lovely and very mild. We have all spent it on deck singing. Had quite a concert with Mr. Millet for spectator.

**Sunday, 10th.** All the morning very pleasant. This afternoon quite a black looking squall came up. Took in main to[p] gallent studden sails now it has blown over and looks very pleasant again. We have made two hundred and sixteen miles today. A year ago today was the last Sunday I spent at home it was a severe snow storm. There is considerable swell on and the wind directly aft so we have been rolling very badly all day. This evening Mrs. Dixey was sitting in the rocking chair with both her children in her arms when the ship gave a sudden roll the chair tiped over and they all went down in the floor in one heap fortunately no one was hurt.

Monday, 11th.     Last night had several squalls of rain and wind took in studding sails. Today has been quite pleasant and very warm. Caught a fine large fish this morning he made a nice dinner, two other's caught the hook but got away again. This afternoon saw the island of St. Domingo at a distance too far off to distinguish anything plainly. We have only made one hundred and ninety-eight miles today.[80]

**Tuesday, 12th.** Today has been very pleasant this morning I saw land from my window[81] has been in sight all day. The island is very high we could see it at a distance of twenty miles. At one time we were only about four miles off could then see things very plainly. This evening just before dark one of the men saw land then the mate and captain and myself saw it but none of the others could see it. Uncle says it is Cuba about twenty miles off. There is a splendid fresh breeze blowing we are sailing about ten knots.

**Wednesday, 13 Jan.** Another splendid day. The high bold coast of Cuba has been in sight all day but we are at too great a distance to see anything plainly. This morning the wind blew fresh from shore so we could plainly smell the orange groves and other delicious perfumes how we all longed to go in close to the shore but Uncle Richard was afraid of getting becalmed.

**Thursday, January 14th.** Today is even warmer than yesterday. We have left Cuba or rather that part visable from the course we are running behind us the wind is very light at times almost calm. It is just a year ago today that we left home how different the weather then it was so cold that it was almost impossible to keep comfortable now it is just the reverse. How I should like to know if another year will elapse before I see that dear old place again. I wonder if any of my dear friends are thinking of me today. I think Grandma[82] will she always remembers dates.

**Friday, January 15th.** Like yesterday intensely warm and almost calm none of us could do anything but seek the coolest spots on the ship and make ourselves comfortable.

**Saturday, 16th.** Another hot day. This afternoon caught a young shark the man had him cooked for supper thought it very nice it had a very large mouth with formidable rows of teeth, and very wicked looking eyes, it made quite a fuss flaping around the deck, but was at last killed by pounding it with iron belaying pins. Also hooked a daulphin got him almost in, when the line got foul with another and he got off. All this afternoon it has been a dead calm. Tonight we can plainly see the light on Capt Antonio.[83]

**Sunday, 17th.** All the first part of the night calm then squally. This morning very moderate. This noon very black and stormy looking, close reefed topsails. In the afternoon a squall of rain pourd down with great fury. This evening shook out reef out of the topsails. The breeze is quite fresh but not fair and the air very cold.

**Monday, 18th.** Today is pleasant but quite cold. The wind ahead and a heavy sea on so we pitch considerably. We are now three hundred and sixty-eight miles from Mobile. If the wind was only fair we would soon be there.

**Tuesday, 19th.** Quite cold this morning the wind still ahead have been beating all day, are far to leward of Mobile and can make but very little easting.

**Wednesday, January 20th.** About the same as yesterday. The wind ahead.

## NEW ORLEANS

**Thursday, 21st.** This morning got far enough along to make the south west pass of the Mis. so Mr. Dixey concluded to run in as far as the bar and send a telegraphic dispatch for orders. Took a pilot soon after dinner were too far to leward to get over the bar without the aid of steam. So anchored outside soon after two steam tugs came to offer their aid but of course it was not accepted. Then Mr. Dixey went[?] in the boat with Mr. Millet and six men to the telegraph office about five miles off. Sent a dispatch to Mr. Brown cannot receive an answer untill tomorrow morning. The steamer Empire City bound to New York is on the bar two steam tugs are trying to get her off. Several ships among whom is our old friend Gov. Langdon Capt. Stone, are on the bar. The Riga has not yet arrived although she sailed several days before us.

**Friday, 22nd.** This morning Mr. Dixey again went to the telegraph office. Found that the line between the city and Mobile was broken down. Received a dispatch from Mr. Beguin[84] one of the owners in New Orleans saying we had better go ahead to Mobile so we got under weigh again with the wind dead ahead. Mr. Dixey left us in the pilot he intends seeing to his business in the city then going to Mobile in the steam boat.

**Saturday, 23rd.** Have been beating all night with a fresh breeze and only made about five miles to windward. Saw a ship going into the S.W. pass this morning took to be the Riga. The wind is blowing very fresh seems like a strong gale. Uncle Richard is sorry we did not wait at the bar for a fair wind.

**Sunday, January 24th.** Today is very rough and stormy. The ship pitching terribly. Reefed topsails this morning close reefed have not made anything on our course today.

**Monday, 25th.** This morning the wind came fair so we made all sail, and went along nicely, at twelve o'clock Uncle Richard marked the course out on the chart found us full thirty miles to windward of Mobile so supposed we had a strong tide in that direction. Altered the course and soon found a pilot who took us in safely though to late for any of the boats as they generally leave about two o'clock.

## MOBILE

**Tuesday, 26th.** This morning Mrs. Dixey, Maria, the children all left in the Natches with Uncle Richard all left for Mobile. Aunt Becca and myself have been very busy cleaning up the cabin looks very nicely now. There are a great many ships in the bay. Capt. Cook and his wife are here I want to see her very much.

**Wednesday, 27th.** This morning Mr. Collamore boarded one of the steamers brought four letters from home for me two for Aunt Becca all the news was good. Have been washing today.

**January 28th, Thursday.** Uncle Richard came down in the boat this morning brought Madam Levert's new work[85] for us to read went up again this afternoon. After he had gone we went to see Mrs. Cook. The mate took us in the boat there was much more sea on than we expected and a very strong tide the boat kept jumping up and down along side the ship so we had hard work to get in but with the assistance of the two mates we succeeded in getting in. I was rather alarmed lest we should tip over. We found Mrs. Cook at home were hoisted up in a chair and had a very pleasant time stayed to tea went home in the evening. Mr. Millet put the lamp in the rigging so we could see it he had began to be anxious about us. Mr. Symonds and the steward went up in the boat. Samuel went to the hospital[86] to try to get cured I am in hopes he will soon be well feel very lonely without him.

**Friday, 29th.** This morning was very cold but grew warmer towards noon. Stayed at home all day working.

**Saturday, 30th.** Uncle Richard came down this morning Capt. Prichard call[ed] to see us. Mr. Millet and a young man the mate of the China took our boat and went oystering. Capt. Cook called to see us took dinner then we all went in his boat to see his ship to spend the afternoon had a very pleasant time. Mr. Millet got a splendid lot of oysters.

**Sunday, 31st.** Today is very rainy and dull. Saw no one out of the ship.

**Monday, February 1st, 1858.** Mr. Collamore left us this morning and a new mate came down he is a very young man has only been to sea six years.

**Tuesday, 2nd.** Mr. Symonds came down this morning went back in the same boat he is going home in a bark bound to Boston. He saw Sam the day before yesterday he had just got comfortably seated could not of course see any improvement as yet. Though I hope he will before long.

**Friday, 5th.** This morning the bark Mr. Symonds is in crossed our stern and went out to sea. He waved his hat as he passed. Received a long letter full of news from Alicia also one from Emma.[87]

**Saturday, 6th.** This morning the mate brought me a letter from Samuel it was dated last Tuesday. So he had only been at the hospital two days.

**Sunday, 7th.** The weather is much milder today than it has been all the week.

**Sunday, February 14th.** We are still in the bay. Have been busy all the week finishing off odd jobs. Aunt Becca thinks to go to town Tuesday to stay the rest of the week. Yesterday Capt. and Mrs. Redman called on us. Mrs. Redman intends going home next Monday week by way of Savanah she wants us to go with her. Aunt has not yet decided which to do. I have had two letters from home this week. Mr. Millet left us last Wednesday. Thursday morning the bark Groat[?] passed us homeward bound all our black boys went in her she carried a large box with some of our Russian curiosities in it. The steward has been down got his clothes and gone up river to a hotel. He saw Samuel the day before with Mr. Millet he was a little better.

**Sunday, September 26th, 1858.** A long time has passed since I last wrote in this book and I have wandered about in various places. Arrived home early in March. After staying in Marblehead three weeks went to Chelsea and the whole summer has been passed in visiting there and the neighboring ... Boston and Medford been passed very pleasantly.

I am now quite settled at home again. When I look back on the past eighteen months with all its danger and pleasures; sorrows and joys; and many many changes, I am almost persuaded that it is all a dream a mere creation of my fancy and that all the while I have been quietly pursuing the even tenor of my way at home instead of wandering so far, so very far away. Those were pleasant times I would they could be revisited[?] but no they have forever passed. I might possibly in future years again visit some of these well remembered places but even if I should everything would be altered I suppose my old friends will be gone married or perhaps dead. I should dearly love to see them again and will hope that even if I never should behold them in this world there is another where we can meet–never again to part.

**Friday, December 31st, 1858.** This is the last night of the year. In a few more short hours the old year with all its joys and sorrows, dangers and temptations will have forever passed away never again to be recalled. I suppose many are tonight like me recalling the past some will look back on time well spent feel that something has been gained that they have been living better lives been more true to their better natures than any preceding year. Others look back to a time spent in vain–see nothing but broken resolutions, slighted advantages, but all who think at all will I believe make new resolutions for the coming year. And if we only remember on whose aid we must rely in order to be able to keep them we shall I trust at the end of another year look back with less feeling of regret than we now do.

\* \* \* \* \*

Rebecca Dixey did decide to return home with Mrs. Redman by way of Savannah, taking a steamer from Savannah to Boston, and Fannie and Sarah Jane of course accompanied her. We don't know whether Rebecca Dixey accompanied her husband again during the remaining twenty months of his life. One reason for thinking she may not have is that life at sea was hard on little Fannie. She was often ailing. In September 1856 Rebecca had written, "She doesn't seem to get rid of her cough . . . I some times think she never will." Fannie died in January 1859 at the age of four and a half.

> Mobile Ala
> August 28th 1858
>
> Dear Sir
>
> In consequence of illness, and the continued depression of business affairs in this place, I have not been able to regain my former position as a Cotton Broker. The short acquaintance that I formed with you while at Mobile, thru the late Capt. John Childe, Engineer, impressed me so favorably, that I have ventured to address you for the purpose of requesting your influence in establishing myself in some way or other, in the Telegraphic Communication that is already established between

*Letter of Herbert C. Peabody, from the Peabody Papers, # 3676z, in the Southern Historical Collection, University of North Carolina Library, Chapel Hill. Used with permission.*

CHAPTER

*9*

# The End of the *Robert H. Dixey*

After the voyage to Russia recorded by Sarah Jane Girdler, the *Dixey* carried four more loads of cotton to Europe, one to Le Havre and the final three to Liverpool. Cotton prices were high, and the profits to the owners were substantial. All the trips were relatively routine—until the last.

On September 4, 1858, the *Dixey* sailed for Liverpool with its seventh load of cotton. Aboard was Horace M. Peabody, nephew of Tom Fettyplace. Horace, age sixteen, had just completed his high school education at the Towle Institute in Mobile.[88] The fairly new Naval Academy at Annapolis (begun in 1845) was of some interest to him, but he was young, and his Uncle Tom suggested he try the "sea life" before committing himself to the Navy. The *Dixey* was in Mobile loading cotton for delivery to Liverpool, and Horace was offered a berth as a "ship's boy" (like a cadet in modern terms). He signed on with great pleasure. The captain later told his father that he did a fine job and would make a fine officer.

The ship docked in Liverpool on October 27, a slow trip. While Horace was in England, he journeyed down to London to see the sights. His father, Herbert Peabody, had written him a letter of introduction to banker and philanthropist George Peabody, a distant cousin, originally from Danvers, Massachusetts. Horace did get to meet his famous kinsman, but not much came of it. Here is the letter:

Mobile Ala<br>August 28<sup>th</sup> 1858

Dear Sir

In consequence of illness and the continued depression of business affairs in this place, I have not been able to regain my former position as a Cotton Broker.

The short acquaintance that I formed with you at Mobile thru the late Capt. John Childe, Engineer, impressed me so favorably that I have ventured to address you for the purpose of requesting your influence in Establishing myself in some way or other, in the Telegraphic Communication that is already established between England and America.

The Cotton Community will need a thorough and reliable system for Transacting business.

A National Board of Trade will ultimately be devised or an Atlantic and Gulf Cotton Inspection and Transit Trade Agency will be organised, in which case I shall be pleased to have my claims properly presented and your influence used in my behalf.

If necessary I can refer to persons and houses with whom I have had extensive Cotton transactions–in England, France and America–– My son Horace Mansfield, a fine lad of 16 years of age, who you may reccollect having seen at the Battle House, is about to sail on the Ship Robert H. Dixey for Liverpool to pass his summer vacation and may probably visit London. If so, I should be glad to have you see him–with sentiments of respect

I have the honor to remain
I am dear sir
Your kinsman
and Ob$^t$ Serv$^t$
Herbert C. Peabody

It is evident that Horace was not enthralled with the sea, and on his return home from this voyage he went to work as a clerk in the office of his uncle Henry K. Fettyplace, marketing coal. He lived with his parents in the Fettyplace country home in Spring Hill until he enlisted in the Confederate Forces two years hence.

Horace would not survive the Civil War. He served briefly with the famous Third Alabama Infantry but was discharged in August 1862 for physical disability.

Returning from Philadelphia in March of 1859, the *Dixey* ran into a tough situation: there was no cotton to buy! Captain Dixey laid off all the crew except for a couple of bosuns/watchmen who lived aboard. The ship swung at anchor in the lower bay for almost six months while the 1859 cotton crop grew to maturity.

In August, Jane Dixey's brother Willie (William Henry Harrison Minge, named after his uncle, the president) returned to Mobile. He was twenty-nine years old and flat broke. In the eight years of his absence, he had sailed as a deckhand, mate, pilot, and captain in the East Indies and India, but he seemed to lack patience and changed jobs frequently. He met Captain Dixey, and he is bound to have admired the *Dixey*, for at the age of four it was still a state-of-the-art clipper. But Willie had lost interest in the sea.

When Willie arrived in Mobile, he found that the family was at the summer home in Point Clear, so he took the *Southern Star* across the bay. By chance a barefoot boy of fourteen met the boat; it was his brother Collie (Collier H. Minge, Jr.). Willie let him carry his bag the few hundred yards to the family cottage, where he greeted his mother and sisters. The following August, at the age of fifteen, Collie would go off to V.M.I. Later he would be deeply involved in the Civil War.

At that time, the *Dixey* was anchored ten miles south of the Point, nearly loaded with cotton. The ship finally sailed for Liverpool on September 9, 1859, with 3,504 bales of cotton. This would be its next-to-last load.

The *Dixey* returned directly from Liverpool, arriving in Mobile on January 16, 1860. By March 9 she had filled the hold with cotton and sailed again for Liverpool.

## THE FINAL VOYAGE

After unloading its last load of cotton, the *Dixey* sailed from Liverpool on May 23, 1860, for New York. After a slow passage and bad weather, the ship arrived and started loading miscellaneous hardware for Mobile.

A visitor in New York was a Mobile bar pilot, Capt. Sam Smyly. He needed a ride home, and Captain Dixey was glad to offer him a trip in return for his services when they arrived at Mobile Bay. The ship sailed on August 15 and, after a rather slow trip, was coming up the Gulf on September 14 with steady west winds. The western sky showed "mare's tails,"[89] and a falling barometer caused Captain Dixey concern. The anchorage in Mobile Bay was pretty secure, so the decision was made to continue. About suppertime, the ship crossed the bar and anchored far up the anchorage. At 10 P.M. double anchors and all chain were put out, with double gaskets on the sails, and all measures to ride out a storm were taken. After midnight the wind dropped, then shifted to the south and turned into a violent hurricane. The anchors held because the shelter of Dauphin Island kept the seas down…but the next day was to be the *Dixey*'s last.

## THE LAST HOURS OF THE *ROBERT H. DIXEY*

The eye of the hurricane passed about 8 A.M., providing only an hour of relative calm; by 9 A.M. violent northerly winds had swung the ship around. The full force of the wind and seas reaching six to eight feet were too much for the anchors and chain. One chain parted, and it was obvious that the ship would be grounded on the west side of the channel. Orders were given to cut away all the standing rigging.

Before this operation was completed, the second anchor chain parted, and the ship quickly pounded southward, where the seas smashed it against the west bank of the ship channel. The crashing of this stout vessel on the shoal broke her ribs, and disaster was close at hand.

The giant seas coming down Mobile Bay, combined with the northwest winds, lifted the ship enough to shift its broken hull across the channel. In the very shallow water that lay to the east of the main ship channel, the *Dixey* was soon pounded to pieces.

The crew of Bahamians who served with Captain Dixey were all nonswimmers, and Captain Dixey was not about to leave them. They all lashed themselves to what was left of the rigging.

Because the ship was wooden and fastened with "treenails" (pegs of locust wood), the breaking of her ribs was like the unraveling of a sweater. Each breaker loosened some more planks, the deck and rails came apart, and the timbers to which the rigging was fastened broke away. The men tied to these shrouds and stays were tossed like rats in a trap. Nothing could be done. Captain Dixey never thought of leaving

# The End of the *Dixey*

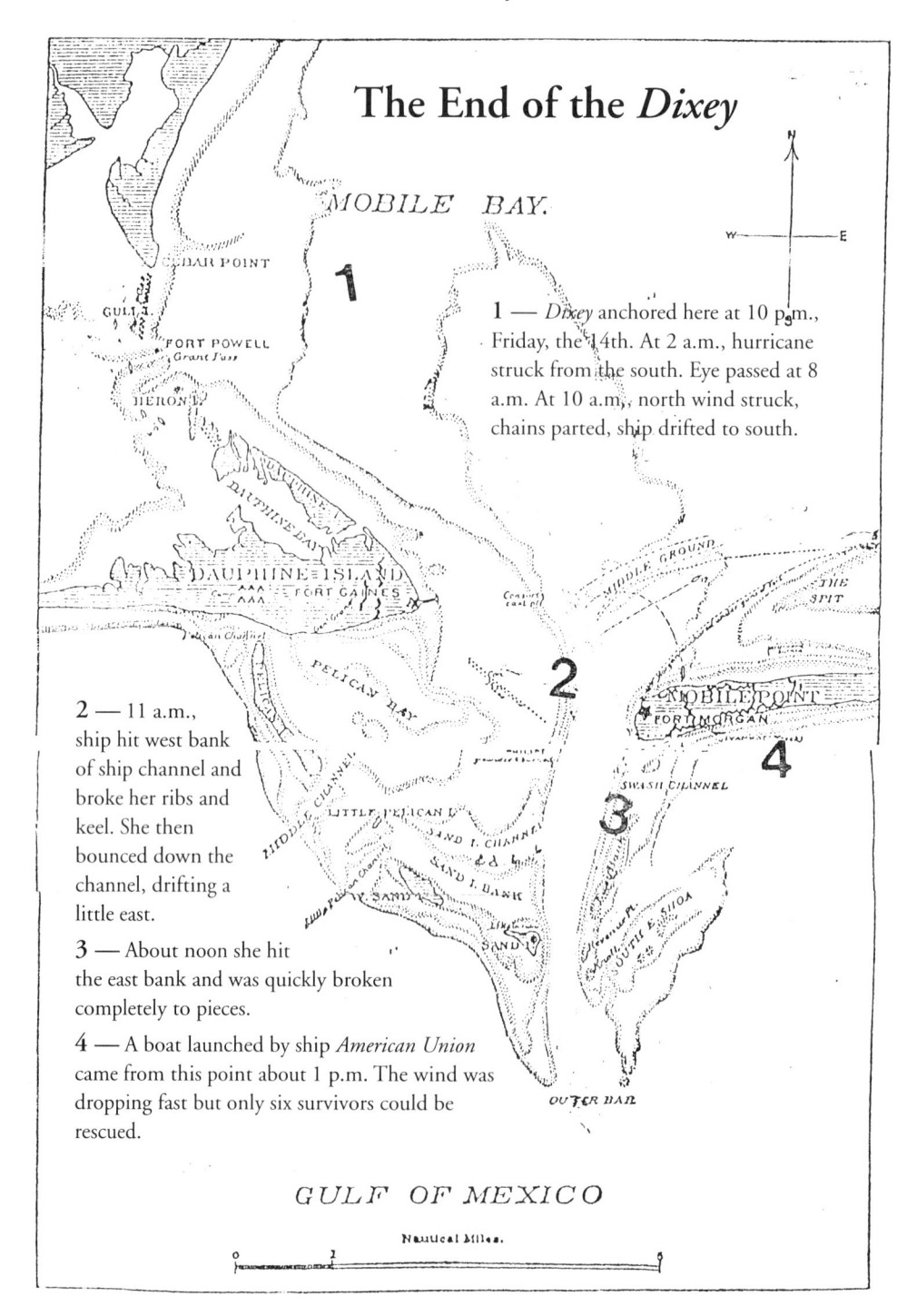

**MOBILE BAY.**

**1** — *Dixey* anchored here at 10 p.m., Friday, the 14th. At 2 a.m., hurricane struck from the south. Eye passed at 8 a.m. At 10 a.m., north wind struck, chains parted, ship drifted to south.

**2** — 11 a.m., ship hit west bank of ship channel and broke her ribs and keel. She then bounced down the channel, drifting a little east.

**3** — About noon she hit the east bank and was quickly broken completely to pieces.

**4** — A boat launched by ship *American Union* came from this point about 1 p.m. The wind was dropping fast but only six survivors could be rescued.

GULF OF MEXICO

Nautical Miles.

them but instead also tied himself on. When his body was recovered, it was still tied to a timber.

Pilot Sam Smyly and five others went up to the bow, which stayed together longer than the center and stern sections. They lashed themselves to a yard that was loose and jumped clear of the ship. The hull was fast breaking apart. The tide was turning at the time of the breakup, and the seas were immense outside Mobile Bay. It was about 1 P.M.

Anchored two miles to the east in forty feet of water was the packet *American Union*[90] from Liverpool with several hundred immigrants aboard. Between rain showers, Captain Macoduck and Bill Lee, the pilot, had been watching this disaster take place from their relatively safe shelter. The land on which Fort Morgan sat provided much protection from the north. Through telescopes they watched men on the forecastle jump clear. In spite of the risk, the sailors launched a boat and were able to pick up the six who survived.

The eye of the hurricane kept moving inland, the wind shifted back to the west, and a tremendous tide flowed back into Mobile Bay. By midafternoon on Saturday, September 15, 1860, all that was left of the *Dixey* was floating back in the bay.

The crew who were lost, eighteen in all, were buried on Dauphin Island in an unmarked grave. Captain Dixey was returned to Mobile, where he was buried in the "new burying ground," now called Magnolia Cemetery. A marker that was placed there has disintegrated, and only the broken stone remains.

An island was created by a later hurricane at the site of this tragedy and was given the name "Dixey Island." It appeared on the charts until it too was washed away in a storm. Today, a shoal area to the north and east of channel buoy 10 marks the "Dixey Bar."

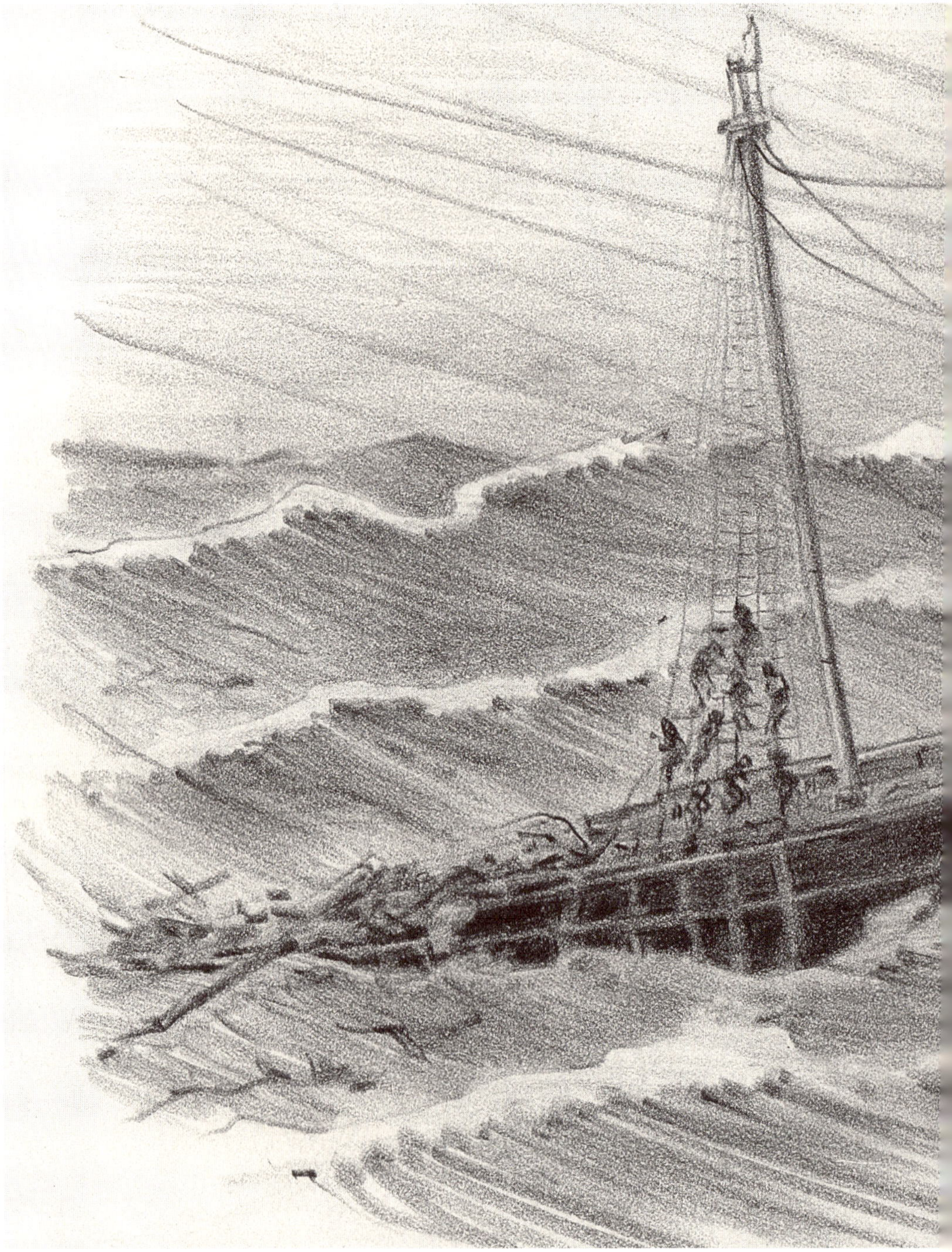

*The break-up of the* Dixey, *as visualized by Ted Brennan from contemporary reports.*

*An Antebellum Life At Sea*

## CONTEMPORARY ACCOUNTS OF THE WRECK OF THE *DIXEY*

The *New Orleans Picayune* for Wednesday evening, 19 September 1860, carried the story of the hurricane and the loss of the *Robert H. Dixey* on its front page. The headlines read "The Gale at Mobile," "Fearful Loss of Life!" "Total Loss of Property Near $1,000,000." Its account of the *Dixey's* demise follows:

> The saddest record of the storm…is that of the loss of the ship Robert H. Dixey, with her esteemed and popular captain, and eighteen of her crew. The ship anchored, on Friday evening [14 September], inside the outer bar, near the west shoal, where she went ashore about 10 o'clock Friday night. The pilot, Mr. Smyly, who had come out as a passenger from New York, urged Captain Dixey to save himself on the top gallant forecastle, which he saw was about to go down, but the captain lashed himself to the rigging and refused to leave his ship. The pilot with the second mate and four men escaped to the shore when the ship broke up, and were rescued by Captain Macoduck, of the ship American Union, who was anchored near, and sent a boat for them.
>
> The Dixey was an A1 ship of 1252 tons, built at Boston in 1855, owned in part by the captain, but chiefly in Mobile. She was valued at $36,000, and was insured in Northern offices. Her cargo was very valuable; we have heard it estimated as high as $300,000, some $28,000 of which was insured here, the rest probably in great part at the North.
>
> Capt. Richard W. Dixey, the late commander of the unfortunate ship, was well known in Mobile, being a regular trader to this city, and was highly respected wherever known. As a sailor, he bore a high reputation, having encountered several severe gales under circumstances which elicited high commendation in Liverpool, Philadelphia and elsewhere. He was remarkable as a successful but mild disciplinarian, and was not unfrequently styled "the Christian Captain." His last words to the pilot were, "Good bye, I hope we shall meet in Heaven." At the time of his death he was about 51 years of age. His remains were brought to the city yesterday, by Capt. W. H. Homer, and were interred from the residence of Col. C. H. Minge. The eighteen unfortunate sailors who went down

with the Dixey, were buried on an island in the bay.

We are unable to obtain a full list of the officers and crew of the ship; we learn, however, that there were in all twenty-four souls on board. Of the sixteen of the crew before the mast, three only were saved. Besides these, the first mate, carpenter and pilot were saved, making only six who escaped a watery grave.

Capt. Dixey was born, and his family lived, at Marblehead, Mass. His wife is at present on a visit to Boston, where the painful intelligence of her bereavement will quite too soon reach her.

Another newspaper carried an account from the ship's pilot:

### Statement of Capt. Smyly, the Pilot

Capt. Samuel Smyly came out from New York on the Dixey as passenger and pilot to take her in over the lower bar. He is well known to be one of the best pilots on the bar and a good seaman. The Tribune obtains from him the following particulars of the loss of the ship.

"On [Friday] evening the ship sailed inside of the bar. The wind was blowing then north northwest. When at about half way between the bar and Choctaw light, it was deemed necessary to let go both anchors[25]; one had a chain of 45 fathoms attached, and the other 50 fathoms, which held fast until [Saturday] morning, when the chain parted and the ship struck. This was about 10 o'clock. The men then went to work to cut away masts and sails, the ship making water for over an hour. The gale continued to increase. The big chain parted, thus leaving no possible chance to save the ship. In a few minutes she bilged, having struck. All saw the danger at hand. The mainmast and mizzenmast came up, and everything was going to pieces, when all hands made for the forecastle and lashed themselves on: 24 men all told. The ship was drawing at the time 17 feet 5 inches, and was loaded with an assorted cargo. The ship and cargo are reported to be a total loss. The value of the ship was, as we learn, $80,000, fully insured in Boston.

"There were eighteen lives lost, all negro seamen. The names of those saved are as follows: George Hamman, a Sandwich Islander; Jas. Brown, Jas. Oddelbridge, Thomas Baker, carpenter, Samuel Smyly, passenger and pilot, and H. K. Lapham, mate. The captain was lost in doing his best to save the ship and crew. There is now not a vestige of the ship left.

"The remains of Capt. Dixey were afterwards found, they having floated ashore, and were yesterday interred in the new burying ground.

"The Dixey was owned by the following persons: Thomas J. Fettyplace, A. M. Godfrey, L. Merchant, Geo. Boyd, Jr. and Capt. R. H. [sic] Dixey."[26]

The *Salem Gazette* for 21 September reported:
"Ship R. H. Dixey, from New York to Mobile, was blown ashore on the lower bar, Mobile Bay, during the gale of 15 inst. and became a total loss. The captain and several of the crew perished. The Dixey was an A1 ship of 1252 tons register, built at Boston in 1855, and owned by R. H. Dixey & Co. of Mobile."

In the *Marblehead Ledger* for Wednesday, 26 September, the notice ran:

"The Ship R. H. Dixey—this vessel previously reported wrecked at Mobile will prove a total loss with all her cargo. Capt. Dixey of this town and 15 sailors were drowned. The mate, pilot and 4 sailors were saved."

It had been a wicked hurricane. On 3 October, the *Ledger* was still commenting on it: "The loss by the late gale to the shipping and on land on the coast from New Orleans to Mobile, a distance of 200 miles, is said to amount to 2 million dollars."

# Epilogue

In the following paragraphs we will try to give our patient readers a summary of the directions that were taken by the people who were a part of the *Dixey* story. In some cases we have little information, and in some cases the lives of these people almost justify another whole chapter or more.

### ROBERT H. DIXEY (1817–1872)

Problems associated with the Civil War quickly caused serious difficulties for RHD. His international operations were greatly restricted by the blockade of the South. By 1862 he had moved to France, taking his family with him. In 1864 he returned briefly to New Orleans to dispose of property he couldn't manage from France. He spent most of his time in Europe until 1866, when he returned to New Orleans and Mobile. He had homes in each of those cities and was able to succeed in business there even during the period of Reconstruction.

In 1872, during a visit to the Dixey family farm in Sharon, Massachusetts, Robert was stricken with "apoplexy" and died quickly. His death due to what we would now call a heart attack was only to have been expected. Cholesterol had not been discovered then, and Robert had always lived "high on the hog" and was much overweight. He lived all his life in the fast lane, reminding me a great deal of Rhett Butler in *Gone with the Wind*.

### JANE MINGE DIXEY (1828–1885)

After she was widowed in 1872, Mrs. Dixey maintained homes in both Mobile and

*Above, Anna Ladd Dixey; Right, Robert H. Dixey, Jr. (Photos courtesy of Mrs. Diane Hailey)*

New Orleans. She was well fixed and traveled often to visit her family in Alabama and throughout the country. When she died in New Orleans in 1885, she was brought home to Mobile. After a large funeral, attended by the cream of Mobile society, she was buried in Magnolia Cemetery near her brother-in-law, Captain Richard Dixey.

## ANNA LADD DIXEY, DAUGHTER OF ROBERT H. DIXEY (1853–?)

Anna never married and lived out her life in the family home in New Orleans. As things got strained financially, she ran a rooming house to make ends meet.

## ROBERT H. DIXEY, JR., SON OF ROBERT H. DIXEY (1855–1910)

"Robbie" Dixey became a cotton broker of reasonable success, with offices in New Orleans and Baton Rouge. He was in business partnerships with his young uncle,

Collier Minge, Jr. He was a socialite and an active gambler at his private club. Of his five sons, three followed him in the cotton business.

## REBECCA GARDNER DIXEY (1820–1896)

Their daughter, Fannie, had died in 1859, and after Captain Dixey was lost, his widow lived in Marblehead with her son, Richard Cowell Dixey. She wasn't well off, but her father, Abel Gardner, helped out. They built a small house on a point overlooking the harbor. Cowell became a music teacher. In 1875, at the age of 30, he married a Miss Ellen Sturgis Tappan, of a wealthy Boston family. He never gave another piano lesson. He moved to Boston, and his mother lived out her life in Marblehead. The house still stands, one of the prettiest on the harbor.

## THOMAS J. FETTYPLACE (1817–1871)

Robert Dixey's closest friend, a principal owner of the ship, and a leading businessman of Mobile, was Thomas Fettyplace. He was a director of banks, insurance companies, and ship chandleries and a partner in numerous ventures, including many ships besides the *Dixey*. He owned much real estate around Mobile County, and his home in Spring Hill was a showplace. Although the house is long gone, it is known to have been on the lot across from the Marshall-Eslava-Hixon house on Tuthill Lane.

*Richard Cowell Dixey (1845–19??), son of Captain Richard Dixey, with his wife, Ellen Tappan Dixey, and their children Arthur and Rosamonde. Photo courtesy of Mrs. Daphne B. Prout, daughter of Rosamond Dixey Brooks.*

Thomas Fettyplace never married. He was very quiet and dignified as compared to his brother Henry, who usually lived with him. He moved back to Salem to live during the war, but kept his business interests in Mobile. Henry died suddenly in Salem in 1869, and Tom suffered greatly from the loss of his brother and closest friend. By the late 1860s Tom was suffering from "bronchitis" (which may have been tuberculosis, angina, or even lung cancer, then unknown by the medical profession), and he died while in Mobile in January 1871. His body was temporarily interred in Magnolia Cemetery and later moved to Salem, where he now lies next to Henry.

## HENRY KING FETTYPLACE (1820–1869)

Henry and Tom were not in the military during the Civil War years, but the conflict was still a strain on both. Henry had been a member of the Mobile militia called the Washington Light Infantry. When it was called up in 1861 to become a Confederate regiment, he resigned his commission. Both Tom and Henry pursued their businesses as far as possible, but as the situation worsened in the South, their Yankee background became an embarrassment. They both moved north during the war.

From his will, we know that Tom made Salem his legal residence in 1866. We assume that Henry did the same. We suspect that Henry's estate passed to his sisters, one of whom was the wife of Herbert C Peabody. Tom's property passed to his estate and was administered in Alabama by Peabody's son-in-law, Louis Stein, for a long time after his and Henry's deaths.

*Henry King Fettyplace (1820–1869), brother of Thomas J. Fettyplace and man about town in Mobile in the 1840s and 1850s. He was a member of the Cowbellion de Rakin Society and a first lieutenant of the Washington Light Infantry, Capt. J. A. Hooper's Company, Alabama Militia. Photo courtesy of Marblehead Historical Society.*

## MARY ANN FETTYPLACE SMITH, AUNT OF TOM FETTYPLACE (1800–?)

After 44 years of marriage and eleven children, Mrs. Smith was widowed in 1865. Mobile records indicate that she must have moved away. Some of her children may know more about her last years, but we don't.

## WALTER SMITH, UNCLE OF TOM FETTYPLACE (1799–1865)

Army officer, banker, editor, general of militia, and Deputy Collector of Customs, Walter Smith was a leader in Mobile in his day. Of his eleven children, three left distinguished records in the Confederate forces. Melancton, for example, (West Point Class of 1843) was an artilleryman with the Mississippi forces. He rose to the rank of colonel and saw heavy action in the South. The most spectacular, however, was Chandler, who enlisted in 1861 as a lieutenant in Mobilian Captain Archibald Gracie's company of Alabama Infantry (the same company in which his cousin Horace Peabody had enlisted in April 1861). They fought with Lee's forces throughout the war. Gracie became a brigadier general and was killed at Petersburg, Virginia. Chandler became a major and surrendered with Lee at Appomattox, one of forty survivors out of nine hundred originally in his regiment.

## COLLIER H. MINGE, FATHER OF JANE MINGE DIXEY (1799–1865)

Collier Minge was sometimes referred to as "Col. C. H. Minge." Perhaps he was a colonel in the Virginia militia, but he doesn't appear to have been in the Confederate forces, He apparently went through the Civil War conducting his regular affairs as normally as possible under the conditions. Perhaps the title derived from a misunderstood abbreviation of "Collier." In any case, he died of natural causes in Newbern, Alabama, right after the war. After his death, his widow lived with her son Willie in Mobile until her death in the 1880s.

*Collier H. Minge (Photo courtesy Mrs. G. P. Russ)*

## SABILLA MINGE, SISTER OF JANE MINGE DIXEY (1840–1892)

Billa, as she was called by her family, lived out her life unmarried. She remained in Mobile and inherited the summer home in Point Clear, which she sold shortly before her death in 1892.

*Above, Maria Minge Adams (Photo courtesy of Diane D. Hailey); Right, Collier H. Minge, Jr. (1845–1915) at age 19, wearing the uniform of a first captain at V.M.I. Photo courtesy of Virginia Military Institute Museum.*

## MARIA MINGE, SISTER OF JANE MINGE DIXEY (1842–1866)

In 1865 Maria married a Benjamin C. Adams. In 1866 she died giving birth to Anna Maria Adams, who lived five years.

## COLLIER H. MINGE, JR., BROTHER OF JANE MINGE DIXEY (1845–1915)

"Collie" left an exciting story. In August of 1860, even before the loss of the *Dixey,* he had entered Virginia Military Institute. He was only 15 years old, but he was ready. By 1864 he was the highest-ranking cadet, the captain of A Company. In the dark days of May, things were so desperate for the South that the 250 cadets of V.M.I. were called out of their classrooms to help stem the Yankee advances. Young cadets of 15 to 19 fought so well that at least a temporary victory was achieved at Newmarket. Cadet Minge led the artillery cadets and was cited for outstanding performance. By the war's end he was a captain of artillery. After the war he became a cotton broker and was a partner of "Robbie" Dixey. He was a leading alumnus of V.M.I. until his death and received many awards and honors for his efforts.

## WILLIAM HENRY HARRISON MINGE, BROTHER OF JANE MINGE DIXEY (1830–1906)

Against the wishes of his family, but lacking any interest in cotton, "Willie" Minge signed on the ship *Ticonderoga* in 1851 and helped take a load of cotton to Liverpool. He sailed the Atlantic for a while, changing ships and jobs constantly, but learning the trade. On a trip to Australia with immigrants, Willie nearly died of fever (yellow?), but survived and continued his seafaring career. Sailing in and around India and Burma, Willie quickly advanced to

*William Henry Harrison Minge (1830–1906). Photo courtesy of Ruth Lyon Russ, one of Willie's granddaughters.*

mate and then captain. He became a licensed pilot at Calcutta.

Between ships and trips, he tried the hotel business, then the restaurant and liquor business, and later dealt in silk cloth, but always kept very busy.

Given his short temper and little patience, his entrepreneurial efforts were seldom very fruitful. He returned to Mobile in 1859 with nothing to show for his career except experience. He was definitely through with going to sea in any capacity.

A New Orleans girl named Mary Jane Gladden was visiting the Butler family next door to the Minge home at Point Clear. In a year she and Willie were married. Her father had been a U.S. Army officer in the Mexican War. He was a cotton factor at this time but would join the Confederate forces as a general and give up his life at Shiloh.

Willie also served in the Confederate forces but saw little action and returned to Mobile. He resumed his restless ways, becoming a cotton weigher, a dairy operator, a commercial merchant, a cotton sampler, manager of the Magnolia Cemetery, a night inspector for the U.S. Customs. Our readers can easily see that Willie bored easily! His searching ended at age 76, when he "left this earth leaving six children and little else."

It should be noted here that the Minge family fortunes suffered badly after the war, as was very common. Most plantation owners were unable to hold on, and things generally got worse before they got better.

## SAMUEL KNIGHT GIRDLER, HALF-BROTHER OF SARAH JANE GIRDLER (1835–189?)

Sam Girdler joined the *Dixey* in December 1857 as a "ship's boy" after hearing by letter that it might provide him a trip home. Sam was Sarah Jane's half-brother and had been going to sea for some years. He was ill suited to it, however, as his health was constantly a problem, and this was to be his last voyage. He got out of the Mobile hospital, returned to Marblehead, and became a clerk in Salem. His descendants are known to live in New Jersey, Massachusetts, and Connecticut.

## SARAH JANE GIRDLER BELKNAP WHEDON (1839–1914)

Aunt Jennie has been profiled earlier in these pages, and we hope our readers will close this with good thoughts of her.

*Sarah Jane Gardner Girdler (1816–1884). Born in Marblehead, she was the widow of Captain John Girdler and mother of Jennie Girdler. She spent her last days with her daughter in Louisville, Kentucky.*

*Aunt Jennie, Sarah Jane Girdler (Belknap Whedon), 1839–1914. This photo was taken about 1890. Photos courtesy of the Girdler family.*

# Genealogies

Following these paragraphs our readers will find three highly structured family trees of the principal characters in our story. We have tried to show how and when these families got involved with the *Dixey*.

Our accounting is limited to the Dixey, Minge, and Fettyplace families who had direct involvement with the ship and whose descendants provided us with the particulars of their association.

When individual "boxes" are ruled with bold lines, it indicates people who were alive during the brief life of the *Dixey* and at least visited her in Boston or Mobile. Many of them made voyages aboard the *Dixey*, some as members of the ship's company. R.H. Dixey and Thomas J. Fettyplace were original partners and still owned shares at the end.

The early members of these families, in almost every case, were men of substance. Their wives, unfortunately, are usually absent from the written record and thus have been omitted here because of lack of information. No slight was intended by the author.

# DIXEY

[1] Descended from Sir Wolstan Dixie, Baronet, of Bosworth Hall. Knighted by Elizabeth I in 1545. Lord Mayor of London. Head of the "Skinners" Guild. Founder of Dixie Grammar School, where Doctor Samuel Johnson was the first librarian and tutor for the Dixey family.

[2] Arrived in Marblehead, Massachusetts, in 1630 from England. Held first franchise to run the ferryboat from Salem to Marblehead.

- Thomas Dixey [1,2]
- Samuel Dixey bb4 1662
- William Dixey bb4 1696
- John Dixey 1714-1746
- Richard Dixey 1743-1800
- Capt. John Dixey 1776-1868 — m 1804 — Rebecca Cowell 1782-1826
  - Rebecca 1804
  - John 1807
  - Hannah 1811
  - William 1814
  - Caroline 1820
  - Elizabeth/Hector 1823
  - Mary 1826

Rebecca Gardner 1820-1896 — m 1842 — Richard W. 1809-1860

Robert H. 1817-1872 — m 1852 — Jane Minge 1828-1895

Ellen Sturgis Tappan — m 1873 — Richard Cowell 1844-1915

Fannie 1854-1859

Anna Ladd 1853-19__

Robert H. 1855-1910 — m 1883 — Mannie Price

- Arthur
- Rosamond — m 1913 — Gorham Brooks
- Robert H.
- Harry
- Collier Minge
- Albert
- Edgar B. — m 1924 — Anna Bentley
- Edgar*
- Diane* — m 1956 — J.W. Hailey

- Shepherd Brooks
- Daphne Brooks Prout*
- Peter C. Brooks
- Violet Brooks McCandlish

*Living "Dixeys" who supplied key facts, documents, and photographs to the author.

(Genealogical data obtained from private family research and from "History of Marblehead to 1850," Essex Institute, Salem, Marblehead Historical Society.)

# FAMILY OF JANE MINGE DIXEY 1828-1885

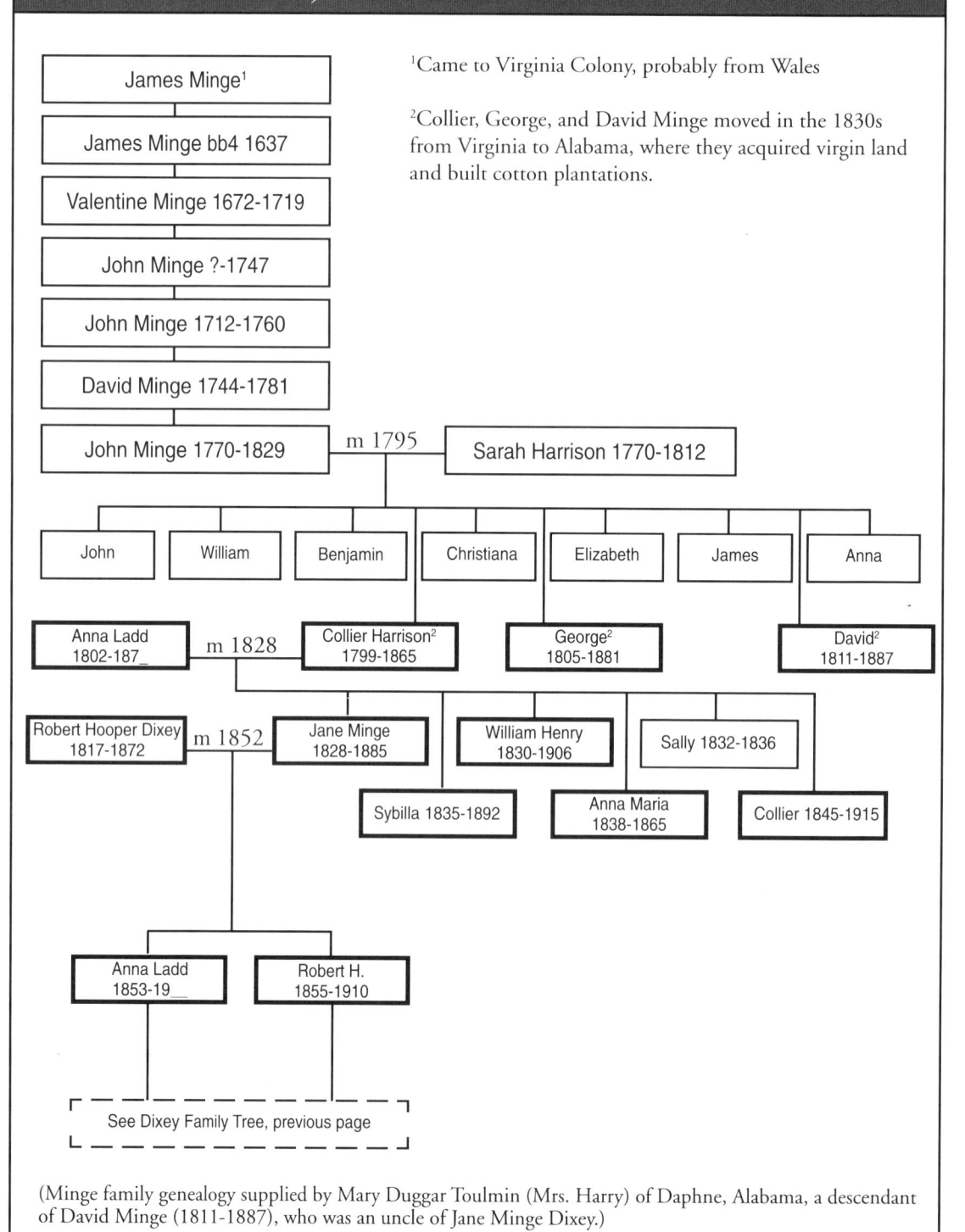

[1] Came to Virginia Colony, probably from Wales

[2] Collier, George, and David Minge moved in the 1830s from Virginia to Alabama, where they acquired virgin land and built cotton plantations.

- James Minge[1]
- James Minge bb4 1637
- Valentine Minge 1672-1719
- John Minge ?-1747
- John Minge 1712-1760
- David Minge 1744-1781
- John Minge 1770-1829 — m 1795 — Sarah Harrison 1770-1812

Children: John, William, Benjamin, Christiana, Elizabeth, James, Anna

Anna Ladd 1802-187_ — m 1828 — Collier Harrison[2] 1799-1865

George[2] 1805-1881

David[2] 1811-1887

Children of Collier Harrison and Anna Ladd:
- Jane Minge 1828-1885
- William Henry 1830-1906
- Sally 1832-1836
- Sybilla 1835-1892
- Anna Maria 1838-1865
- Collier 1845-1915

Robert Hooper Dixey 1817-1872 — m 1852 — Jane Minge 1828-1885

Children:
- Anna Ladd 1853-19__
- Robert H. 1855-1910

See Dixey Family Tree, previous page

(Minge family genealogy supplied by Mary Duggar Toulmin (Mrs. Harry) of Daphne, Alabama, a descendant of David Minge (1811-1887), who was an uncle of Jane Minge Dixey.)

# FAMILY OF THOMAS J. FETTYPLACE[1] 1817-1872

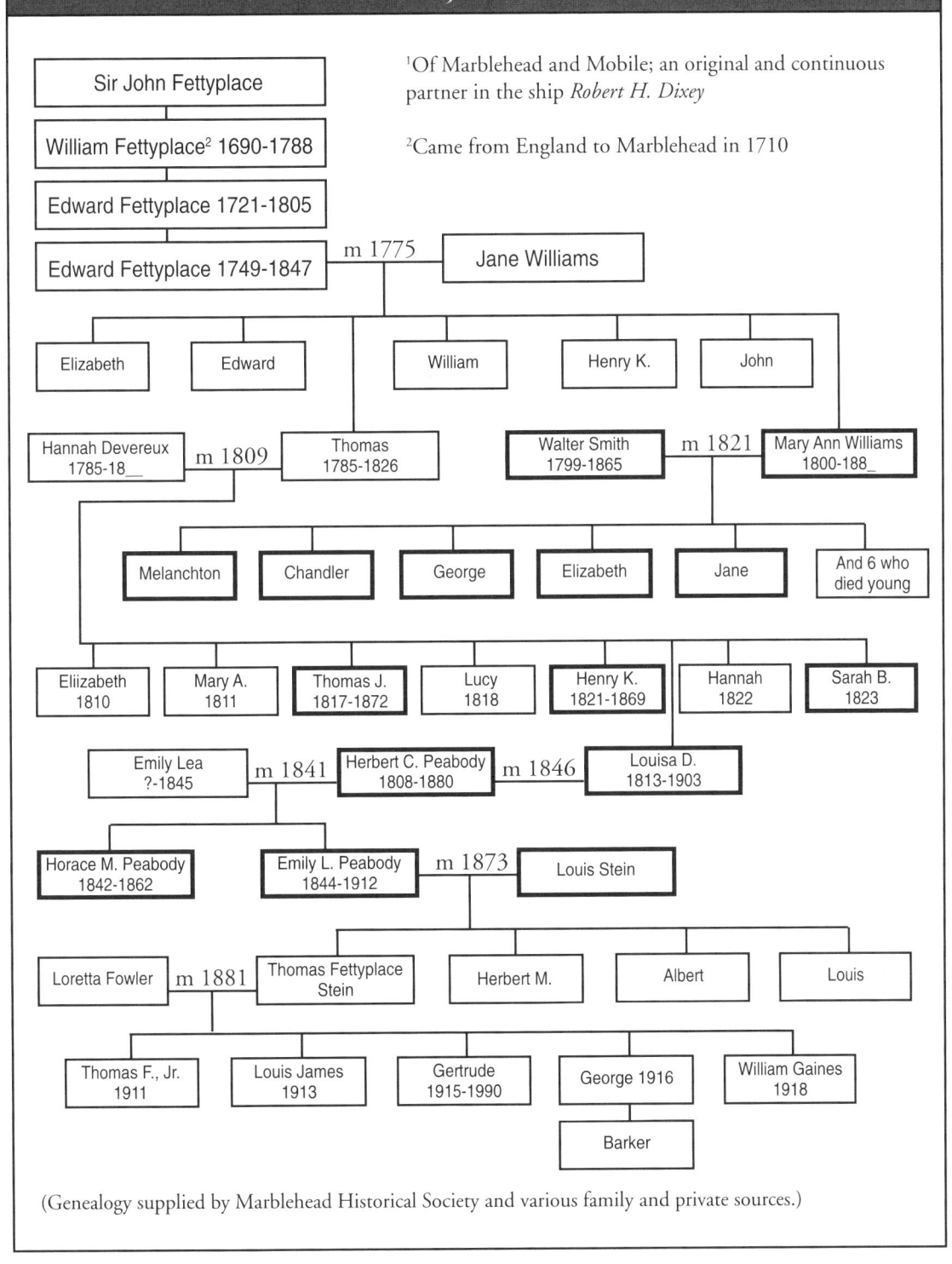

[1] Of Marblehead and Mobile; an original and continuous partner in the ship *Robert H. Dixey*

[2] Came from England to Marblehead in 1710

- Sir John Fettyplace
- William Fettyplace[2] 1690-1788
- Edward Fettyplace 1721-1805
- Edward Fettyplace 1749-1847 — m 1775 — Jane Williams

Children: Elizabeth, Edward, William, Henry K., John, Thomas 1785-1826, Mary Ann Williams 1800-188_

Hannah Devereux 1785-18__ — m 1809 — Thomas 1785-1826

Walter Smith 1799-1865 — m 1821 — Mary Ann Williams 1800-188_

Children of Walter Smith and Mary Ann Williams: Melanchton, Chandler, George, Elizabeth, Jane, And 6 who died young

Children of Thomas and Hannah Devereux: Eliizabeth 1810, Mary A. 1811, Thomas J. 1817-1872, Lucy 1818, Henry K. 1821-1869, Hannah 1822, Sarah B. 1823

Emily Lea ?-1845 — m 1841 — Herbert C. Peabody 1808-1880 — m 1846 — Louisa D. 1813-1903

Children: Horace M. Peabody 1842-1862; Emily L. Peabody 1844-1912 — m 1873 — Louis Stein

Loretta Fowler — m 1881 — Thomas Fettyplace Stein; Herbert M.; Albert; Louis

Children of Loretta Fowler and Thomas Fettyplace Stein: Thomas F., Jr. 1911; Louis James 1913; Gertrude 1915-1990; George 1916; William Gaines 1918

Barker (child of George 1916)

(Genealogy supplied by Marblehead Historical Society and various family and private sources.)

APPENDIX

*A*

# Dixey Letters

The following letters are arranged in chronological order. They don't all fall within the lifespan of the *Dixey,* but they all add to an understanding of the people and the times. Much of the previous narrative has been extracted from these pages and the facts contained therein.

Our loyal readers will find some of these pages tedious. Some are incomplete because the fragile and faded originals just couldn't be read. Our notes and comments are meant to increase our readers' grasp of how these people thought and talked a hundred thirty years ago—actually, not too differently from the way we talk and write today.

## LETTER FROM CAPTAIN JOHN DIXEY TO REBECCA COWELL DIXEY, HIS WIFE, 14 MAY 1817, ANJER (JAVA HEAD)

The envelope reads: "Capt John Dixey, Marblehead, Massachusetts."

There is a cancellation stamp on the letter reading "Sep 14," which may be the date of receipt at Marblehead, some three months after it was written at Anjer.

Staates [?] Sunday
Anjer[1]
May 14 1817

My Dear girl

We Arrived here to day after a passage of 108 days–102 to the land–we have had a tolerable pleasent passage & Very Agreeable–We have a fine Ship[2] good Officers & Crew–I hope we shall have a quick passage to Manilla[3]–I hope this will finde You & the family well–Kiss all the little ones for papa[4]–tell them I long to see them–we shall return to Urope where I hope to here from You–pray write when Your Unkle Hooper[5] does–he will send your letter with his–tell me all the news you have–how Hooper & Russell comes on–Keep all the children to school winter & summer–I Shall write every opertunity that offers–I Steal three or four minutes to write this as we have just come to Anchor —  If there is any addishion to the family let me know & if you have given the name we talked of–my love to all our Brothers & Sisters & all friends–tell Hannah I here John is at Batavia–I shall write him By this Conveyance in Batavia–I hope Hector is got Home by this time–I hope Peter is got some Employment before this–If you should want any thing apply to your Unckel Hooper–I Shall be vexed if you do not–do not want nor let the Children for any thing if I thought you would I should be very uneasy–I never felt worse in leaving home in My life–I felt very anxious about you–I hope every thing turns out well–I have Enjoyed Excellent Health ever since I left home–Commiting you & the Children to almighty Protection––I remain Your

Affectionate Husband

John Dixey

Recolect I am in grate haste or I should write more–I have nothing about M[r] Hooper as he has wrote my Officers & Crew are all in good health.

## JENNIE MINGE DIXEY TO HER AUNT

Brest—Monday 14th December/52

My dearest Auntie–I had a letter all written to you in New York & was about sending it when Mr Dixey came up to tell me he was going to leave the next day for Havre & if I could get ready I could go with him as he expected

*An Antebellum Life At Sea*

to be gone some time–That drove every other idea out of my head & I threw aside everything to commence packing immediately–Sat up till 12,0ᶜ that night & had all ready to start next morning at 10–In a previous letter home I have described my trip across the big pond & our travel from Havre to Brest where we are located for the next month or six weeks–but from a few days experience I am fully satisfied it will require at least that much time to see this place–Rain is as certain every day & in fact all days as that the sun rises & sets–Umbrellas are as common & as indispensable as a hat–or shoe–for the sun if it [?] comes out never shines more than five minutes at a time–& half of that it will have rained–seldom a hard sousing[?] rain–but an incessant drizzle–The [?] classes men, women & children wear a sort of large clumsy wooden shoe–that are called sabots & the women wear [?] real old fashioned caps like Aunt-Cherry's some of them with very wide frills around the front are only as deep as the cap itself–the noise of the shoes on the stones sounds exactly like the tramping Polly would make with a pair of brogans on or the tramp of a body of cavalry–The people never confine themselves to the sidewalks but the street is thronged with dogs–carts–horses (like sheep) with panniers on each side of them sacks & men women & children jogging along indiscriminately. The sun does not rise until 8 o'clock altho it is light at 5 & the whole place is astir with market people–& those on their way to & from Mass–We have [?] two meals a day breakfast at 9 or 10 o'clock–dinner 4 or 5 o'clock as we please & what is the strangest thing of all, they charge extra for a cup of coffee at breakfast 10 cents to each person but furnish a bottle of claret free of charge. We have taken all our meals in our room ever since we came–as at the table d'hôte there are a [?] [?] common frenchmen that would stare a lady out of countenance–so that in the morning I sleep till about half an hour before breakfast is made–get up & make my morning toilette which is my dressing gown, & sack till about 1 or 2 o'clock then by that time Mr Dixey has been down town–seen the ship–attended to all the business for the day & comes home to go out walking with me–wet or dry it makes very little difference just so it is not pouring–I always wear india rubbers & hold up my dress indifferent to showing my ankles as it is quite the fashion–I can't tell how many times I have seen up above a ladies knee–only she has on a nice pair of drawers fastened with a band at the top of her shoe—We have seen a good many curiosities in the various shops & Mr D—scarcely ever comes in without some thing new he has picked up—We expected to have come by land from Havre to Brest through Paris & by that means seen a great portion of the country but on our arrival at Havre Mr D found there was a steamer going to Morlaix which would only give us 45 miles of land travelling & also learned that the land route is very fatiguing & slow so that we would save 2 days by coming by water—As it was the 45 miles diligence[92] travelling which was [three illegible words] night in a close pinched up place like to have killed me so that we chose mud the lesser evil of the two—when we leave here it will be to go to Nantes or Angers by diligence and from either place by railroad—I wish you & Bettie were along with us—I am sure you would enjoy it & Bettie would be delighted besides being very much improved. Propose to Uncle [Cyrus?] to bring you to Paris & visit us there in Feb or March & then take the trip down to Marseilles—all you have to do is take the Humboldt to Havre & there is a direct railroad from there to Paris. I hope to see the coronation[93] & be there also at the time of the Emperor's marriage with the Princess of [?] who I am told [is?] pretty beside being quite young. I shall think of you all at Xmas [four illegible words] which will be about the time you receive this & as you ought to be in Mobile if you are not I will send this there as being of more [line missing on copy] [?] of a married couple—but either I am unusually amicable or Mr Dixey is or both—anyhow we will both be contented to pass the rest of our lives as pleasantly—now & then he gets piping mad with me for eating candy—or pickle[94] & says I have no more control over myself than a child—which I retaliate by [?] him for not having more command over himself than to give up the use of tobacco as he has promised. He has fattened up tremendously—so that you would hardly know him & I think looks happier than he ever did in his life. There seems to be very little enthusiasm among the people for the Emperor or Empire—nobody seems in favor of it but are submitting with as good a face as they can put on—I don't think I ever saw a sadder looking set than formed the procession at Havre & here they say Vive l'Empereur was only shouted by the command of the General of the troops—not the voice of the people at all—They have an Opera here twice a week—Thursdays—& Sundays so of course I shall attend but never on Sundays certainly—although I understand the best plays are generally [?] for that evening–The view from the port is splendid & the whole place is thronged with soldiers–every other man you see has the red stripe on his pants & the military cap. There is not a decent vehicale in the place so we have to walk wherever we go–whatever the weather is–we foot it. The houses are old & smoked looking & very narrow–some six stories, some three; four, & some only two, which gives the place rather an irregular appearance. The men almost all wear large cloaks with hoods to them & generally have them pulled over their caps which shelter them from the rain but gives a very grotesque appearance to their [?]. We formed acquaintance with a Naval Officer–a Captain Somebody & his wife who was an English lady. They are in the same house with us & the only persons we know in the whole city. The Captain has been in the South of the United States–Gulf of Mexico & Pensacola & speaks a little English. They expect to be in Brest six months or more perhaps & are looking out for lodging a furnished suite of rooms–so that will be one place we shall have to visit–he has promised to take us all through the arsenal which is an immense place & well worth seeing also to the Base where convicts [three illegible words] for life, others a certain number of years, they are made to work on the docks & in all other ways a certain part of the day & the rest of the time they work for themselves–some of them carve [?] beautifully in ivory, or cocoa and wood–make pipes, boxes, & all such things & sell them–some times they do the most beautiful work in straw that I ever saw–Mr. D –bought me a box the other day that is a perfect curiosity–The French are great in all gimcracks, bonbons[?], & fancy things, but entirely primitive in locks, shovels & tongs &c. I never saw such bolts & locks as they have on their doors–old scrap must have been used [?] & the tongs are antiquated beyond every thing–Uncle Armistead could beat the pr I have in my fire place all to pieces–they are made precisely like a pr of sugar tongues–a little flattened at the top & one little brass [?] to [?] the middle–the contrast between the andirons, fenders & tongues, and the ornaments on the mantlepiece is laughable–Imagine all that is rusty[?] & dirty about iron and brass–then all that is fine–of gilt & fancy clocks–and artificial flowers & most elaborate gilt frames & mirrors & you will form a very correct idea of a french chimney piece–for a clock is as certain a piece of furniture in a corner as a bed; chair; or a table–I expect you will all be quarreling with me when I come home for putting your eyes out with my letters–but I prefer writing in this way to the stiff thin paper that is new[?] here for the lines on one side destroy those on the other & you cant read either–I have found out a new medicine that is given here for derangement of the stomach or any such bad feeling–you couldn't guess what it is–we have it with us in great quantities but I am sure I never heard of its being used in that way before. A tea made of the blooms of the Linden tree are dried and kept all winter like you would sage. I had some prescribed for me a few nights ago & found a great deal of relief from it–simply a few of the blossoms steeped in boiling water & sweeten to your taste–there isn't much taste to it–but very soothing & the french keep it always in their house–Live and learn–I have been hearing from all quarters that Bettie is to marry cousin Joe–Now if it is so–dont let it take place before I get back–tell her I saw she had better wait and let me bring [?] & dresses & all sorts of pretty things from Davis–Mr Dixey says let him put in [line missing on copy] very astonishing as to have the sun out for an hour perhaps & no mist or drizzle through the day–We have both concluded it is a most astounding climate although there is always so much humidity in the atmosphere yet we have the window open during the night–in the morning there will be no dampness on the window or even percetable on any thing in the room. The natives have most beautiful complexions–fresh, clean & fair as lillies with all the couleur de rose–that you can imagine as to [?] make it appear that they are ridiculously rouged but I am told that persons unaccl... are apt to be much indisposed so that I am rather in dread–although they tell me it is so fine for the complexion. Everything is so green and as fresh as the spring and we are eating all sorts of nice vegetables–lettuce the tenderest & freshest I ever ate–also chicori–selery & cressy which the french are very fond of–besides since spinach–sorrel–radishes & all sorts that you can imagine–I reckon dearest Auntie you think you have eaten artichokes in perfection from your own garden–so you have in quantity–but could you see some that we had for dinner yesterday you would declare you never saw their like before as tender as the most delicate leaf–large as an orange at the bottom & such leaves, or [?] whatever they are called as astonished me–I measure ours–broader than three of my fingers & so long–the choke part is so large & tender that dearly as I love them I could not eat but two & made my dinner off of them—We had them for breakfast one morning—a sort of course prompted by our waiter, but I did not relish them much—it was too much out of the natural order of things—Havn't you heard the old saying "throwing smelt[?] to catch [two illegible words] well this morning we breakfasted on [smelt?] I found out they were small delicate looking fish, not larger than an anchovy & very nice—I suppose I must have eaten a dozen or more before I had enough—We have been feasting [four illegible words] & expect to have some fresh sardines as soon as the season permits—On Sunday morning we went to the Church of the Marines to hear a mass of music—where all the Officers, belonging to the Navy attend & have most of the service sung & played by the Marine band that forms the choir—The music could not fail to be fine, but hardly repaid me for being crowded & jammed up between a crowd of men & women with coarse muddy shoes &c—Having no pews makes you liable to all sorts of annoyances & ever so common & crude a person can come & crowd in right beside you—We heard in the afternoon that there was a small protestant Chapel & services every Sunday morning between 9 & 10, so we shall find it out next Sabbath—I had a visitor Sunday—all dressed in white vest & kids[95] & what think you of our receiving him in our bed room—In a french hotel (in this part of the world, I mean) there is no reception room only a large dining room—[not?] intended for any one except at meal times—usually a narrow filthy staircase & the rooms apportioned to the guests some with parlors & others not—we have but one room—which Mr Dixey was dissatisfied with at first—but I told him what was the use of paying for a room perhaps to have one visitor during he month we staid & be the consigne[?] of the Ship. So that I persuaded him out of that idea—Yesterday our travelling friend & [his wife] who turns out to be a Commodore of one of the finest frigates in the French [?] called to take us to see the Port & Arsenal—It appeared [?] like one huge canal where ships of any tonnage might [two lines missing on copy] our way back we walked through the [?] & afterwards saw[?] the Bague[?] or what we would call Penitentiary. It is where all the convicts are sent & imprisoned some for life & others for 20, 10- or 5 yrs according to their crime—The building is included in the grounds around the Port & the convicts or forcats[?] as they are called are made to work for so many hours of each day & are [five illegible words] Those who are very [?]

& troublesome are chained together two & two [two illegible words] looking watch–& the green cap they wear means for life–a yellow for 10 years–red for 5–& so on. Those [who] have escaped [?] & have been retaken have two different colored sleeves & as they work 20 or thirty together are guarded by 2-4 or 6 armed soldiers that looked as hardened in their misery as the poor forcats themselves. They sleep on the hardest kinds of boards & on that account are not required to work more than one or two hours a day–The rest of their time they employ in working for themselves & [?] of their [?] most exquisitely in ivory & cocoanut & their things are placed in a show room for sale–

As we walked through the room, some were hard at work–some reading–playing back gammon & one poor fellow was trying to write a letter– At night they are chained by their feet to their beds. But the authorities [?] ...ing away with such places of which there are only two now one at Toulon & this one–but they are breaking them up by sending them away to a colony & excommunicating them forever–[?] Mr. D– came in this morning he brought me a letter from Mother written the 17th of Nov & which was received five days after I left N.Y.–How it gladdened my heart to hear from [?] Can there be anything sweeter than a letter when abroad from home. Nothing–Mr D did not receive the one that she said Father had already sealed for him–supposes it was opened at the office thinking it was about freight & kept till he returns as they frequently do. I have written twice home since I left N.Y. which was three weeks this last Saturday 11th Decem–I shall try & send [?] every week if not oftener–if I wasn't afraid of postage being too high there is such a difference–Tell Mother I didnt get Bill's[96] cape or Colly's[97] clothes or in fact anything scarcely–I came off so unexpectedly–but that I want to bear all the expenses of such little things if I had[?] & her dress was not to [?] & did not cost her anything–but that the forty dollars was laid out entirely on the sofa & curtains for which I hope she dont mean to scold me–If she does tell her I thought that was what the sofa sold for & I had a right to spend it–Mr Dixey is so much taken up with business & had so many sort of letters to write, that he says his ideas are all confused among freights, charters, repairs with all hast &c–but that as soon as he gets his [?] a little cleared–he means to write as nice a letter to his Mother[98] as is in his power–Give my love to every body that inquires after me [?] bless me for having been so unpardonably wordy[?]

[line missing on copy; complimentary close also lost]
Across the top of the first page, a line which is indecipherable, followed by:

[?] have a large fireplace–burn wood & use old fashioned bellows, have [?] no dry wood but burn oak altogether–when we are eating our breakfast at 9 o'clock you all are sleeping soundly. Mr Dixey sends lots of love.

## JENNIE MINGE DIXEY TO HER FAMILY IN MOBILE

I hope my dear sweet Colly did not get another broken head
New Years Day–Brest–1853
To the dear folks at home.

Mr. Dixey hopes to get the Ship off the last day of the week–say Thursday or Friday & I can't tell you how much I am tempted to jump aboard of her–take a french maid for company & be landed in Mobile in thirty days leaving Mr D to travel about as he Chooses–but for Mother Eves[?] curiosity predominating[?] I think I would. How differently I am passing this Day to what we did this time last year–The first thing I did this morning was to jump up dress quickly & go to market for a bouquet to deck off my room come home to a poor breakfast as the chief cook had been out spending the New Year to the neglect of his culinary duties. Last year Auntie & I had to bounce out of bed to ice a huge cake by the fire that wouldn't get dry & gave Mother the "Narvous"–dont you recollect it. I told Mr Dixey of it this morning & asked him what were his recollections of N.Years Day & Evening? The Proprietor of the Hotel gave a grand dinner to day to all his guests at the Table d'hôte & our waiter is dreadfully put out because we wont go down–says we will miss all the nice things by having ours served as usual an hour earlier than the regular dinner hour–the [?] huge fish–turkey au truffles &c, but we prefer our nice cozy table in our room to all that–as there are few ladies in the house & it is any thing but agreeable to eat with a whole table full of Frenchmen looking at you. My Christmas & N.Years presents were a handsome set of [?] candelabras and clock to match–which you must promise to give house room & take care of for us until we a snug little cottage of our own. Mr D treated himself to some antiques in the way of pictures–which came from the sale of furniture belonging to an old antiquarian & which he [two illegible words]–In the box area[?] *[A line appears to be missing here.]* mementos for one or two friends– as curiosities from Brest. Christmas day as we were walking round looking round in all the shop widows I spied a sort of segar case that struck my fancy & exclaimed "oh there is something that would suit Mr Weekes[?]" I wish I had that" & we passed on–that evening when Mr D walked out to smoke his cigar–he came back with the case, for [?] which I wished I could transfer across the big pond that sight with Colly & Jim. It is not a year yet that we have been married yet it seems to me *three*! (and that I have been married & found the time[?] long" [?] I am not going to say that) but it seems to me *three years* since I saw you all in Mobile–It is because we have been going about so much [?] the mean time–travelled over so much space. Every minute I was wondering to myself what you are all about if Aunt Bettie ...ing [?] with you receiving calls & if Mother was ready in time–Here the custom is for the gentlemen to visit their & certain[?] friends & only leave cards among their acquaintances which seems to be quite sensible–for then there is not so much [two illegible words] I sent down & invited the Captain up there this evening to drink egg nog with us. I was determined to have some[99]; forgot about it Christmas but have been waiting for New Year but dont think I will be as successful as Billa & [?] used to be last winter certainly shan't be enough as to make Mr D measure his length on the floor again.[100]–The streets are thronged with people–peasants in their holy day dress who have walked miles & miles to the city & this is the great day for beggars to turn out as some persons give this day of the year and not oftener–The Mayor and Admiral & persons holding such offices also give to all who present themselves. I shall be delighted to leave Brest for I am almost tired to death of the place– one day of last week we took a carriage with the Commandant & his wife & went to a little village called [le] Folgoët about 21 miles from this city to see a very elaborate old church built in 1423. They tell a story about it of an old man who [line lost here] water of a spring which was the spot & lived on bread he would get well & he said he would stay there until a church was built–it seems he did [?] his mind but died soon after & King John 1st of Britany hearing of it ordered a church commenced–he died before it was finished & John II^d carried it on condition his image was to be between the two altars– The carving is most exquisitely done all in solid stone & sure enough the statue of John 1st & his queen & one of John II^d are there–During the revolution in Britany the Churches were very much mutilated & the carving is shamefully broken in many places. John's [statue?] is gone & the painted glass windows are defaced & broken but enough of them remains to testify to their antiquity & magnificance–we left here at _ ten & arrived at _ one at the church–saw the fountain which is at the back of the Church just under the main altar & a basin of stone constructed so as to let the water flow in & out continually–Over the main entrance is represented in bass relief the accouchement of the Virgin & God in the figure of a man holding the infant Jesus in his arms–In one little church that we stopped at in a village about ten miles from here were the skulls of individuals who had been sainted and their heads perserved, in little wooden boxes some ten or twelve of them on each side of the vestibule–We had to ride _ of a mile farther to a village

*Photo courtesy Mrs. Daphne B. Prout*

called Les [?][101] to get our dinner as there was no place of entertainment at Folgoët. When we drove up to the main door on one side was a large kitchen & on the other the diningroom & right before the door in the passage were all the meats suspended from the wall–– beef mutton–– fowls of sorts–– chickens geese & turkey already picked & the gentlemen ordered such & such a piece cooked for our dinner–every time the diningroom door was opened there hung the meats like a butcher store right before our eyes. I expected it would take away my appetite but I have seen so much of such things [?] all was so hanging that I could have eaten anything they [two lines missing from copy] got home about _ eight–tired as I could be–On our way home the Com$^d$ called our attention to a rainbow caused by the sun[102] a sight I never saw before. We had seen it in the morning when the sun was shining a good many times–but that night it was a silver color like the moon, instead of the [?] How do you account for that–it was not around the moon in a circle or anything of that kind, but opposite to it in the heavens strangely[?] from end to end–Dearest Mother, the above was written a long time ago think we would get off that week but here is the 12$^{th}$ & we are no nearer than we were then–I hope however that this Ship will at least go to sea tomorrow & we may be detained a day or two after on account of [?] bills not being all in yet– The other evening while Mr D was reading his paper I threw myself down on the sofa & as I did, said, oh how I wish I could run home for half an hour & see what they were all about & that everything was going on right–I had no sooner got asleep than I dreamed I was at home–saw myself lying on the sofa fatigued from the journey & you & Aunty sitting by me telling me the news & answering all my questions Was n't it natural for me to say "how are the Hopkins, shall I run over there now or wait till tomorrow morning" & you said to me "They are all gone to Church now but you might go over for a few moments when they come back for they want to see you. (It is Sunday evening that I dreamed it) & I woke myself up saying "Mother does Mrs Barney[?] live in the same place"? Mr D– answered my question by saying he could n't tell me–(that night I dreamed of seeing Mrs W– & Neely–& we talked about their dear mother until I woke up with the tears streaming down my cheeks–the second time that I have done this same thing–Nobody but you knows how I loved that dear old lady, not like a friend–but a blood relation–there were so many ties that made her dear to us—Say to Mrs Dabney[?] that if she will accept of the two [?] in the box which I wore travelling she is perfectly welcome, as I found it inconvenient to have an open dress. I have buttoned it up & they are of no further use to me but if she will use them for [?] I will be very glad to have her do so—Tell Bea the pair of brown gaters[?] seem too narrow & [?] in the instep for me but if she can wear them to do so—& if you can alter the blue [three illegible words] of them I wish you would as I shant want it again—it will be spring before I get home—& [?] them can have a good [two more lines and the closing cut off in copying]

## CAPTAIN RICHARD W. DIXEY TO CAPTAIN JOHN DIXEY, HIS FATHER

New York—Feby 16th 1853

My dear father,

We expect to get ready for sea abt. Saturday next, if naught prevents. Rebecca & Cowell are well & so am I, for all which I hope we feel thankful to our good Heavenly Father. 'Tis blowing a gale from the South, and rain. The carpenters have been working round the head under a sail. Think they will not do a great deal this afternoon however. Hope is 'tis Gods will to have a good passage out to San Francisco. Hope above this, to be submissive to Gods will, and if my anticipations are not realized, [?] still believe that all things will work together for good to them who love God. Dear Father, I wish I could send on some handsome present but I find it takes abt. all I can raise in NYork to fit me away. If Robt.[103] were at home I could get from him, as he owes me abt. $200 & father Gardner[104] has abt. $240 more of my money at interest. So if you should at any time get pinched, pray use this in either case, & I shall be glad if it is useful to you. I have been very busy since the accident to the ship and have not called on Messrs. Harbeck & co. So that I dont know when Robt. intends coming home. I have commenced a letter to him and intend to finish it this evening if naughts prevents. If I return again safely, I shall be able to have some of the girls[105] here, as I shall be better able to afford it, and want them to hear Mr. Beecher[106] with me. I do think he is a wonderful man. He has given me impetus, I trust, in the way heavenward. He is a spiritual man, I believe sincerely. I am writing this on board the Houqua. The joiner is widening my berth, as tis rather narrow to accommodate double. Hope I shall see Bro. Hector[107] in California. Cowell had a letter from cousin Theodore today, with some of his drawings included. He will make a good drawer I have no doubt. Wish he could have been here part of the time at least. He would be delighted with NYork. So many things to see. Cowell seems to secure the good graces of all the ladies. He makes it a point I believe to get acqt. on their first arrl. I think you would be pleased with Mrs. Kimball, I like her much. She is very sensible, and good natured. Please give my love to Mr. and Mrs. Lawrence, and to any of my friends who you may see. Tell Elisa I hope she has got bravely o'er all her California Fever. Please say to Robt. on his return I want him (among the rest) to write me to Cal[a]. direct, care of F. C. Sandford Esqr. Hope the girls will not forget to write me, Rebecca, Hannah, Carrie, Elisa & [?]. Of course you will answer some of my letters if you feel well enough, as I have not much doubt you will, by the time I arrive at San Francisco. Love to all in abundance. Please tell W[m]. B. Brown[108] I shall certainly expect a letter from him and if I do not get one, shall feel disappointed. May God bless you dear father, and all our dear family, here upon earth, and make us all content with our lot, and thankful and finally, when done with us here, receive us all in His Heavenly Kingdom, through Jesus our Redeemer, Amen. Your affectionate and loving son, Richard W. Dixey.–P.S. Rebecca and Cowell would send love with mine did they know I were writing.–Pray for us. Your own son, Richard W. D. The M.h.d.[109] boys are all well. R.W.D.

## JENNIE MINGE DIXEY TO HER MOTHER

Sunday–AM–Paris–91 Champs Élysées
July 24th/1853

This dearest Mother is the 3[d] day I have been sitting up in a large "Fauteuil Mechanique"[110] in which I stretch myself out at full length–am now by the window looking out on all that is passing when they rolled me to window from bed–so dont be uneasy fearing I might undertake too much–Indeed if you could only see how exceedingly & very attentive, particularly Robert is you could feel no uneasiness whatever–On the 8th day[111] the D$^r$ of his own accord told me I might sit up for a short time for fear in this warm weather of [?] my back too much–(So Robert who was in town when the D$^r$ made his visit) would not believe me when I told him & actually kept me in bed. In the same way he told me I might eat a small plate full of Rasberries so I told R– & he declared he did not believe he had said a "small plate full" so brought me six the first day & 8 the next–The old D$^r$ is one of the nicest of physicians I ever knew–he asks me what I like & tells me I may eat it–The other day he enquired did I like fruit–of course I told him I did–had lived on nothing else scarcely for last 6 or 7 months–well then he said you can have now & then an apricot & a few rasberries but I asked "wont it hurt the baby" "Oh! said he never mind the baby–never mind her"–eat what you like only a little at a time with plenty of sugar–& accustom her to it early–she lived on it before she was born & thrived & she can but do the same now!! So it is with meats & vegetables & in fact any thing I fancy he says I [?] liberty to try only be careful & not overload the stomach–I have plenty of milk & the nurse says the richest & sweetest she ever saw & it runs away[?] so continuously that I am never dry although I wear[?] glasses most all the time–so I have had [line missing from copy] Two evenings I had a little tight nervous feeling over my left eye & that is every ailment I can remember since the 14th–then I had enough to last me my life time–I have had several visitors every day nearly– Cousin Octavia & Diddy[?] were the first–a Mrs. Moeller whom I met at the Hotel another–Helena Coad is another who came to see me the day they returned from the Rhine & yesterday I was quite in luck Cousin O & D again accompanied by who do you think? John Scott & in spite of [?] strance–Mr Dixey would bring him in and I was glad enough to see him I assure you. Afterwards the Dr came & brought Mrs. S... to see me who I found an exceedingly pleasant woman & afterwards–who do you think had to see me? I would give you three guesses but I know you could not tell–Miss DeValcout[?]– looking prettier than ever–she is living a short distance out of town with her Mother & made me promise to drive out & see them as soon as I was able to ride out–saying I should lay on the sofa till I was rested enough to come back–she enquired most afftly about Bea–Rea & both you & father–also Miss Tarlton[?] & seems to have recollected all the names of those she met at the Pt[112] with wonderful accuracy–We will leave here as soon as I am able to travel as the Picardy[?] is expected at Lpool by the 10th August & Robert says he must be there as soon after she arrives as possible–in fact he ought to be in Bristol now attending to the HH–but tell father I have given him leave to go–but he will not–If the Picardy should arrive as soon as expected he will go over for a few days & return for his family–In the mean time will take rooms [?] at West Dinby[?][113]–4 miles out of Lpool & near the cousin of Mrs Babcocks– the Mrs Frank Babcock I spoke of who was with us for a week–& an exceedingly pleasant fine woman–Helen told me they had changed their plans & were going [line missing on copy] we may come together after all–but if Robert is able to get off before, you may depend we wont wait for any body– My baby is the sweetest little black eyed girl you ever saw looking just like a little gypsy or Indian baby she has such black hair and brown reddish looking skin. Doesnt cry any scarcely & loves to be washed has not suffered from the cholic at all–has now & then what the Nurse calls a little pinch from the wind & all she has ever taken was the usual spoon full of oil & a little sugar & water with some fleur-d'Orange in it–Mrs. H is gentle & quiet–& very attentive to both me and the baby & seems to understand the management of infants so well that I shall be relieved of a load of responsibility by having her with us. Dear Mother you dont know how glad & grateful I feel to think it is all over. I have dreaded it for so long–You must tell me how you like the name we have chosen I first called her as you know Anna Mary[?] then it occured to me that would be after Aunt A. & not you & as none of us had your maiden name or your first name either I concluded to take the two–I am sure she will be in every way worthy of it–besides the hair I sent you–Robert sent Sister Hannah quite as much & I have put some away for a locket & yet we have not made her bald indeed what we have taken cannot be missed–but dont imagine she has even half the quantity Mrs Tucker's baby ever had down at the Pt–I wouldnt have it such a fright as that for the world–This morning[?] when I had her I stuck her with a pin & did not [know] what made her scream out so & she was so good about it & so soon over that we could not find the place & began to think I had only pressed her against it until I took her a second time

& found where the point had gone right deep into her dear little arm & made the place quite purple–but Nurse [?] it & she is now fast asleep in the bed for you must know her cradle is the chair I am [line missing on copy] pillows & little [?] & that which [?] wants me [?] have to let her go for while Miss Anna is asleep–Did you ever think to have had a Parisienne Grand daughter–She has taken two or three french lessons already–Robert is making such a fuss about my writing too much that I find I must stop

Written on the edge of the letter in Robert Dixey's hand:
25th
All well & Jennie sitting up chatting as fast as ever
Truly yours
RHD

# REBECCA GARDNER DIXEY TO SARAH JANE GARDNER GIRDLER

Cadiz–September 3d 1856[114]

Dear Sister Sarah

Rich$^d$ wrote a few weeks ago to John Gilley telling him of our safe arrival here and that we were loading for Boston–last Saturday we received orders to go South instead of B. We all felt much disappointed, & more especially Rich. & the boys[115]–however they are getting more reconciled–I never saw Willie so much disappointed about any thing–tell Bethia.[116] I think it will be a good thing–as this seems to be the first time that he is inclined to be tired of the sea, & even goes so far as to say if he gets home, he hardly thinks he shall go again. We shall probably touch Mobil for orders whether to discharge our salt there or go to N. Orleans. Do write before you hear of our arrival, & direct to the care of C. H. Minge, & Co Mobile, and should we go to N. Orleans, he will forward them. Had I have known the Ship was going South I should have stopped in Havre, as I think it would have been better for me–but knowing the ship was coming to B. could not resist the temptation of coming, & then again I wanted to make some arrangement of our house, & furniture–should I have gone back with R. There does'nt seem to be much use in keeping house while Rich. is running in this trade and yet I do'nt know how we can arrange matters without coming home. If freights are good this winter I suppose there will be no prospect of the Ships returning until another summer. I wish you would write, & give Fathers opinion, & your own, what is best to do, & we will write from N. Orleans or Mobile, any ~~thng~~ things that you want, in any of our own families take them, it will do them good.

Now I suppose you would like to know something how Fanny gets along. I think she likes the Ship better than any other place–she grows more and more knowing every day–but still does'nt talk much–a few days since she commenced calling herself Sis–so now when we ask her what her name is– she says Sis. tell S.J.[117] she will be obliged to give up her name. She continues to sing Grandpa's tune, & we think sings it more, & more like him–she remembers you all, & loves dearly to have me talk about you. While in Havre we had some little girls at the house who sang, & danced sweetly. Fanny was charmed–one piece they sang I took quite a fancy to–after some weeks she commenced humming it, having never heard it but once.

She has just come to kiss this letter–so I said, you want to send a kiss to Aunt Sarah? She said yes–then in a little while she began stomping her foot for me to look–saying Loo, Loo, Loo, I said Lewis?[118] She said yes, so here it is– ––. her eye, & stomach teeth are all through but she does'nt seem to get rid of her cough as I would like to have her–I some times think she never will–it seems to be something natural to her–but I must hope for the best–Cowell is well, & sends love to all. When do you expect Rich$^d$? I have been on shore several times–but do'nt see much to interest–it is very warm and dusty–we have plenty of grapes, & fresh figs besides several other kinds of fruit so you see we do not suffer for good things.–if we had come to Boston we should have brought a nice lot of olives, & some wine sherry for Mother. Last week we went to the salt pans, and there Rich. got a donkey for Cowell to ride–but his father thought he would try him first–then C. Mounted and had a nice ride–we could find no side saddles–but as we were away from the town I was determined to try him–so I mounted with R–he to guide the donkey, & I to hold on him–as the donkey began to trot I found myself slipping and finally had to spring to save myself from falling–I then sprang on with Cowell, & rode some time. I think with a side saddle I should enjoy it much–Fanny rode some ways with her Father, & seemed highly delighted.

 How is Father, & Mother, & all our dear friends at home. How is Bethia? poor child, she has been greatly afflicted. I do hope we shall have some good long letters from home, when we arrive South. I have no one with me as yet– we were hurried away so from Havre that I had no time to look after girls– however I get along better at sea than in Port as there I am obliged either to stay at home, & take care of her, or take her with us–how many times I have wished I had taken Sarah with me–although I suppose she would have been homesick by this time–if we had stopped at Havre I think she would have enjoyed it, as everything is so different from home. I should'nt have stopped in the city, but just out of it on a very high hill called the Le Cote. The situation is so delightful, & called very healthy–Sarah is making so much money now[119]– I suppose she would not leave at any rate–tell her I am much obliged for her letter, and if we had come to Boston I should have taken her with us that is, if she would have come. I have something for her and if Willie comes home shall send it by him. Willie sends love–says he wants a letter waiting for him when he arrives South–all the boys are well–but I believe none have written home. Rich[d.] Thinks with me that our stoves if left in the house through the winter will rust badly, & if any one wants them–to sell them at a reasonable price–I think I mentioned them in Bethia's letter–perhaps it would be well to consult Wm. B.[120] as he is in the habit of making bargains–how is Carrie[121] my love to her–tell her I shall expect a letter on arrival out[?] South. kisses also to all the children. I wish you would all write long letters–we have heard nothing later than 22[d] july the last letter from Robert dated Aug. 26 and 28th said they were all well in Paris. Mary[122] had met Nat. & Lizzie Hooper[123] at their house. Do hope to arrive in safety, & get a good freight–R has done very little since leaving the black sea–we shall sail to morrow if nought prevents. Rich[d.] Cowell, Fanny self send love in abundance to you all, & kisses to the children. hoping to see you soon I am your affec. Sister

 R. B. Dixey[124]

APPENDIX

*B*

# Letters of Sarah Jane Girdler

The letters that follow were written by Sarah Jane to her mother, the lady pictured on page 167. They will give you another perspective of her trip on the *Dixey*.

At Sea–February 3, 1857
My dear Mother,

If the wind holds we expect to get into Mobile Bay tomorrow, so I thought I would write and have a letter all ready to send when we arrive.

I've got so much to say that I don't know where to commence or what to say first, but suppose I had better begin at the day I left Boston. Fannie Collemore, the young lady you saw on board the ship, and myself staid on deck most of the afternoon in order to catch the last glimpse of Boston. All the islands were covered with snow, and great fields of ice were floating all over the harbor, so that it looked very dreary. We went to bed early as we were very tired. I had some trouble in getting into my berth which is the upper one, but after having attained my position their, was rocked to and fro and slept as soundly as I would have at home. The next morning I awoke, instead of feeling sea sick as you all thought I should, I was just as smart as ever. I sat up in my berth and looked down, there I was perched up ever so high with no way of getting down. If the ship had been lying still, I might have succeeded, but it was rolling so that I expected to go out head first in a much quicker way than I wished. At last I had to call Uncle Richard to the rescue, he rigged a board for me to slide down on, and then by holding on to the berth, I managed to get my clothes on. At the breakfast it was about as much as I could do to hold onto my cup and plate. It snowed hard all day and as night approached, to blow a perfect gale, but the wind was fair. It seemed so stormy that Aunt Rebecca took Fannie into her berth, and I slept on the lower one, and well it was for me that I did, for the ship rolled so that I could hardly keep in the berth, and as it was Uncle Richard had to put a lee board in. We had severe thunder and lightning. In the middle of the night we shipped a large sea, which came into the cabin window and poured down into the upper berths. I was in a lower one so I did not get wet, but Aunt Rebecca got completely drenched. Just as I had got over this fright, I was destined to a still worse one. The wind was blowing furiously and splitting the main topsail, making a noise when it parted, which to my inexperienced ears, seemed like all the masts going over board. I was never more glad to see daylight in all my life, for I had not closed my eyes for all night, and of course was tired lying in bed. You would have laughed if you could have seen me trying to get into the cabin. I got as far as the door, and then fell flat on the floor, and finding it hard work to get up, sat there while I combed my hair, and then crawled on my hands and knees to breakfast, after which I got to the door and sat down on the step[125] to look at the waves, and certainly I never emagined any thing so magnificent. I have often heard of the waves rising mountain high, but could never realize that they really did before. The ship would rise to the top of some huge wave, then sink down until it seemed as if it would never rise again, and deck would slant so as to be almost perpendicular. I was never tumbled around so before, even Uncle Richard and the men who were used to such rolling could not walk without holding onto something. The rough weather continued for several days, as long as it lasted I had a pretty bad time as I would generally fall down every time I'd try to walk. I guess I've got about twenty black and blue spots on me.

But after about a week the weather grew milder and then my troubles ended. It has been as warm as it is at home in summer. Just think, today is the third of February and it is so warm on deck that it is really uncomfortable. It does not seem possible that it can be so cold at home. I have enjoyed myself finely all the passage. Like going to sea full as well as I expected to. I suppose you will think we have had a very long passage. Last Friday we were going at the rate of twelve knots an hour and expected to get in the next day, but suddenly a squall came up, and we had a bad thunder storm all night, and the wind has been dead ahead since untill this morning, when it became fair again.

Oh Mother: if you had been here that night you would have been frightened enough. I sat up in my berth and looked out of my window. The lightning was very sharp and so frequent that it seemed like one continued flash. At last some one shut my shutter so I could not watch the lightning any longer, then the rain poured down making such a noise that I could not hear anything else. All at once there was a very large flash instantly followed by a tremendous crash of thunder, which seemed to strike very near us. At first I thought it was the main mast that was struck, and expected to hear the men cry fire, but there was a dead silence, then I thought perhaps every one on deck is killed. At last I heard the mates voice giving some orders, so I knew that all was right. Soon Uncle Richard came down. He said that everyone on deck was slightly affected by the lightning, two men were knocked down but not hurt badly. In the morning we found that we had had a very narrow escape. The lightning had struck the lightning rod on the main mast and passed down breaking the chain that was in the water. If we had not had a rod on the mast, in all probability the ship would have been struck and burned up. How greatful we ought to be that we were saved from such an accident. We have got the drollest set of sailors I ever saw not half of them know one rope from another. Last evening Fannie Collemore and myself were on deck walking. I saw Mr. Symonds[126] and asked him to get a Spaniard, one of the crew, to sing. I have not heard such good singing for a long time. He sang several Spanish songs for us. Then Albert, another of the sailors, played on his violin. so you can see we have no lack of music. How is Richard's[127] leg now? I hope he is a good boy and trys to learn. Tell Lewis[128] that he need not be afraid of Fannies forgetting him, for she talks about him every day. She speaks about all of you very often, particularly Grandpa and Grandma and Mammy Taddy [?].[129] How does your school flourish?[130] Well, I hope. Give my love to all the folks. Tell Grandma I shall write to her soon. Tell Cissie[131] I shall write to her soon. You must send her this letter so she can have a slight idea what I have been through. I hope I shall have letters from her and Emma when we get to Mobile, as well as from the rest of the folks youself included. While I've been writing I heard quite a commotion on deck. On going up to hear the cause of the noise I found we were in the middle of a large school of porpoises, the first I have seen. They were splendid large fish. Mr. Millet[132] was in the bows of the ship trying to harpoon one but they were all around the stern–he did not find it out till we had almost passed them, so we did not catch any of them. Remember me to Hannah.

Give my best love to Richard Evans[133] and family, tell him I use the desk every day and have written my journal regularly & I think of him whenever I use them. I don't know how I should get along without it. Tell Hattie Haskell[134] not to forget to write to me and tell me all the news. Tell Willie Turner I wish he was here.[135] It would be so much company. I heard Dan[136] saying that he missed the boys very much. Sometimes Fannie takes me to the room the boys used to have and says Willie all gone. There is another Willie on board the ship[137] but Fannie doesn't seem to think so much of him as she does of her Willie. Give my love to all the folks and accept a large share for yourself from your affectionate daughter.

    S. J. Girdler

I have not written half that I wanted to, so I must keep it till next time. I have finished my dress. It sets very nicely. I was very sorry to find that I had left those kid gloves. I wish I could get the dark ones. I don't care so much for the white ones.


Off Elsinore—May 24, 1857

My dear Mother,

We are now lying at anchor in the sound, waiting for a fair wind to go up the channel to Elsinore. I suppose you saw by the papers, that we left Mobile the 18th of March. We have had a tremendous passage, had to beat most of the way. When[?] the fair wind would come, it would be so light that we could not do much. We have had several severe storms, or rather long gales of wind but as I am now more used to the sea, I did not mind them as much as those we had on our way to Mobile. We were off the English Channel twelve days beating and longing[?] for a fair wind to get in. The thirteenth of this month the wind changed, and we got into the channel, then it came about again, so we had to beat all the way up. The first day we had any number of pilots on board who wanted to take us up, but Uncle did not want them. I never saw such begging in my life, first they would ask for some tobacco, then beef, pork, bread, tea, sugar and everything else they could think of. They never seemed satisfied, but would keep on begging as long as they got anything.

    The pilot that took us up looked like Lewis Evans, only he was not as good looking as Louis. The air was quite clear all the way, so we had a fine opportunity to see the land. The coast of England is quite high–very unlike our coast–there being no rocks only tall white chalk cliffs. Oh Mother I wish you could see the Isle of Wight, it was so refreshing to see its hills covered with natures carpet of green, and the pretty little towns nestled under there sides. I saw a tall tower on top of one of the hills. The whole island seemed like a beautiful garden, everything looked so neat and well kept. We passed a large number of towns, on the English coast. It seemed so nice after being on the water so long–to see the pretty little towns nestling down under the hills, with there clean pretty streets wandering among the green fields, and the hills rising in gentle undulating waves being all covered with verdure, interspersed with patches of cultivated grounds and dotted over the villas, and country seats of the English gentry–There was an old ruined castle on the side of one of the hills which gave quite a romantic air to the scene. We had been short of coal for some time so when we got opposite the town of Hythe, as it was a dead calm we dropt anchor and sent a boatman, who came along side, to the town for coal, fresh beef, butter, eggs, vegatables &c. He got back about eight bells, and as there was a slight brease springing up we got under way again. The pilot entended to anchor us that night in the Downs but the wind died all away, so we were obliged to drop anchor off Dover so we had a fine opportunity to see that place. It is quite a large town, built under the hill on which is the castle, which is a very large fort surrounded by strong fortifications. I should think it would be an utter impossibility to take it.

We were so near shore that we could, with the aid of a glass, plainly see the soldiers marching round the fort, could even hear the drums beating–and see the people walking in the street. When it came night, the town was brilliantly lighted, also the two light houses and the head, and the Calis light on the French coast. The next morning the pilot left us. There was scarcely a breath of air, but towards night the brise freshened, and we went on finly.

The 18th of the month we passed a Dutch fishing vessel–They asked us to throw them a line, but they did not catch it, and before we could throw it again we had passed them, but they called in such a pitious tone, "Cap-i-tan, vater, vater," that Uncle ordered the men to back the main yards, and in a few moments they were along side. They had been out much longer than usual, owing to the calm weather, and were out of water, and provisions. Uncle gave them beef, bread, rice and water. They gave us in return some very nice fish, Sole and turbot, they are the nicest fish I ever tasted. There was a little fat faced white haired boy on board who looked just like our Louis[138] only his face was not as clean as I hope Louis always is. The poor child had not had anything to eat for a long time and when he saw the beef and bread comming over the side, he grinned just like Lou. He like all the others on board had on great wooden shoes that looked so clumsy that I dont see how they managed to get round in them. During the day we suplied three other boats which we found in the same predicament as the first. They all seemed very thankful for what they received, and did not keep asking for more like the English people. There boats are the queerest looking things I ever saw, the bows and stern are just about as round as a tub. We are laying at anchor at the mouth of the channel, and about eight miles from Elsinore–wind and tide both against us so we shall either have to wait for a fair wind or take steam. There is a large number of vessels of every discription lying around waiting, like us, for a fair wind. On one side of us is the coast of Sweden on the other Denmark. The coast of Sweden is high and rocky something like our coast. Denmark is lower and more fertile. The pilot says a month ago the ground was covered with snow but now every thing looks green and flurishing. The reason every thing advances so rapidly is because the sun is shining so much longer than it does at home. The sun does not set till about nine o'clock and it is day light all the time. It seems very strange to be able to read after ten o'clock at night.

I wish the wind would change so we could get up to Elsinore. I like the sea as well as I did at first. Think I should like to go all the time.

Is Richard at home?[139] If he is I hope he goes to school and tries to be more of a man and not plague you as much as he used to. I expect Louis is quite a scholar by this time–tell him I hope he goes to Mr Valentines school before I get back. Fannie talks about him a great deal–she always calls him "Janes[140] Loo-Loo." She says almost anything now–is a regular little "chatter box"–she is the cunningest little thing I ever saw, and she grows prettier every day–Almost every day she wants to see all the miniatures, and kisses them and talks to them. Sometimes she puts on her shaker[?] and goes to see Nanpa and Nanma, Mammy Taddy, Lalice[?][141] and Loo-Loo. Then comes back and tells us about them so you see we hear from you all very often.

I dont suppose I shall be able to write as often as I did in Mobile as the postage is so much more. Aunt Becca wrote to Cowell last week–told him to write to you as soon as he received [?]. I suppose he will. Fannie can sing some of the sailors songs such as "Haul the boline," [?] bunch [?] come down &c." The other morning Aunt Becca found her sitting in bed, with her night cap on her foot, pulling the strings and singing, "Haul the boline [?] We have two little black kittens on board. She has one of them in her arms almost all the time when she is on deck. She talks a great deal about her "doing darling Dick."[142] There is not the least bit of danger of her forgetting any of you.

How does your school prosper, as well as usual? How are Grandpa and Grandma. Give my best love to them. How I should like to see you all–I dream about some of you every night. So does Aunt Becca. She sends love to all of you–she wants[?] to see you very much.

Wednesday, 27th. Dear Mother, I wish you could see us now we are laying at anchor about three and a half miles from Elsinore perfectly surrounded by vessels of every discription and nation. The ship next to us is so near that I think we could converse very well speaking in an ordinary tone of voice.

Yesterday morning a steam tug tried to tow us up to town but the wind and tide were so strong against us that they had to give up the attempt. Uncle Richard went up to town in a boat Monday–he came back at night very much pleased with the place. He had made the acquaintance of an English gentleman named Cary liked him and family very much. Mr & Mrs Cary wanted us to come up to town as soon as we could and stay there but we have had no chance to get up.

This afternoon the wind came fair so we got under way. We went along nicely for some time passing all the ships that were ahead of us. There were about five hundred, but when we got up to where we now are the winds died away and the tide turned the ship around and as she would not mind the helm, we had to drop anchor again. We came very near running into two ships, managed to clear them and thats all.

As soon as we anchored Uncle Richard went up to town in a sail boat to try to [?] a steam boat to tow us up. The wind is fair so I dont suppose we shall [?] in Elsinore more than twenty hours just to get water &c. So I dont know whether we shall go on shore or not.

Thursday 28th. The steam tug is towing us up to town. We are almost up. [We] are going on shore a little while. The ship is only going to stop long enough to get coal & water, unless the wind dies away–I cannot stop to write any more. So Good Bye.

Love in abundance to all my friends except a very large share for yourself from your loving daughter.

Sarah J. Girdler

PS–Tell Lizzie Stevens[143] I must to have answered her letter in Mobile but put it off till too late–will write from Cronstadt.–my best love to her and Emma.

Sarah


Bordeaux–––Dec–8th/57

My dear Mother

Uncle Richard has just returned from town says a steamer is comming tomorrow to take us down the river–the wind is fair so if it continues I suppose we shall soon be a sea again.

I am glad we are going to leave this place but feel almost afraid when I think of the rough time we had on our former passage and the possibility of its being repeated but I hope and trust that the same power that enabled us to ride out that awful gale in safty will guide us across the wide ocean again.

Samuel is here–came quite unexpectedly last Thursday night. We had all been envited to dine at Mr. Martiques[?] but only Mr. Robert Dixey's family went.

Aunt Becca and I were in the forward cabin ironing some collars and undersleeves when in walked Sam. He had received my letter saying the ship would sail the middle of the week the Monday before and started the next morning the land route through Paris and arrived as I before said Thursday night.

He looks rather slim but his finger is much better. It was so late when he arrived that he had no place to sleep so Mr Millet (good soul that he is) made him a bed on his and Mr Symonds chests. I covered him with my long shawl and he slept very comfortably. The next morning he went on shore to get his chest then helpt the carpenter build him a berth in the after hatch house. The [?] Willie [?] to [?] in and then went to work as though he had always lived on board. There are two other boys that live in the house with him. I often pay them a short visit. This morning I found him just at breakfast–he was sitting on his clothes bag, with his chest for a table, eating[?] his food from a tin pan with his knife and lead[?] spoon. He said Sis, this is rather different from taking my breakfast at the Hospital, in bed, and having all the choicest bits put aside by the cook for me, but "Variety is the spice of life." So you see that he has not lost his habit of taking every thing easy. He likes every thing so very well and think he will continue to do so. I dont see any reason why he should not.

Poor little Fannie has been very sick since I last wrote. I believe I said then that she had a bad cold–she continued growing sicker untill at last we grew frightened and sent for Mrs Dixey's doctor a [?] but very skillful. He pronounced her very sick with "inflamation of the lungs" and a high fever for over a week she continued very sick none of us had any sleep, scarcely. She had blisters and mustard plasters on her legs leaches too–all of which with the medicine had the desired efect and about a week agoe she was pronounced out of danger. Today she has been dressed for the first time since her sickness. She is quite well but very week. She tried to walk but tottered and would have fallen had not I caught her. She did not know what ailed her but said "I can't walk with these shoes Jennie–put on my nither ones." She has a good appetite now so will pick up her strength fast.

Mr Millet tels me that he wrote his wife that we were going to New Orleans–instead of that we will start for Mobile so please tell her that she may direct her letters as before to the Care of C. H. Minge & Co. He was very much disappointed at not receiving her letters from home when Mr Symonds did. He is very well and as pleasant and [?] as ever.

Sam tells me that Mrs Hammond is dead–how the family must miss her–she has been sick so long and suffered so much.

He speaks very highly of Willie[144]–Says he is as smart as a steel[?] trap and was very kind to him. I hear through him also that Louis is growing very stout and is likely to become the "pope of the family"–how I should love to see the dear little fellow. I expect by the time I get home he will be grown so that I shall hardly know him. I hope he loves his books now better than he used to. And how is Richard getting along–well I hope.

How I should like to see you and hear how you are getting along and what you are doing–it seems such an age since I heard any [news?]–you know you wrote your last letter in such a hurry that there wasn't time to write much. But I must wait patiently and I suppose I shall know all in due season.

Give my love to Lizzie–Emma–Hattie–Alice and other friends–tell them I shall expect letters from them all on my arrival at Mobile and shall be sadly disappointed if there are none. Tell Em. that she must not be so much taken up with Thomas that she cant find time to write to me. I shall try to answer Richards letter on my arrival at Mobile if I am fortunate ever to get there.

Give my best love to Grandpa–Grandma–Lewis and all other friends and please dear mother except a large share for yourself from your loving daughter

Sarah

You must excuse the shortness of this as well as the errors which you will find plentyfully dispersed all over it as I did not commence writing untill late and it is now long after ten, and both my back and hand aches

Mobile Bay–Jan. 25th, 1858

My dear Mother

We are again anchored in safety in the bay–arrived this afternoon about five o'clock, too late for Mrs. Dixey's family to go up in the boat so they will be obliged to stay until tomorrow when they will all leave us. We shall miss them very much and be very lonely when they are gone.

Aunt Becca has not decided about comming home–will not make up her mind untill she hears from home which will be I hope in a few days, as soon as Uncle Richard can go to town and come back again. Oh, how disappointed I shall be if he brings no letters. I am so anxious to hear how you and all the other dear ones are. But I suppose you will want to hear about the passage so I will tell you. The first week out was rough and the wind ahead–then we got in the north East trades and had delightful weather very warm too. Christmas day was more like the fourth of July, so warm and pleasant. I thought about you all then a good deal and imagined you, having a nice time at home. We passed it like any other, only commemorated it by killing a pig and giving all on board a nice dinner. We saw the island of St. Domingo and Cuba very plainly–could even smell the orange groves and other delicious perfumes. But after passing them the wind came ahead so we were obliged to beat– and coming through the Gulf of Mexico got far down to leeward of Mobile with the wind in such a position that we could not get up. After beating about for several days and without success, Mr. Dixey concluded to run into the mouth of the Mississippi and telegraph on to Mobile so we went in and anchored just outside the bar. Mr. Dixey went inside to the telegraph office but it was too late to receive an answer so the next morning he went again, found the wire broken between New Orleans and Mobile so his dispatch had not gone through. He then telegraphed to Mr. Begouen one of the owners in New Orleans who advised him to go to Mobile–So we got under weigh much to the disappointment of every one on board myself included. Mr. Dixey left us and went up to the City, to see to his business there. For three days we tried to beat up to the windward but every time we would strike in towards land, there would be the south-west [wind?] in the same old place. This morning however the wind came fair, so we got in. We had forty days passage which is quite good for this season. Capt. Freeto in the Riga[145] sailed five days before us, had a fair wind blowing all the time too, but had not arrived in New Orleans when we were there.

Poor Sam has been all this passage and is now quite sick. When he came he had besides his sore finger an irruption all over his body–it itched dreadfully and he used to scratch himself so it made sores all over him. After suffering a good deal that way it came out in the shape of boils all over him–sometimes he would have twenty at one time aching dreadfully too. He suffers everything as one could easily see by looking at him for the poor boy is so thin and as pale as can be. The boils are now getting better but the little pimples are coming back worse if possible than before.

He has kept about all the time, notwithstanding all his diseases. Sometimes he is so stiff that he can scarcely move one foot before the other. I really feel quite anxious about him. One thing I am certain of–and so is he–that is if he goes to sea another voyage it will quite kill him. Sometimes he feels very low spirited then again he will be quite merry about it–he calls himself Lazerus a [three illegible words]. When you see Uncle[146] do tell him about him. I suppose when he writes he will put the best side out. He says he shall go to a hospital as soon as he can get there–which is I think the best thing he could possibly do. Aunt Becca thinks like me that the sea is not a fit place for him–the salt air and provisions bring out his humor and will if he continues going down kill him. I wish Uncle could get him some place in Boston no matter how small the salary is and send for him to come home and fill it. It would be the best thing he could possibly do. He would be much shoked to see Sam now–he looks so sick he would hardly know him. I believe if he had been on board [other?] ships he would have been dead before this, but now he is allowed to stay in when he felt sick, and had the privilege of taking any medicine he wanted–besides Mr. Millet and Symonds are very kind to him. I shall always feel under great obligations to them for it. They are both well. I believe Mr. Symonds is coming home. Mr. Millet is not going to decide until he hears from his wife. He desires to be remembered. Oh, how I long to hear from you all. Do tell me all the news even the slightest events that happen. I hope Lizzie and Emma have each written me long letters. Is

Emma going to be married this Spring? How funny it seems to think of her being married.

Is Richard still at Mr. Woods?[147] I hope he satisfies him. What school does Lewis go to now, Mr. Valentine's I hope? Tell him sister wants him to study hard and make a very wise and good man. How I long to see the dear little fellow. Sam was delighted with him–thought him very smart. I hope he helps Grandpa, does all his errands and so on.

Fannie looks remarkably well–has gained considerable flesh since her sickness. I expect she will miss her little cousins[148] very much for she plays with them all day long and therefore must be very lonesome when they are gone. We shall stay down on the ship at present–dont know whether we shall stay any time in town or not.

Tuesday morning–I have not time to finish this dear mother as the steam boat is along side so will write again soon–love in abundance to all the dear ones except a very large share for yourself from your loving daughter

Sarah

APPENDIX

# C

# More Dixey Letters

### ROBERT HOOPER DIXEY
### TO HANNAH GLOVER DIXEY[151]

This letter was written three weeks after the loss of the *Robert H. Dixey* and its captain. The envelope reads: Miss H. G. Dixey, Sharon, Mass[tts]

New York–-Oct–3/60

My dear Sister–

I rec[d] only to day your favor of 26th having been laid up with a severe sprain to my foot & can only just hobble now–it comes rather hard as we are preparing to go South[152] & I thought to profit by a few days to spend[?] with Father and Sisters but fear now it will be impossible. Jennie & the Children & Billa[153] all have colds & are coming to town this week for a few days before starting out–I rec[d] letter from Cowell[154] to day–poor child he says he cannot yet realize his loss & that it seems as if his Father was still at sea. Gods providence is inscrutable for some nice purpose no doubt our dear Brother was taken from us & I hope Father & all of us will bow in resignation & resolve to seek our peace with God & endeavor to so conduct ourselves as to make it sure of meeting our Sainted Brother in Heaven. Tell Father not to be worried about means to get along. I shall be able to send him all you need & shall send some before leaving New York. I wrote Cowell I hope he & his Mother[155] [will?] visit Sharon as often as possible to cheer up Father–I shall try & find something for Hct[?][156] at New Orleans instead of going to sea[?], as it will be far preferable.

Write often & with much love from us all to Father and Sisters believe me your afft Brother

Robert

## ROBERT HOOPER DIXEY TO HIS FATHER, CAPTAIN JOHN DIXEY, AND SISTERS

The envelope reads: Capt. John Dixey, Sharon, Mass[tts].

New Orleans
May 26th–1861

My dear Father & Sisters–

I rec[d] some days since letter from Sister Hannah & was glad to hear you now all well. Hector wrote me he had requested M[r] Appleton[157] to pay you some funds on his a/c–suppose this is at Mhead. I also wrote Messrs. Harbeck & Co. to send you a check for $100 & if not sent soon you can write to them at N.Y. Jennie & Anna & Bobby are about starting for Bladon Springs Ala. to pass a month & I shall go up there for a few days next week. You say that I am on the side of the South & this is true, for a more righteous cause than ours was never known & I trust the evil counsels & opinions that now prevail at Washington will soon be dispelled by returning reason & allow us to take care of our own affairs–all we ask is to be let alone–seeking no conquest or agression. I fear now that as Federal troops have invaded Virginia we shall soon hear of serious battles. God in his mercy avert and quell these fearful scenes of Civil War. There is not a solitary Union man in the whole South & its worse than useless to try & compel a Union against such opposition –

I hope Father will not worry himself about funds or any thing. My business[158] has been quite prosperous since I arr[d] here & shall be able to furnish all he requires. When you write to Elisa[159] tell her I have been writing her for [two illegible words] but could not recollect her name or rather Mr. Moodys[?] exact initials & know there were several others of same name at York. Love to Carrie,[160] W^m & the children & all the friends you may chance to hear or see. Write soon as I expect the mails will soon be stopped but as there will be occasional parties going north will write when good opportunity offers by private hand.

Trusting that Peace may soon smile upon both countries ere long—I remain D^r Father & Sisters

Your aff–Son & Bro
Robert

# Notes

Notes to the Letters on Pages 64-68

6 An advertisement in the 1856 Mobile city directory for Bladon Springs, in Choctaw County, Alabama, a "well known watering place," makes it clear that "Bladon water" was a mineral water regarded as salutary. The ad compares the water to that of "some of the best Springs in Europe, such as Seltzer, Spa, Pouges, and Aix La Chapelle" and boasts cures "in cases of Rheumatism, Dyspepsia, Dropsy, Cutaneous Affections, Scrofula, Ulcers, &c, &c, many of them of long standing, which had defied the skill of the most eminent physicians." The secret of the water's efficacy, according to Professor Brumby, of the University of Alabama, is that it is "an *alkaline acidulous* beverage"!

7 Collier Minge's son William Henry Harrison Minge, about 25 at this time. He was off training to be a sailor-captain.

8 Robert and Jennie's two-year-old daughter.

9 "Oh Lee": this was the name by which baby Anna called Leana Preston (wife of John Preston), a slave of the Minges. Sophia was another slave.

10 Evidently the family name for Anna's grandmother, Jennie's mother.

11 This was the ferry or "bay boat" from Mobile to Point Clear, most likely the *Southern Star*, captained by Captain John P. Carson.

12 Messrs. Harbeck & Cie., the French company with which they did business.

13 Richard Dixey had been master of a ship called *Montreal* in January 1847 for a run from Norfolk, Virginia, to Cork, Ireland, but this ship, built in 1850, appears to be a different one.

14 Richard W. Dixey, captain of the *Robert H. Dixey*.

15 His oldest son, William Henry Harrison Minge (1830–1906).

16 He did get a charter and ship and never left the Atlantic Europe trade.

17 A "packet" of the Spackman Line between Philadelphia, Liverpool, and New Orleans or Mobile.

18 I.e., Bladon Springs mineral water.

19 The Lyons were another family transplanted from Virginia. The Minge plantation in Faunsdale was

near Demopolis.

20 Another reference to the *Southern Star,* the new ferry to Point Clear.

21 Mr. Withers was the mayor of Mobile at the time.

22 This is evidently a nickname for Jennie's sister Maria (pronounced Mar"eye"ah).

23 The ships were the *Robert H. Dixey,* Boston, and the *Nuremberg,* New Orleans.

24 The ships were currently having their bottoms coppered.

## Notes to Sarah Jane Girdler's journal, beginning on page 70

8 This may have been the daughter or some other relative of Dexter Collamore, the first mate. She left the ship in Mobile to return to her home in New Orleans. Perhaps she had come on the ship to Boston to visit relatives there.

9 The raised poop deck must have been at least the length of the cabin.

10 Great Abaco, one of the Bahama Islands.

11 As we have said, the *Dixey* was fast; the reader will be interested to note how many times Sarah Jane records her having passed other ships going the same direction.

12 By the time of the *Dixey,* quite a bit was known about the laws of electrical discharge caused by thunderstorms. The modern protection from lightning aboard sailing ships is remarkably similar to the system used on the *Dixey.* A copper rod atop the highest mast was clamped to an iron shroud (cable) running down to the main deck "deadeyes" (a type of turnbuckle used to tighten the cable). A length of chain was fastened to the shroud, and to its lower end was fastened an iron bar. During thunderstorms, the length of chain was lowered into the sea alongside the ship. The electric current in the lightning strike was supposed to pass down the copper rod, the iron shroud, the chain, and the iron bar into the water, thus "grounding" the charge without damage to the ship. Strangely, it usually worked! Jennie's journal is excellent proof of the efficiency of that rather crude system.

13 Square-rigged ships, even the best, don't go to windward very well. Only a point or so (11_°) with the wind, they excelled!

14 The crew list given at the beginning of the chapter lists an Allen and an Alex but no Albert.

15 A dance of plantation Negroes in the South accompanied by complexly rhythmic hand clapping and slapping of the knees and thighs.

16 A strip of land at Marblehead Harbor.

17 Fort Morgan, at the tip of the peninsula extending into the mouth of Mobile Bay from the east. The fort is a popular tourist attraction today, and the officers' quarters mentioned in the next sentence were restored in 1985.

18 83 N. Royal Street.

19 Collier Minge's 18-year-old daughter.

20 Almost certainly Christ Church, which was within easy walking distance of their boarding house.

21 This could have been Little Zion A.M.E. (NE corner of Dearborn and Church or the State Street Methodist Church (north side of State Street between Lawrence and Cedar).

22 An international banker from New York, in Mobile to purchase cotton for St Petersburg. He brought credit for "hard money" from Czar Nicholas I of Russia, and RHD worked for his firm.

23 Although this may seem a curious choice of words, it is possible that Jennie used *splendid* in its original sense of "gleaming, bright, brilliant." This theory is somewhat belied, however, by her later

reference to a "splendid bouquet of flowers." It is obvious that the fire was regarded by the ladies, at least, as a form of entertainment!

24 March 3, 1857, was "Fat Tuesday" or Mardi Gras day that year.

25 This may have been the "Strykers" or perhaps the Cowbellion de Rakin Society, of which Henry K. Fettyplace was a member. Mrs. Ward was probably the chaperone. Sarah Jane had arrived in Mobile at a very social time of the year. While the season was not yet being referred to as Mardi Gras, secret societies were being formed and balls were being held. The Minges and Fettyplaces and the Walter Smiths were most anxious to entertain Captain Dixey and his family. Although the entries in Sarah Jane's journal make only brief reference to her social activities, we can be sure that these former Marbleheaders and Virginians would live up to the high traditions of the "Deep South" as to entertaining visitors. These families were very active in Mobile society. In addition to their town residences, most of them had country and summer homes as well. Things were good in Mobile in the spring of 1857.

26 Now Old Shell Road. Spring Hill, now a lovely residential area of Mobile, was once a country town to which well-to-do families migrated in the summer to escape the danger of yellow fever in the low-lying downtown areas of the city.

27 General Smith's house at 49 Government Street was across from the home of Dr. Henry LeVert and his well-known wife, Madame Octavia Walton LeVert, which stood on the site currently occupied by the old Mobile County Courthouse. At this soirée were all the Marblehead and Salem members of the Fettyplace family who were then in Mobile. It must have been a lighthearted group, as the price of cotton was high and the *Dixey* was headed for Russia with its fourth load. All those present that night were directly or indirectly involved with the story of this ship. Walter Smith, at 57, was prominent in Mobile business and society. His wife, Mary Ann Fettyplace Smith, 57, was Tom Fettyplace's aunt. Their guests, in addition to Captain and Mrs. Dixey and Sarah Jane Girdler were: Thomas John Fettyplace, 25 percent owner of the ship and a close friend of all the Dixeys; Tom's sisters, Sarah Fettyplace, 35, and Louisa F. Peabody, 44; Louisa's husband, Herbert C. Peabody, 47; and Henry K. Fettyplace, 38, Tom's brother and business partner.

28 Government Street Presbyterian Church, the "mother church" of Presbyterianism in Alabama, located then and now at 300 Government Street. Dr. Mandeville died a year later.

29 Dan Simons, the third mate, from Marblehead.

30 This is presumably a Portuguese man-of-war, an extremely poisonous jellyfish, though the reference to "feathers" is puzzling.

31 The southern right whale (*Eubalaena glacialis*), now nearly extinct in the North Atlantic through overfishing.

32 *Thrasher whale* is another name for the killer whale (*Orcinus orca*), a "fierce carnivorous gregarious whale" that feeds on other whales.

33 The northern gannet (*Morus bassanus*), a goose-sized white sea bird with black wing tips that fishes by plunging from the air.

34 The name *drum* is given to several fishes of the order *Sciaenidae* that are capable of making a drumming noise. These include channel bass (red drum), black drum, and freshwater drum.

35 One of Sarah Jane's cousins in Marblehead, Lewis Girdler Evans, son of Captain Richard Evans and Elizabeth Girdler (sister of John Girdler).

36 A famous anchorage fifteen miles east of Dover near the mouth of the River Thames.

*An Antebellum Life At Sea*

37 Baptized "Lewis" after his grandfather Girdler. Jennie evidently thought the French spelling more stylish.

38 The Danish town of Helsingør.

39 A large ship's boat, probably about twenty-four feet long.

40 Daniel Symmonds, the third mate.

41 The ship's boat, which was kept on top of the midship deck house (the forecastle), was rigged for both sailing and rowing and could hold ten or more people.

42 It is not surprising that Sarah Jane has trouble with the spelling of this word (which she later spells "studden sails" as well as the correct "studding sails") since the usual nautical pronunciation is "st…n(t)s…l." The studding sail is "a light sail set at the side of a principal square sail of a vessel in free winds to increase its speed."

43 This was undoubtedly a portable writing desk, the sort whose writing surface, usually covered with felt, lifts up to reveal storage for stationery and supplies.

44 The spencer, a very short fitted jacket, has a curious history. Lord Spencer (George John, 2d earl Spencer, an English politician) claimed that fashion was so absurd that he himself could concoct a ridiculous, impractical style and it would become the rage. He cut the tails off his own coat and went for a stroll. In two weeks, all London was wearing the "spencer," and soon fashionable men, women, and children of the Continent and the colonies were wearing the same little jacket. It filled a need for the women of the early nineteenth century, who had previously been limited to capes and shawls.

45 Gogland, a Russian island in the Gulf of Finland.

46 Melodeon, also called "American organ," a type of reed organ similar to a harmonium except that air is drawn through the reeds by a suction bellows rather than being forced through by a pump bellows. In *Aunt Jane's Travels,* Jennie refers to it as a "parlor organ."

47 The Alexander Column, "erected by Nicholas I in memory of his brother, after a design by Auguste Richard Montferrand. A huge pillar…eighty-two feet high stands on a pedestal hewn out of a single piece of granite. In 1832 it took more then 2,000 soldiers and 400 workmen, using an intricate system of ropes and pulleys, to erect the Column on its high base, where it still stands without any additional support." (Fodor's)

48 A modern guidebook gives the figure of 100 kilos, or about 220 pounds, so perhaps something was lost in the translation!

49 Presumably this was a *kolaska,* the Russian equivalent of a *calash* or *calèche*—a light carriage with small wheels and a folding hood.

50 Although this word can mean "warehouse," it is probably used here in the sense of the French *magasin*—an emporium or department store.

51 The *Caroline Nesmith,* an 832-ton ship built in Maine in 1848 by J. Drummond, has a significant part to play later in the story of the *Dixey.*

52 Samuel Knight Girdler was born to Capt. John Girdler and Emma Knight Girdler, Captain Girdler's first wife, who died in childbirth, on June 24, 1835; he was thus Sarah Jane's half-brother.

53 Frank Millet, the second mate.

54 Vyborg, though now in Russia very near the Finnish border, is in an area that frequently changed hands. It was captured from the Swedes by Peter the Great and remained Russian till 1812, when Finland gained autonomy. It remained Finnish until 1939–40, when it was retaken by Stalin.

55 Probably not colored wax crayons (like the familiar Crayola) but chalk or clay mixed with graphite.

Although colored crayons had been a natural development from the introduction of aniline dyes in the 1850s, what is probably meant here is chalk, charcoal, or "Conté crayons," which are produced in black, sanguine (dark red), bistre (brown), and white.

56 Although there was an Alex Brown on the crew list when the ship left Bordeaux, there was no Brown listed in the crew at this time. This could be William Butlier, who dyed in Vyborg on 15 July according to the crew list.

57 Captain Dixey's son, Richard Cowell Dixey, born 1844.

58 Presumably this is the same person as Mr. Seseman.

59 According to Webster, "a long narrow light-draft Dutch merchant ship carrying a mainmast and a jigger with a mainsail having a long foot and short gaff."

60 Born in Marblehead on August 15, 1854, Fannie must have been conceived aboard the *Houqua* in December 1853, en route from San Francisco to Foo Chow, China, then back to New York.

61 The promontory of Kent extending into the Strait of Dover (north of the English Channel).

62 The Gironde.

63 This is undoubtedly Lormont, a town on the Garonne northwest of Bordeaux.

64 Mrs. Dixey's sister Maria Minge, from Mobile.

65 Robert H. Dixey, Jr.

66 A stagecoach, possibly on rails by 1857, though still horse-drawn.

67 There is no explanation of how the *Caroline Nesmith* came to recover the stolen boat, but that is what this must be. It indicates, however, that the Danish authorities were supportive and efficient!

68 At the mouth of the Gironde.

69 Readers are referred to Sarah Jane's letter of December 8, 1857, to her mother (to be found in the Appendix).

70 Becca's sister, Bethia Gardner Turner, mother of Willie Turner, who traveled as a companion for Cowell on one of the *Dixey*'s voyages.

71 The Azores; San Miguel was 60 miles west at noon on December 23. Captain Dixey turned south to miss the islands by a wider margin (see the chart on the endpapers).

72 Samuel Knight Girdler, Sarah Jane's half-brother, age 22 (born about September 27, 1835), who came aboard December 8 as one of the crew.

73 For Christmas dinner.

74 This must have been removable to permit access to the cargo.

75 This must be a new quarter boat, as the original was crushed in the hurricane in the Bay of Biscay.

76 From the entry for February 1, 1858, it is evident that this is the first mate, listed in both crew lists as Dexter Collamon.

77 From the next entry, it is evident that this was Morrison Blair.

78 The *Dixey*'s average speed was just over nine knots this day and ten knots the previous day.

79 Over the British at the Battle of New Orleans, January 8, 1815, the last battle of the War of 1812, fought in ignorance that the Treaty of Ghent had been signed on December 24, 1814.

80 It is obvious that Jennie has gotten used to *speed:* even to make "only" 198 miles in a day, the *Dixey* had to average nine knots.

81 From this it is evident that Jennie's cabin was on the port side of the ship, which was passing north of

Haiti; later it sailed south of Cuba.

82 Jane Bray Gardner (1788–1866).

83 Cabo de San Antonio, the westernmost tip of Cuba.

84 Mr. Begouen of Brown & Begouen in Mobile.

85 *Souvenirs of Travel* (published 1857), by Mme. Octavia Walton LeVert, a well-known Mobile personality and international socialite. Wife of Dr. Henry LeVert, she was also the daughter of George Walton, Mayor of Mobile in 1837, and a granddaughter of a Signer of the Declaration of Independence from Georgia.

86 Undoubtedly the Mobile City Hospital at 850 St. Anthony Street. Built in 1830, it was operated by the Sisters of Charity, who struggled to keep it going through the Civil War to serve Confederate soldiers. It fell into disuse in the 1960s but was restored in the mid-1970s to house the Mobile County Department of Pensions and Security.

87 More Marblehead cousins.

## Begin Chapter 9 Notes

88 A private institution founded by a former Barton Academy instructor, Amos Towle. It later became the Julius T. Wright School, now merged with the former University Military School to become UMS-Wright.

89 Ragged high clouds; sailors say "Mare's tails bring torn sails."

90 This ship, like the *New World,* which Captain Dixey had commanded earlier, was of the "Blue Swallowtail Line." It was on a special charter to Mobile.

## Notes to Samuel Smyly Statement, Chapter 9

25 It was necessary (and prudent) because the barometer was falling rapidly. Incidentally, Smyly must have estimated the ship's position on the basis of his experience, since the Choctaw light was undergoing repairs and was not burning at the time.

26 A natural confusion between R. H. and R. W. Dixey; R. H. Dixey never sailed as captain. All the listed owners lived in Mobile at this time.

## Begin Appendix C Notes

1 Anjer was a village at Java Head, that part of Java opposite Prince's Island.

2 John Dixey was master of the *Ganges* and owned a share of the voyage with John Hooper and Robert Hooper, Jr. The ship had sailed [illegible] in January 1817. It would return from Bremen, its last port of call, on 14 October 1819 with miscellaneous cargo and pay $1,771.80 duty—not a very rich cargo for a 300+-ton ship.

3 Dixey and the *Ganges* arrived at Manila on 24 June 1817 according to the Custom House Records at Baker Library, Harvard University.

4 The "little ones" were Rebecca (b. 1804), John (b. 1807), Richard (b. 1809), Hannah Glover (b. 1811), and William (b. 1814). Robert Hooper Dixey (b. 19 February 1817) was the anticipated "addishion to the family" and cause of Dixey's anxiety. Hector C. Dixey, another son, was born 2 June 1813. He is mentioned by RWD in a letter of 16 February 1863 to his father. Hector appears in *Ocean Life in Old Sailing Ship Days* as captain of the schooner *Eagle.* His crew deserted in 1850 because of a

difficult mate. Elizabeth Hooper Dixey was the twin of Hector C. Dixey.

5 This was Robert Hooper, Jr., one of the most important Marblehead merchants in the immediate post-Revolutionary period, who had married Mary Glover, Rebecca Cowell Dixey's aunt.

92 Stagecoach.
93 Of Emperor Napoleon III, who married Eugénie of Spain.
94 Jennie was pregnant at the time and evidently starting to get "cravings."
95 Presumably kid gloves.
96 Her oldest brother, William Henry Harrison Minge (b. 1830).
97 Her younger brother, Collier Harrison Minge, Jr. (B. 1845).
98 Since RHD's mother drowned in 1826, Jennie may have meant to say "father," but more likely she is referring to *her* mother (RHD's mother-in-law), whom she has just been talking about and whom RHD quite possibly called Mother.
99 Mrs. Dixey was at this time one and a half months pregnant with her daughter Anna Ladd.
100 Mr. Dixey was a man who liked to eat and drink well—sometimes too well!
101 Possibly Lesneven.
102 It is evident from what follows that she means "moon."
103 Robert H. Dixey, his brother.
104 Abel Gardner, his father-in-law.
105 Later identified as Rebecca, Hannah, Carrie, Elisa, and one other.
106 Henry Ward Beecher (1813–1887), the well-known New England clergyman and social reformer. He was a forceful orator who spoke out on social and political issues, including slavery.
107 Hector C. Dixey, born June 2, 1823.
108 Husband of Caroline ("Carrie") Dixey, Richard Dixey's sister.
109 Presumably "the Marblehead boys," i.e., members of the crew from Marblehead.
110 Literally, "mechanical armchair." It seems to be a sort of wheelchair.
111 After the birth of Anna Ladd Dixey on July 14, 1853.
112 The Minge home at Point Clear.
113 Possibly W. Kirby?
114 Aboard the *Robert H. Dixey*.
115 Cowell Dixey and his cousin Willie Turner.
116 One of Rebecca and Sarah's four sisters.
117 As seen in Sarah Jane's letters to her mother, this was her name for her cousin Alice Bray Goodwin.
118 Presumably Lewis Girdler, Sarah's son and Jennie's brother.
119 By making shoes.
120 William B. Brown, husband of Caroline Dixey, Richard Dixey's sister.
121 Caroline Dixey Brown, born August 2, 1820.
122 Maria Minge, Robert's sister-in-law.
123 Nate (b. 1827) and Lizzie (b. 1825) Hooper are a brother and sister, contemporaries of RHD and

neighbors in Marblehead. They were wealthy people and were probably just traveling.

124 That is, Rebecca Bray Dixey, Bray being Rebecca Dixey's middle name before she was married. At this time, women tended to drop their maiden name but keep their middle name on marriage.

125 This indicates that the poop deck was raised and the cabin with it.

126 Daniel Symmonds, the third mate.

127 Richard Girdler, her brother.

128 Her younger brother.

129 Abel and Jane Bray Gardner. Mammy Taddy may have been a servant.

130 Sarah Girdler had started a "dame school" for small children after her husband died in 1853.

131 Probably Alice Bray Goodwin, daughter of Priscilla Gardner Goodwin. Earlier she is known as Sis. Sarah Jane and Alice were nine years apart but for a period of time they had lived together in the same house and probably felt toward each other quite like sisters.

132 The second mate, Frank Millet.

133 This is the Sarah Jane's cousin, the son of her uncle Captain Richard Evans by his first marriage. It would seem that he gave her a notebook in which to keep a journal during the voyage.

134 Harriett G. (Hattie) Haskell was the young sister-in-law of Richard Evans above. When the federal census was taken in 1850, Richard Evans and his wife Mary had been living with her father, William Haskell. Curiously, William Haskell's son William Thomas Haskell had married Richard Girdler's daughter Sarah Elizabeth. Living in the same house at that time, but in a separate part of it, was the daughter of Lewis Girdler, Jr., Abigail Girdler Green!

135 Her cousin William H. Turner, who had been with the Dixeys on their previous voyage as a companion for Cowell Dixey. It was summer vacation and they traveled to Mobile, made a trip to Le Havre, Cadiz, New Orleans, and Boston.

136 This seems unlikely to have been the same person previously referred to as "Mr. Symonds"; perhaps Daniel Short, the cook?

137 Possibly William H. Steele, a ship's boy.

138 Her younger brother, Lewis Girdler. The family spelled the name both ways, indiscriminately.

139 Her brother, Richard Girdler, who had been sent to sea.

140 Fannie Dixey may have been the first to call Sarah Jane simply "Jane."

141 Possibly cousin Alice Bray Goodwin.

142 Sarah Jane's brother Richard.

143 Ten years later, Sarah Jane writes about visiting Lizzie Stevens and her parents in Louisville, Kentucky. It may be through them that she met Dexter D. Belknap, an up-and-coming young businessman from Canada, whom she married.

144 Probably Jennie's cousin Willie Turner.

145 Francis Freeto of Marblehead, born August 8, 1791. The *Riga* had been launched at Marblehead December 12, 1856. See Benjamin Lindsey, *Old Marblehead Sea Captains*.

146 Richard Girdler, their uncle, living in Boston at this time. He had just recently resigned from his position at Massachusetts General Hospital and would soon find a new post as captain of the school ship *Massachusetts*. It was undoubtedly felt that he had many contacts on the Boston scene. He did not fail his family. In the 1858 Boston City Directory and for several years thereafter, Samuel K. Girdler is listed as living at the same address as Richard Girdler, his occupation given as "bookkeeper."

147 After those very tender years at sea from the age of 12 to 14, Richard Girdler seems to have stayed in Marblehead. Mr. Woods might have kept a private school of some sort in the area. He was not at the public high school, as its principal at that time was James Batcheller.

148 Anna and Robert H. Dixey, Jr., children of RHD and Jennie Minge Dixey.

149 Although the ship's party spent almost a month in the St. Petersburg area (including Cronstadt), they were in St. Petersburg itself for only a week (June 11–17). Since Jane wrote this with reference to her journal, it is unclear why she exaggerated the visit. Perhaps the days were so packed with visiting and sightseeing that, in retrospect, the time seemed longer.

150 Maria Minge, nineteen-year-old sister of Jennie Minge Dixey (Mrs. Robert H.), with whom the Richard W. Dixeys were staying.

151 His older sister, born August 13, 1811.

152 To Mobile.

153 His wife, Jennie Minge Dixey, and children Anna and Robert; Billa is Jennie's younger sister, Sabilla.

154 Richard Dixey's son. He would have been fifteen years old at the time.

155 Rebecca Gardner Dixey.

156 Hector Cowell Dixey, the youngest son of Captain John Dixey. He was a master mariner.

157 This could be Thomas Appleton, Jr., of Marblehead. He was probably part of the Boston Appleton commercial group, which would have had offices in New York City.

158 He was a commercial merchant, ship agent, and ship owner.

159 Probably Elisabeth Hooper Dixey, Hector Cowell Dixey's twin sister. She evidently married a Mr. Moody.

160 RHD's sister Caroline, Mrs. William B. Brown.

# FOR FURTHER READING

The volumes listed below constitute a partial record of historical and other works that the author searched in an effort to look more closely at the 1855–1860 period in America. We looked especially at cotton, the commodity and the sailing ships that carried it, particularly the ship *Robert H. Dixey,* to which we feel a strong bond and of which we have acquired a close knowledge.

    Amos, Harriet. *Cotton City*, University of Alabama Press.

    Beach, Capt. E. L. *History of the U.S. Navy*, Henry Holt & Co., 1986.

    Bowditch, N. *American Practical Navigator* (2 volumes), U.S. Hydrological Office, 1984.

    Bradlee, F. B. C. *Marblehead Foreign Commerce*, Essex Institute, Salem, Mass., 1929.

    Brantley, *Banking in Alabama*, Mobile Genealogy Library.

    Campbell, George. *China Tea Clippers*, International Maritime Pub., 1974, 1990.

    Chapelle, H. I., *History of U.S. Sailing Ships*, Bonanza/Norton, 1935.

    Mobile City Directories, 1830–1890, Mobile Genealogy Library.

    Cohn, *Life and Times of King Cotton*, Mobile Genealogy Library.

    Tax Records of Mobile County, Mobile County Courthouse, Alabama.

    Fairburn, *History of American Sail* (six volumes), Mobile Library.

    Family papers of Fettyplace and Dixey families.

Gosnell, H. A. *Before the Mast in Clippers*, Dover Books, 1937, 1989.

Levert, Octavia Walton. *Souvenirs of Travel*, Vols. 1 & 2, Guetzel & Co., 1858 & 1959.

Lindsey, B., *Old Marblehead Sea Captains and the Ships In Which They Sailed*, Marblehead Historical Society, 1915.

Lord, P., and Gamage, V. Marblehead: *The Spirit of '76 Lies Here*, Chilton, 1972.

*Marblehead Vital Records* (2 volumes), Essex Institute, Salem, Massachusetts, 1904.

Minge Family Papers (looseleaf), courtesy of Mary Toulmin, Daphne, Alabama.

Norbye, M. *Leningrad (St Petersburg)*, Passport Books, 1992.

Peabody, H.C. "Peabody Letters" (unbound), Wilson Library, University of North Carolina, Chapel Hill.

Pratt, Fletcher. *Civil War In Pictures*, Garden City Books, 1955.

Roads, *History of Marblehead*, Riverside Press.

Sullivan, Charles L., *Hurricanes of the Mississippi Gulf Coast: 1717 to Present*, Gulf Publishing Co.

U.S. Census 1840, 1850, 1860, Mobile Genealogy Library.

Villiers, Men, *Ships & the Sea*, National Geographic Society.

*War of Rebellion* (many volumes), Mobile Genealogy Society.

Whidden, *Ocean Life in Old Sailing Ships*, Little, Brown & Co.

Whipple, *The Challenge,* William Morrow & Co.

Watkins, James L. *King Cotton.*, Negro University Press, 1908.

# INDEX

## A

A. A. Low & Bros., 50
Abaco Island, Bahamas, 73
Academy of Arts and Sciences, St. Petersburg, 110
Alexander Column, 109
Allenson, Charles, 132
*American Union*, 153, 156
Appomattox, 163
Australia, 165
Azores, 134

## B

Bahamian crew, 35, 61, 151
Baker, Thomas, 157
Baltic Sea, 100
Barker, B. Devereux, 26
Barnhill, Suzanne S., 17
Baton Rouge, 160
Battle House, 10, 11, 149
Bay of Biscay, 13, 26, 48, 49, 127-
Beachy Head, England, 124
Beck, Richard, 35
Begouen, Mr., 142
Belknap, Dexter, 43
Bethel, 12, 79-80
birds, 85, 87, 89, 99
Bladon Springs, Alabama, 64
Blair, Morrison, 132; beating of, 136-137

Bordeaux, 125-127, 129, 131-132
Boston, 16, 22, 40, 41, 43, 45, 61, 62, 70, 145-146, 156, 161
Boyd, George, Jr., 157
Bowden, Hammond, 16
Brighton, England, 91
Brooks, Rosamonde Dixey, 161
brothel, 12
Brown, Alex, 132
Brown, James, 157
Brown, Nicholas Harleston, 45
Bryant, Edward H., 132
Bunker, Capt., 113
Burma, 166
Butler family, 166
Butlier, William, 62, 132

## C

Calcutta, India, 65-66, 166
Callamore, Fannie, 62    see Collamore?
Careforend, 132
Carey family, 122, 123
*Caroline Nesmith*, 112-114, 127
Carson, John P., 65
Chase family, 111
Childe, John, 149
China, 14, 51
*China*, 144
Christ Episcopal Church, Mobile, 60
Christmas (1857), 135-136

churches, 81, 84, 103, 105, 108, 109, 110, 114, 135
Civil War, 150, 159, 162-163, 165-166
clipper ships, 44-50, 55, 89
*Clothilde*, 59
Collamon, Dexter, 62, 132, 136, 142
Collamore, Fannie, 62?, 73
Colman family, 117, 119-120
Commerce Street, Mobile, 58
Conception Street, Mobile, 41, 61
Constantine, Duke, 111
Conti Street, Mobile, 60, 61
Cook, Capt. and Mrs., 143-144
Copenhagen, Denmark, 100, 122
coppering hulls, 61
cotton, 10, 11, 12, 23, 27-28, 31, 37, 40, 43, 57-59, 61, 64, 103, 111, 148, 150, 165
Cotton Exchange, Mobile, 58-59
cotton warehouse fire, 82
Cowbellion de Rakin Society, 40, 83, 162
Cowell, Richard, 30
Crimean War, 61
Crondstadt, Russia, 102, 112-115
Cuba, 141
Curtis, Paul, 26, 45-47

## D

Daughdrill, Annette, 18, 39
Dauphin Island, 22, 151
Dauphin Street, Mobile, 10
Davis, Terry G., 70
dead calm, 133
Delaney, Caldwell, 9, 17, 58, 79, 83
De Meaux, Edward Bergoren, 45
Demopolis, Alabama, 37, 67
Denmark, 95-100, 121-122
Deshon, Daniel, 45
Deshon, George, 45
Devereux family, 40
Dixey family, 23
Dixey family home, 35

Dixey, Anna Ladd, 32, 60, 65, 127, 132, 134, 143, 160
Dixey, Arthur, 161
Dixey Bar, 153
Dixey, Cowell, 14
Dixey, Dan, 16
Dixey, Ellen Tappan, 161
Dixey, Edgar, 17
Dixey, Fannie, 34, 62, 71, 82-84, 86, 98-100, 106, 109-111, 113,116, 123, 132, 134, 145-146
Dixey Island, 153
Dixey, Jane Oliver Minge, 32, 60, 125-128, 132-133, 143, 159-160
Dixey, John, 30, 31
Dixey, Rebecca Cowell, 30, 31
Dixey, Rebecca Gardner, 13, 14, 15, 33, 43, 59, 62, 71, 74-75, 82-83, 89, 98, 105, 106, 110, 111, 113-114, 116, 127, 130, 132, 143, 145-146, 161
Dixey, Richard Cowell, 34, 120
Dixey, Richard William 13, 15, 16, 21, 28, 33-36, 44, 47, 49, 51, 54, 60, 62, 70, 74-75, 80, 82-84, 89, 91, 96-98, 103, 105, 106, 113, 116, 127, 132, 134-136, 139, 143-144
Dixey, Richard William, death of, 151-153, 156-157
Dixey, Robert Hooper, 16, 17, 28, 31-33, 38, 39, 44-45, 56, 60, 61, 64, 67-68, 125-127. 132, 139, 159
Dixey, Robert Hooper, Jr., 32, 126-127, 132, 143, 160-161, 166
*Dixey (Robert H. Dixey)*, building of, 45-50
*Dixey (Robert H. Dixey)*, crew list of, 62, 132
*Dixey (Robert H. Dixey)*, dimensions of, 45, 54
*Dixey (Robert H. Dixey)*, hurricanes encountered by, 13, 22, 26, 128-131, 150-158
*Dixey (Robert H. Dixey)*, painting of, 17, 26, 27, 40

*Dixey (Robert H. Dixey)*, wreck of, 150-158
*Dixey (Robert H. Dixey)*, speed of, 139-140
*Dixey (Robert H. Dixey)*, voyages of, 63, 112 (map)
Dixey/Minge letters, 16
Dixie, Thomas, 30
Dixie, William, 30
Dixie, Sir Wolstan, 30
Dobbs, Rev. N. H., 60
double topsail rig, 26, 47, 49
Dover, England, 92, 124
drowning, 30
Dungeness, England, 124
Dutch boats, 93-94
Dutch galliot, 122-123

## E

Elsinore (see: Helsingor)
*Elvira Harbeck*, 50
*Empire City*, 142
English Channel, 91, 124
*Europa*, 87
Evans, Lewis Girdler, 91

## F

Fairhope Public Library, 17
Falconet, Etienne-Maurice, 108
Fetchko, Mr., 16
Fettyplace family, 23, 38-40
Fettyplace, Edward (b. 1721), 38
Fettyplace, Edward (b. 1748), 38
Fettyplace, Hannah Diamond, 38
Fettyplace, Henry King, 39, 40, 41, 150, 162
Fettyplace, Mary Ann, 39
Fettyplace, Mary Jane Williams, 38
Fettyplace, Sarah, 40, 83, 84
Fettyplace, Thomas, 39
Fettyplace, Thomas J. (Tom), 26, 28, 32, 39, 40, 41, 45, 56, 61, 83, 148, 157, 161-162
Fettyplace, William, 38

Finelly, Lewis, 132
Finland, 115
fire companies, Marblehead, 25
Firemen's Day, Mobile, 11
Fitch, Edward, 69
*Flying Cloud*, 47, 50
food, 90, 93, 95, 105, 120, 122-123, 126-127, 136, 141
Forbes, Robert Bennett, 47
*Forest Eagle*, 121
Fort Morgan, Alabama, 39, 61
France, 92
Franklin, Daniel, 132

## G

Gabbard light, 124
Galloper light, 124
Gardner, Abel, 13, 42, 43, 161
Gatling, Eva, 18
*George E. Webster*, 42
Gibson family, 120
Girdler, Emma Knight, 42
Girdler family, 23
Girdler, Jane Bray, 43
Girdler, John, 13, 42
Girdler, Lewis, 13, 26, 42-43
Girdler, Reynolds, 16, 64
Girdler (Belknap Whedon), Sarah Jane (Jennie), 14, 15, 23, 26, 29, 33, 34, 42-43, 59, 62, 64, 132, 148, 166-167; journal of, 14-15, 22-23, 29, 36, 47, 69-146
Girdler, Sarah Jane Gardner, 13, 42, 43, 132
Girdler, Samuel Knight, 42, 113, 132, 134, 139, 144, 166
Girdler, T. M. III 26
Girdler, Tracy, 15, 64
Gironde, 129
Glash, Allen, 62
Glash, David L., 62

Gracie, Archibald, 41, 163
Griffith, Capt., 113, 122
Godfrey, A. M., 157
Goodman, Duke W., 33
Gosling, Marion, 16
Gulf of Finland, 101-103
Gulf of Mexico, 74

## H

Hailey, Diane Dixey, 16, 18, 160
Haliard, Janais, 62
Hall, Isaac, 62, 132
Hamman, George, 157
Harbeck and Co., 31, 81
Harris, Robert, 62, 132
Harrison, Nancy Girdler, 14
Harrison, William Henry, 38
Helsingor, Denmark, 95-100, 121-122
Hermitage, 106-109
Hobart, John, 62
Homer, W. H., 156
Hooper family, 30
Hooper, J. A., 162
Hooper, Robert, 31
*Houqua*, 14, 50-51
Hubbard, John W., 132
hurricane 13, 22, 26, 128-131, 151
Hutton, Marjorie Post (Mrs. E.F.), 52

## I

India, 65-66, 166
Isle of Wight, 90, 124
Isaac Church, 108-109

## J

Jackson, Ariel, 62, 132
Jackson, Henry, 62, 132
Jenkins, Charles, 62
Juba (dance), 78, 135
July 4th Celebration (1857), 116

## K

Kamiesch, 61
Kate, Horatio, 62
Kenny, Susan, 112, 114

## L

Lapham, H. K., 157
Lee, Bill, 153
Lee Mansion, 16, 25
Lee, Robert E., 41
Le Havre, France, 61, 148
LeVert, Octavia W., 10, 143
*Lindsay*, 114
Little, William H., 132
Liverpool, 148-150, 165
Lormont, 125, 127
lottery, 25
Louisville, Kentucky, 43

## M

Macoduck, Capt., 153, 156
Magnolia Cemetery, Mobile, 38, 40, 153, 160, 162, 166
malachite, 107, 110
Marblehead, Massachusetts, 16, 23, 24-27, 30, 31, 35, 38, 39, 42, 104, 145, 156, 161, 166, 167
Marblehead Academy, 32
Marblehead Historical Society, 16, 31
*Marblehead Ledger*, 158
Mardi Gras, 9, 40, 83
Marseilles, 26, 61
Marshall/Hixon house, 41
Martin, Richard, 16
Maury, Lt. M. F., 34, 35, 55
Maury Log, 129
McKay, Donald, 50
Merchant, L., 157
*Mercury*, 31
Millet, Frank, 62, 92, 113-114, 123, 127,

130, 132, 134-136, 139-140, 142, 144-145
Minge, Anna Maria Ladd, 37
Minge, Benjamin Harrison, 37
Minge Bible, 18
Minge, Collier Harrison 28, 33, 37, 61, 64, 81, 84, 156, 163
Minge, Collier Harrison, Jr., 150, 164
Minge, David, 37
Minge, George, 37
Minge family, 23, 36-38
Minge home, 46
Minge, James, 36
Minge, Jane Oliver (Jennie), 33, 38
Minge, Maria, 125-129, 132, 133-134, 143, 164
Minge, Mary Jane Gladden, 166
Minge, Robert, 62
Minge, Sabilla, 66, 81, 84, 163-164
Minge, Sarah Harrison, 38
Minge, Virginia, 17
Minge, William Henry Harrison (Willie), 17, 37, 65, 150, 163, 165-166
Mobile, 9-12, 13, 15, 17, 27-28, 33, 37, 38, 39, 45, 57-59, 60-61, 62, 80-85, 142-146, 148-150, 159-163, 166
Mobile *Advertiser*, 39
Mobile Bay, 21, 22, 65, 78-80, 104, 151-153
Mobile Bay, map of, 152
*Mobile Daily Register*, 65
Mobile Point, 21
Mobile Public Library, 17, 62
Monrepos villa, 126
*Montreal*, 50, 66
Mulligan, William, 62
Museum of the City of Mobile, 17, 35, 40, 65
music, 78, 80, 81, 92, 103-105, 114, 116, 118, 135, 161

## N

*Natchez*, 61, 84-85, 143
nautical terms, glossary, 76-77
New Orleans, 38, 41, 43, 45, 58, 142-143, 158, 159-160, 166
*New Orleans Picayune*, 153
*New World*, 50
New Year's Day, 138
New York City, 31, 33, 41, 50, 66, 150
Ninth Alabama Militia, 39
Ninth of April, 11
North Sea, 90, 93

## O

Oddelbridge, 157
Old Maid (card game), 81
*"Old Ironsides"* sketch, 35
oystering, 144

## P

Pauillac, France, 124-125, 127-128, 131
Peabody Essex Museum, 16, 23, 51, 69
Peabody, George, 149
Peabody, Herbert Cheever, 40-41, 147, 148-149, 162
Peabody, Horace M., 40, 41, 148-150
Peabody, Louisa Fettyplace, 40-41, 83
Pendley, Levin, 62
Peter the Great, 107
Peter the Great, statue of, 108-109
Petersburg, Russia, (see St. Petersburg)
Petersburg, Virginia, 163
Philadelphia, 150
Pierce, Winnifred, 13-15, 16, 62, 63, 64
Point Clear, Alabama, 65, 150, 163, 166
Preston, John, 38
Preston, Leana, 38, 65
Prichard, Capt., 144
Prout, Daphne Brooks, 16, 26, 34, 51, 71

## Q

*Queen Mary*, 52
Quina, Charles F., 62

## R

Redman, Capt. and Mrs., 145-146
Relley, Alex, 62
Rice, George, 62, 132
Richard, Tom, 132
*Riga*, 142
Rinyers, Sam, 62
Rogers, Isaiah
Roux, A., 26
Roux, F., 26
Royan, France, 127, 131
Russ, Ruth Lyon, 17, 37, 165

## S

sails, 47-50
St. Albans, 90
St. Domingo, 140
St. John, Samuel, 41
St. Michael Street, Mobile, 9, 58
St. Petersburg, Russia, 105-111, 113-114, 120
Salem, Massachusetts, 16, 23, 40, 41, 51, 69, 162, 166
*Salem Gazette*, 157
San Francisco, 42
Sand Island lighthouse, 21
Savannah, 145-146
Schell, Sidney, 18
Schiff, Adolf H., 132
Schroeter, George
sea chanteys, 104
*Sea Cloud*, 52
sea sickness, 127, 133
Seliger, Augustine, 62
Seseman family, 118-121
Setegill, August, 121? (see Careforend), 132 (see Seliger?)

*Sharon*, 121-122
Sharon, Massachusetts, 31, 38, 159
Sherreff, Adolph C., 62
shipbuilding, 45-47
ship chandlers, 105, 161
Short, Daniel, 62
Siberia, 110
Simons, Dan, 85
slavery, 33, 36-37, 59
Slate, Horatio, 132
Smith, Chandler, 163
Smith, Franklin, 132
Smith, Mary Ann Fettyplace, 162
Smith, Melancton, 163
Smith, Walter, 39, 163
Smyly, Sam, 21, 150, 153, 156-
*Southern Star*, 65, 150
Sparks, John, 132
Spinks, Sarah, 106, 109-111
Spinks family, 106
Spinks, Maggie, 110-111
Spring Hill, Mobile, 40, 41, 83, 84, 150, 161
spencer jacket, 101, 124
square rigging, 26, 55
steam engines, 44
steam boat, 84, 115, 119-121, 124, 130-131, 142
Steele, George, 62
Steele, William H., 62
Stein, Albert, 41
Stein, Barker, 18
Stein, Emily Peabody, 40-41
Stein, Louis, 41, 162
Stein, Thomas Fettyplace, 41
Stein, Thomas Fettyplace, Jr., 18
Stinkle family, 117-118
stowaway, 117
studding sails, 101, 133, 139, 140
Suddeth, Betty, 17
Sullivan, Charles L., 17
Sully, T. W. painting, 37

Sweden, 95
Swinston, James, 62
Symmonds, Daniel, 62, 98-99, 112, 132, 144

### T

*Talbot*, 30
telegraph, 142, 149
*Ticonderoga*, 165
tobacco, 90, 95, 124
Toulmin, Mary, 17
Towle Institute, Mobile, 148
Thanksgiving (1857), 131
theater, 9, 82
Turner, Bethia Gardner, 132
Tyler, John, 36, 38

### U

University of North Carolina Library, 41, 147

### V

Virginia, 23, 27, 36
Virginia Military Institute, 150, 164-165
Virginia Military Institute Museum, 164
Vyborg, 115-121, 132

### W

*Waltham*, 114
War of 1812, 31, 140
Washington Light Infantry, 162
Watts family, 120
Weyanoke plantation, 37
whales, 86-87
Whidden, John D., 104
White, William, 62
Williams, George, 62, 132
Wilson Library, Chapel Hill, North Carolina, 41
*Windsor Forest*, 114, 121-122

### Y

Young, Emily S., 18

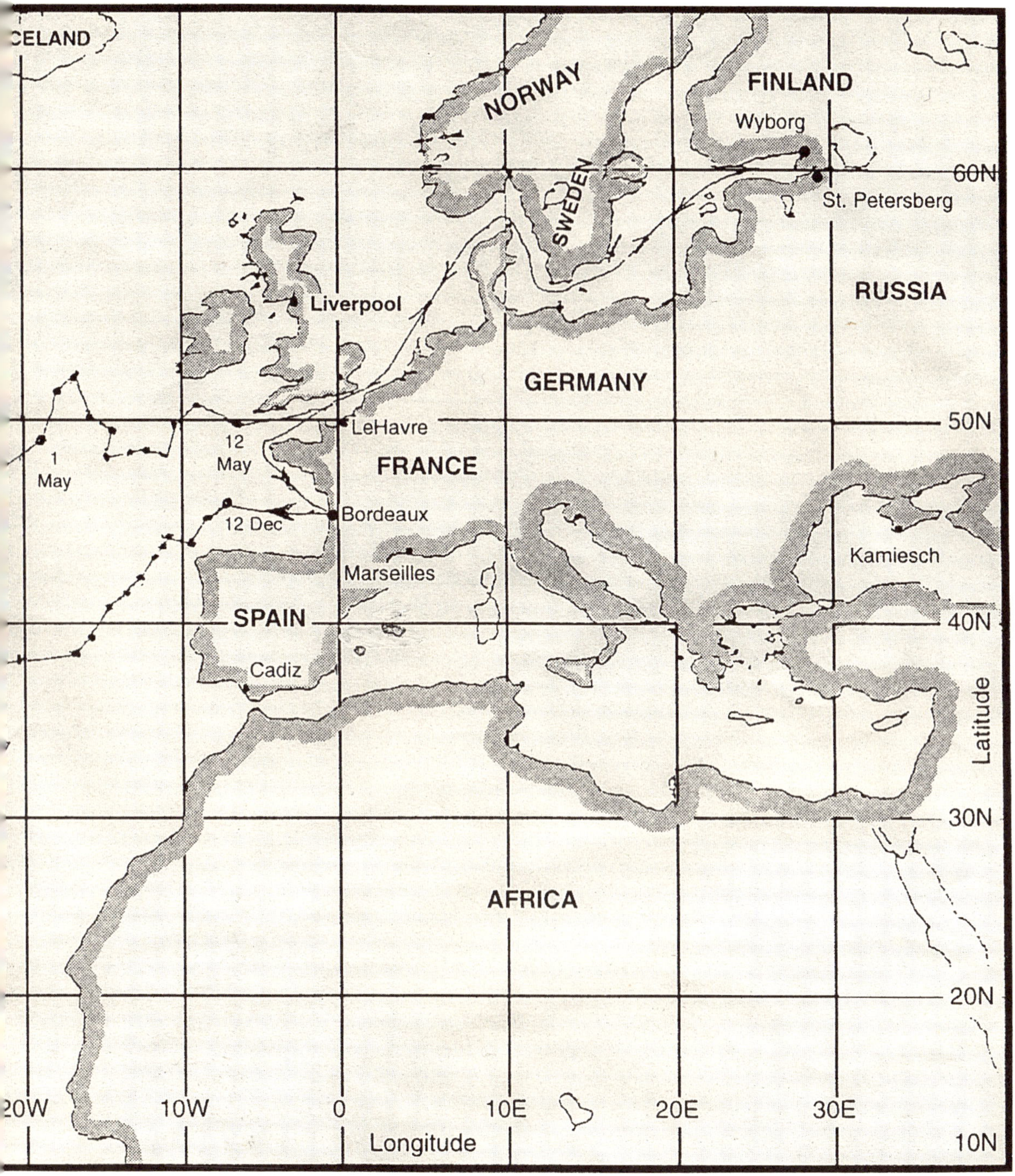
CELAND
NORWAY
FINLAND
Wyborg
SWEDEN
60N
St. Petersberg
Liverpool
RUSSIA
GERMANY
50N
LeHavre
12
May
1
May
FRANCE
Bordeaux
12 Dec
Kamiesch
Marseilles
SPAIN
40N
Cadiz
Latitude
30N
AFRICA
20N
20W
10W
0
10E
20E
30E
Longitude
10N